Agile Learning and Management in a Digital Age

This book offers a detailed theoretical analysis of the fields of learning and management in the digital age. Taking an interdisciplinary approach, it opens a dialogue between agile management theory and agile learning theory.

The book argues that there is a tension between participative and action-orientated approaches on the one hand and neoliberal enclosure of the actor on the other hand. It takes this as an opportunity for interdisciplinary dialogue between learning theories and management concepts. With contributions from a range of international experts, chapters discuss the need for suitable theoretical, epistemological, and ethical foundations as well as practice-orientated methods for learning and management to implement appropriate strategies and meet educational challenges.

This highly topical book will be of great interest to academics, postgraduate students, and researchers in the fields of digital learning, educational theory, management theory, and communication studies.

David Kergel is Professor of Social Work, IU International University of Applied Sciences and Director of the Center for Diversity and Education in the Digital Age, Germany.

Birte Heidkamp-Kergel is the Leading Coordinator of the E-Learning Centre, Rhein-Waal University of Applied Sciences, Germany.

Hanne Nørreklit is Professor of Management Accounting and Control, Aarhus University, Denmark.

Michael Paulsen is Associate Professor at the Syddansk University, Denmark.

Perspectives on Education in the Digital Age
Series Editors: David Kergel and Birte Heidkamp

The process of digitalization is leading to a fundamental social change affecting all spheres of social life. In the pedagogical field there is a need for re-structuring key concepts such as learning, teaching and education that considers socio-economic and cultural changes.

Perspectives on Education in the Digital Age explores the process of coming to terms with socio-economic and socio-cultural shifts arising from digitalization and discusses this process with reference to its effects on education. The Series provides a forum for discussion of critical, integrative analyses of social transformations in the digital age, drawn from different fields such as the humanities, social sciences and economics. The aim of the Series is to analyse the implications of cultural change on education in the digital age by bringing together interdisciplinary dialogue and different theoretical approaches.

Foreign Language Learning in the Digital Age
Theory and Pedagogy for Developing Literacies.
Edited by Christiane Lütge

Smart Campus E-Readiness
A Framework for Cyberspace Learning Strategic Management
Sayed Hadi Sadeghi

Nordic Childhoods in the Digital Age
Insights into Contemporary Research on Communication, Learning and Education
Edited by Kristiina Kumpulainen, Anu Kajamaa, Ola Erstad, Åsa Mäkitalo, Kirsten Drotner and Sólveig Jakobsdóttir

Agile Learning and Management in a Digital Age
Dialogic Leadership
Edited by David Kergel, Birte Heidkamp-Kergel, Hanne Nørreklit and Michael Paulsen

For more information about this series, please visit: www.routledge.com/Perspectives-on-Education-in-the-Digital-Age/book-series/EDUDIG

Agile Learning and Management in a Digital Age

Dialogic Leadership

Edited by David Kergel,
Birte Heidkamp-Kergel,
Hanne Nørreklit and
Michael Paulsen

LONDON AND NEW YORK

First published 2023
by Routledge
4 Park Square, Milton Park, Abingdon, Oxon OX14 4RN

and by Routledge
605 Third Avenue, New York, NY 10158

Routledge is an imprint of the Taylor & Francis Group, an informa business

© 2023 selection and editorial matter, David Kergel, Birte Heidkamp-Kergel, Hanne Nørreklit and Michael Paulsen; individual chapters, the contributors

The right of David Kergel, Birte Heidkamp-Kergel, Hanne Nørreklit and Michael Paulsen to be identified as the authors of the editorial material, and of the authors for their individual chapters, has been asserted in accordance with sections 77 and 78 of the Copyright, Designs and Patents Act 1988.

All rights reserved. No part of this book may be reprinted or reproduced or utilised in any form or by any electronic, mechanical, or other means, now known or hereafter invented, including photocopying and recording, or in any information storage or retrieval system, without permission in writing from the publishers.

Trademark notice: Product or corporate names may be trademarks or registered trademarks, and are used only for identification and explanation without intent to infringe.

British Library Cataloguing-in-Publication Data
A catalogue record for this book is available from the British Library

ISBN: 978-1-032-03731-8 (hbk)
ISBN: 978-1-032-03732-5 (pbk)
ISBN: 978-1-003-18872-8 (ebk)

DOI: 10.4324/9781003188728

Typeset in Bembo
by Apex CoVantage, LLC

Contents

List of editors and contributors — vii

1 Introduction — 1

PART 1
Learning to manage the digital turn — 3

2 Agile cognition and the age of transformation — 5
LENNART NØRREKLIT

3 Revisiting enabling formalizations of remote work: learnings for short-term and long-term impacts — 38
TEEMU LAINE, TUOMAS KORHONEN, AND NATALIA NIINA MARIA SAUKKONEN

4 Digital technologies, management, and big data: a way to a "living" or a "dead" (school) life? — 56
FINN WIEDEMANN, DION RÜSSELBÆK HANSEN, AND MICHAEL PAULSEN

5 Paranoiac versus agile management of universities — 70
LENNART NØRREKLIT, LISA JACK, AND HANNE NØRREKLIT

PART 2
Learning and management in the digital age — 97

6 From agile management to agile-orientated teaching and learning: a heuristic analysis — 99
DAVID KERGEL AND BIRTE HEIDKAMP-KERGEL

7 Moving forward in social constructivist theories
through agile learning in the digital age 107
INGRID NOGUERA

8 The magic of digitalized educational projects 126
NIKOLAJ KURE

9 *Lightschools®* space and freedom for the co-creation of new possibilities,
opportunities, and valuable solutions 140
BRITT VAN MENSVOORT – IN CREATIVE COLLABORATION
WITH MAR CANO MESA

10 Agile learning and management in times of crisis
in the digital age: actor-reality construction in the
COVID-19 pandemic 159
TUOMAS KORHONEN, FABIO MAGNACCA, OSSI HEINO, TEEMU LAINE,
JAKOB LIBORIUSSEN, AND HANNE NØRREKLIT

PART 3
The digital management of the lifeworld 177

11 From the fordist self to the entrepreneurial self:
self-management in times of digitization 179
DAVID KERGEL

12 Between romance and market: the construction of
partnership on dating platforms 190
ANNICK ANCELIN-BOURGUIGNON AND HANNE NØRREKLIT

13 Conclusion 214

Index 215

Editors and contributors

Annick Ancelin-Bourguignon, PhD, is Emeritus Professor at ESSEC Business School, France. Her research addresses psychological, sociological, ideological, and ethical dimensions of management systems; organizational change and creativity; psychosocial risks; and teaching methods.

Dion Rüsselbæk Hansen is Associate Professor in the Department for the Study of Culture at the University of Southern Denmark. He is the leader of the Pedagogy, Culture, and Leadership research program. His research interests lie in educational policy, philosophy of education, psychoanalysis, and critical research in education.

Birte **Heidkamp-Kergel**, MA, is the coordinator of e-learning at Rhein-Waal University of Applied Sciences, Germany. Her research interest is in the interface between teaching and learning, media pedagogy, and e-education.

Ossi Heino, PhD, is currently working as a postdoctoral research fellow at Tampere University on a project concerning the resilience of health systems. His research interests lie at the intersection of critical infrastructures, preparedness, and terrorism.

Lisa Jack, PhD, is Professor of Accounting, Portsmouth Business School, UK. She is a former president of the British Accounting and Finance Association. Her research interests lie in management information for decision-making, including accounting communication, accounting, and social theory. She has a special interest in accounting in agri-food industries.

David Kergel, PhD, is Professor at the International University of Applied Sciences Dortmund, Germany. His research includes qualitative educational research, media education, diversity in the digital age, and teaching evaluation. He is a coordinator of the research group "Diversity and Education in the Digital Age."

Tuomas **Korhonen**, PhD, is *Associate Professor* of Profitability Management *at* Tampere University, Finland. His research interests lie in studying the potential of management accounting in contributing to various types of managerial work, including balancing of different types of values.

Nikolaj Kure, PhD, is an associate professor at the Department of Business Communication, Aarhus University, Denmark. His primary research interests include new public management reforms, organizational paradox, and organizational change.

Teemu Laine, PhD, is Professor of Profitability Management at Tampere University, Finland. His current research interests include management accounting and decision-making in service business and R&D management. He is also heavily involved in developing the interventionist research approach.

Jakob Liboriussen, PhD, is a postdoctoral fellow at Norwegian School of Economics, Bergen, Norway. His current research interests include management accounting in the public sector and management accounting communication.

Fabio Magnacca, PhD, CA, is a postdoctoral researcher in Accounting and Business Administration at the University of Pisa, Italy. He tends to conduct interventionist research, and he is interested in understanding and developing performance management practices within organizations, mostly adopting a pragmatic constructivist approach.

Britt van Mensvoort has a master degree in Health Psychology from Tilburg University, Netherlands. She is the founder and initial creator of Lightschools and the author of the book Living Is Learning.

Mar Cano Mesa has a master degree in Research and Change in Education from Barcelona University, Spain. She is interested in multiple educational ecosystems around the world and in learning from innovative educational systems, institutions, pedagogies, and methodologies.

Ingrid Noguera, PhD, is a lecturer and researcher at the Department of Educational Theories and Social Pedagogy of the Universitat Autònoma de Barcelona, Spain. Her research interests are teaching and learning in digital society and innovative teaching methods.

Hanne Nørreklit, PhD, is Professor of Management Accounting and Control, at School of Business and Social Sciences, Aarhus University, Denmark. Her research areas include performance management and control, management rhetoric, and validity issues in accounting and management. She is the coordinator of the research network on pragmatic constructivism (see http://mgmt.au.dk/research/organisation-strategy-and-accounting/osa-research/networks/actor-reality-construction/).

Lennart Nørreklit, PhD, has been Professor of Philosophy and Management at Aalborg University, Denmark. His research interests are the concept of reality, cross-cultural philosophy, methodology of social science, and philosophy of the "good life." He has developed the philosophical basis of pragmatic constructivism.

Michael Paulsen, PhD, is Associate Professor and Head of Intercultural Pedagogy Studies at the University of Southern Denmark, Department for the Study of Culture. His research focuses on the ontology and axiology of education. In particular, he has an interest in "Bildung theory" and pedagogy in the Anthropocene.

Natalia Niina Maria Saukkonen, PhD, is a funding expert at St1 Oy. Her research interests cover investment decision-making and emission control.

Finn Wiedemann is Associate Professor at the Department for the Study of Culture, University of Southern Denmark. His research interests are science of education, school development, and leadership.

Chapter 1

Introduction

Digitization alters the media upon which learning processes and management processes are founded. Learning as knowledge management and management as knowledge about the organization of social processes are coined by an ambivalence. This ambivalence unfolds between participative and action-orientated approaches on the one hand and control and test regimes and neoliberal enclosure of the actor on the other hand. This challenge is also an opportunity for interdisciplinary dialogue between learning theories and management concepts. Modern learning theories like "'connectivism," which is discussed as a learning theory of the digital age, consider learning as a self-directed management process. On the other hand, the so-called "agile management" reproduces epistemological aspects of socio-constructivist learning theories. In other words, organizational processes are located at the interface between learning and management. It is precisely this transdisciplinary analysis that makes it possible to open a dialogue between management research and learning research. An interdisciplinary analysis of organizational processes can be an essential point of orientation for interdisciplinary organizational research and project management practice in the digital age. This is particularly against the background of the digital age's challenges and the questions of information competence, autonomy, and efficient action age. Based on these considerations, the book provides an interdisciplinary to the fields of learning and management in the digital age.

For this purpose, the volume is divided into three sections.

- In the first section – "Learning to manage the digital turn" – the influence of digitization on epistemological and conceptual aspects of management discourse is analyzed and discussed.
- The second section "Learning and management in the digital age" focuses on management in digital teaching and learning processes.
- The third section "The digital management of the lifeworld" deals with digital self-management in the private sphere.

This structuring provides an overview of the digital age's complex and multilayered interaction of management and teaching/learning processes.

DOI: 10.4324/9781003188728-1

Essentially and simplified, learning can be defined as a sustainable change in behavior or behavioral potential. The fact that people learn throughout their lives is a product of their need for education or learning. Thus, learning is based on repeated experiences that a human being makes. Humans change as a result of experiences. Learning, like disease, growth, or aging, is a process of human change.

In contrast to disease, growth, and aging, learning involves acquiring knowledge based on experience. This knowledge acquired through learning leads to a lasting change in behavior or behavioral potential. From a normative perspective, learning is characterized by the unfolding of exploratory curiosity and self-efficacy expectations. Digitality requires new adaptations of knowledge or new learning strategies. Concerning this question and against the background of digitalization and forms of communication in the digital age, the terms polyphony (multiple actors compose a text) and polydirectionality (multiple actors communicate with each other in different directions) become relevant. These terms describe the media structure of digital communication. In other words, digitization changes the culture of communication or the world. World appropriation must be reorganized or managed. Thus, a heuristic thesis of the volume is that learning in the digital age must be adapted to the media's ecological infrastructure. At the same time, organizing or managing must be redesigned or relearned under the influences of the digitization of processes. This insight interest forms the focus of the volume.

Part I

Learning to manage the digital turn

Chapter 2

Agile cognition and the age of transformation

Lennart Nørreklit

Dilemma and challenge

IT and transformation

This section addresses the challenge of transformational change and the idea of an agile response. The IT revolution transforms the actor–world relational systems. It has accelerated the change of human relations – family, work, and political relations, so that they are turning into something different from what they used to be. We are entering a society in continuous transformation that was unimaginable a few decades ago, very much caused by the power of IT. There have always been changes that involved transition from one state to a different one, and some of these changes create real transformations as in a metamorphosis. The transformation we address here is, however, different. It is the constant formation of new types of phenomena, new forms and patterns, something that constantly makes the future qualitatively different from the past, which is being disrupted. Already many practices have been transformed – for instance, states and institutions, including research and education, have been transformed to modern forms of business. Although the institutions still have the same names, their functions are different.

The effect of IT is due to its special nature as communicative systems, based on a digital language that is exact and which has great calculative power. The translation from user to machine-language forces augmentation of precision, which is essential for control, but also rigid and unnatural. Further, as a tool in research and technology, it has created endless results that further accelerate transformation. Even if someday IT is "fully implemented," this will not stop but only strengthen the process of ongoing transformation in the foreseeable future. New technology has always replaced human work, but it has also created new forms of work. Labor has increasingly transformed to control the equipment that performs the work. Progress created new technology and the skills to control it. At the beginning of the IT revolution, it followed a similar pattern. People augmented their work by using IT. However, now IT systems control and manipulate everybody, not only employees but also professionals and managers. AI-based systems can control themselves: in addition to running the machines, they can develop their own software. It can read orders, produce the product, find the delivery route, deliver the product, and write a report. The controlling workforce itself is being replaced by technological systems that control themselves. This creates a new outlook on how to organize work and social life. IT technology causes autocratic techniques and the accompanying institutional setup to become outdated because the kind of work that management traditionally aims to control is being replaced by the work of very efficient IT. As work gets outdated so does that of traditional management. It is in the process of being replaced by something else. New forms of work and organization are emerging. To make them productive, a mindset is needed which is capable of generating and realizing new ideas. Management for industrial production and service and the corresponding forms of education for classical democracy are being rewritten to enact a human mindset that is more humane and less paranoiac than autocratic forms of teaching and governance that, despite great achievements, also produced fake truth, conflicts, as well as unnecessary damage of the ecosystem. Family members, workers, leaders, and teachers need a new mindset to fulfil their role to contribute and help others to perform under new conditions. Transformation implies that things get a new meaning and new values, that new types of phenomena enter the environment, new tools, and new institutions, that the relational system changes character, and that new possibilities emerge. All of this calls for new methods and practices.

Nevertheless, people also experience that IT can produce the most powerful autocratic control instruments the world has ever seen. These tools are used to do the opposite of what was mentioned earlier, using a variety of techniques such as systems of enforced self-regulations, manipulative algorithmic-based control, and more. The emerging irrelevance of this control over productive work is, however, the overall replaceability of such uncreative human work through IT. This development dissolves the traditional "master–slave" basis for organizational hierarchies. In the past, there has been an economic need for the hard and undesirable work that created master and slave relations. This basis is disappearing. Consider an industrial management-work hierarchy: a manager issues commands to workers, who then press the adequate buttons on the machine that consequently does the physical work. This model is getting outdated. Soon there is no more need for this manager–employee relation. Workers and middle managers can be replaced. Consider a service management-work hierarchy: a manager commands employees to interact with customers to finalize a transaction. This hierarchy of the service society may appear less vulnerable to becoming outdated because employees and customers appreciate dealing with human beings. Nevertheless, increasing parts of service functions are being taken over by IT. Bureaucratic hierarchies have similar prospects – administrative bureaucratic tasks can be performed by IT systems that communicate with customers and employees without support from live administrators and secretaries. This also applies to management technologies – as, for instance,

NPM-based management that follows procedures based on self-regulation by the employees. They can be enforced more consistently by IT systems than by live managers. All professions are targets. IT-based accessibility of knowledge is already augmenting people's cognition and transforming professional-client relations from autocratic domination to agile cooperation. In this situation, the task for management and teaching is to revolutionize themselves and replace an industrial mindset with an approach that augments people's ability to thrive and contribute. Although autocratic management uses IT to manipulate people, using Big Data for panoptic surveillance to influence behavior, this practice does not need autocratic rule. This is a structural dilemma: on the one hand, IT systems have augmented the control systems to force people to align to simplistic behavior – whether in work, buying, or voting. On the other hand, IT makes these control systems irrelevant and negative – irrelevant because they control work that should be done by robots, and negative because they prevent people from being creative and pursuing innovative projects. Augmenting agile cognition solves the dilemma. Actors create transformation and IT bots work for them. Future work and social life do not need autocratic rule and subjugation because the very reason for work is changing due to IT. Undesirable, hard, and monotonous work will be performed by efficient, precise, and reliable IT systems. This increases the productive capacity to serve the population. To imagine future forms of human work, one might identify what kind of work cannot be performed by robots – if there is any. IT systems may take over all quantifiable processes including undesirable, hard, and boring labor. IT technology is after all an embodiment of quantification and calculation. What is left are qualitative activities – in so far as they are not translated into quantifiable processes. And if nothing should be left, then the machines may do all the unattractive and inhumane work. Human work then becomes the kind of activity people want to do because they like it.

The challenge of transformation

> "I finally was able to master things, and my performance was agile and great. Then transformation came, everything changed. Now, the skills that I acquired are irrelevant. Transformational change is unpredictable – how do I live with it?"
>
> People develop networks to survive. But how strong are these relations in time of transformation, where relations are brittle?

There is change in every system, and there is transformation. With change, we shall mostly refer to transitions in a system that is stable, where stable means that the same type of phenomena recurs time and time again. Such world is static.

Transformation, however, is a form of change during which something new appears and replaces the old forms that do not recur. While change – consisting of movements in space and changes of qualities – can be analyzed with the given conceptual framework, transformations cannot be analyzed with the given conceptual framework. It needs the conceptual framework to be changed and reformed. Innovative mental activity of cognition is needed to cope with transformation. The power of IT systems unleashes innovation and productivity that transforms the nature of the world from being something specific and recurring to being something in ongoing transformation.

Prior to IT, the world was experienced as basically static despite its dramatic events. Philosophies and mythologies outlined visions of the world and its forces. The life of children resembled that of their parents. Skills in demand at the beginning of life were still in demand at the end. There were improvements, but rarely something radically new. Change was change *in* the world, which remained the same. However, sometimes a profound change, a transformation, took place. This was an occasional change *of* the world. Systems broke down, and there was a need for new ideas. After the transformation had taken place, people found themselves in a new stable world, and changes were once more changes *in* the world. The transformations were occasional radical leaps ahead – qualitative dialectical leaps. They implied that controlling conceptual framework had to be replaced because the old framework had broken down, which would lead to chaos, if it is not replaced. Presently, however, the world *is* transformation. Life is transformation. It is the norm. One cannot solve problems to establish a new stable normality. Today a problem is not that things change. A problem is if things are stuck and cannot change. The world has no stable structure. Its transformation appears to make relations unstable and brittle. Because the world tomorrow is different from what it is today, people cannot even really know what it is today. In this situation, it may not be clear what framework controls practice, because frameworks also change. People feel that speed accelerates, and that society reacts with hurry and stress. This reaction is inadequate. It would be adequate if it was a reaction to the speed of change. If things speed up, then people need to hurry to keep up. However, if things transform, then people need to concentrate to discover the situation that is emerging and react to that. They need to be calm so that they can concentrate on that which is emerging. To cope with transformation requires a different mindset than speed and stress, one which can innovate its conceptual framework and cope with the new world. In the world of transformation, the best survivors are those who can change and transform the environment. If the environment is stable and unchangeable, then a person needs to adapt to the environment to survive. But if the surroundings transform, then they must create change within their environment, a new habitat with which they can survive. People need a mind that thrives in and contributes to transformation. The conditions to thrive and survive include being actors who can transform their environment and adapt it to themselves.

Transformation often renders preceding efforts of people irrelevant to their survival. This is a tough experience. Under the premise that everything is equal and that the world is stable, persons make themselves a master of things through learning and hard work. But then transformation comes, and they are lost. They feel betrayed by society. They trusted its advice and they became masters. But they did not learn to master transformation. They focus on mastering a profession and becoming an agile performer made them ignore the signals of emerging transformations that disrupted their profession. Society still deceptively teaches, trains, and advises people as if the world was static. But there is no more "everything is equal." The rewriting of the human mind is in process, although social ethos is sluggish and tries to resist. This analysis addresses one aspect of the challenge of rewriting the human mind: how to conceptualize a world that is in continuous change. We coin the term "agile cognition" to signify such a state of mind. It is characteristically human. It is driven by value and a sense of meaning, and aims at good quality; it is skilled, smooth, and flexible; and it works in a process of flow (Csikszentmihalyi, 2014). Further, it is a rewarding state that people enjoy. This is the kind of work people like to do no matter whether a machine could do it better. It is the skill with which human beings innovated and conquered Earth. It is the work of a master, not a slave. In the world of transformation, cognitive agility is a reflective mindset that develops and mobilizes persons' resources to make them perform, contribute, and thrive.

Agile manifesto

Agility is to possess nimbleness, move with ease and grace, be quick, smart, and clever, and have a resourceful and adaptable character (e.g., Merriam-Webster). The concept migrated into research in social fields with the attempt to renew and invigorate it (Parson, 1978; Parson et al., 1953), in educational theory through interactive, collaborative, and personal learning (Vygotzky, 1978), and in manufacturing with focus on responsiveness, speed, flexibility, and customer values (Lehigh report, 1991). In 2001, the *Agile Manifesto* (Beck & all, 2010) was formulated to outline values and principles of agile teamwork in software development. This manifesto is a reference point in agile management and our point of departure for the analysis. It illustrates how the very software developers who create the powerful controlling systems avoid being sidelined themselves by the transformations they cause. The *Agile Manifesto* lists four value preferences and 12 principles as constituting agility which we shall briefly discuss.

The four value preferences are (my phrasing) as follows:

1. individuals and interactions   over   processes and tools
2. functioning product   over   comprehensive documentation
3. recipient collaboration   over   contract negotiation and
4. responding to change   over   following a plan.

The value preferences augment agility. They do not define the concept of agility, nor do they explain what agility is. The focus on individuals and interactions over processes and tools, preference 1, is the basis for creating relations that generate performance synergy as well as intrinsic value. According to preference 2, one might think that it is the actor's performance that is agile; for instance, that for a software engineer the functioning software constitutes the agile performance. This is misleading. A product is not agile because it functions but because it has special qualities of brilliance. The agility here must be the way the actors work to develop the product. For software developers, it is the way they work, their attitudes and procedures. However, the point of the attitudes and procedures is the *cognitive process* that these attitudes and procedures facilitate. The four values are means to augment the cognitive skills and energies activated in agile performance. So although these values do help create agile performance, it is not true that a performance *is* agile because it follows these values. It is agile because of the underlying cognitive processes. The value preferences are therefore instrumental to agile performance. They are shared by a team of actors to augment their performance. The value preferences are likely to function as intended. It is, however, possible that the performance is still not agile despite the actors having implemented the value preferences. For actors to deliver an agile performance, a deeper value commitment than instrumental value preferences is needed. They need intrinsic values that give them intrinsic motivation to deliver an agile performance. The four instrumental values create cognitive space for deeper intrinsic values to control their activities.

The Agile Manifesto further lists 12 principles. In my simplified rephrasing, they are as follows:

1 highest priority is to satisfy the recipient
2 welcoming change in requirements during development
3 delivering working components frequently
4 cooperation with recipient
5 build projects around motivated individuals and support them
6 face-to-face communication works best
7 components that work are the best measures of progress
8 constant pace in the development process
9 continuous attention to technical excellence
10 simplicity
11 self-organizing teams create the best design
12 regular reflection in the team on how to improve effectiveness.

The principles outline procedures and attitudes to augment the customer values. They do not inform what an agile product or agile work is. There may be performances that are not agile despite following these principles. Many other factors influence agility in addition to the mentioned value commitment: skill and insight of the actor, work discipline. A special sign of agility in their work is the state of flow. The principles of agility are significant to every profession that is affected by ongoing transformation. The principles focus on people, values, and workflow. Principles 1–4 focus on satisfying the recipient's value, emphasizing the significance of the team's ongoing cooperation with the recipients, and adapting to changing conditions and delivering components regularly. Principles 4, 5, 11, and 12 focus on values related to the team and its members. Again, there is the formation of working relations due to face-to-face communication and interaction between individual actors – producers and recipients. This is, we shall see, the basis for generating intrinsic value and synergy. Furthermore, teams are self-organizing. The absence of hierarchical structure and autocratic leadership is significant. Principles 6–9 including also 3 and 4 are work principles which lead to intrinsic motivation driving the work. The manifesto's welcoming of ongoing change, cf. principle 2, signals its understanding and assimilation to the condition of ongoing transformation by the adaptation of the activities to changing preconditions.

The manifesto's values and principles do help actors and teams to develop agility. However, to call a practice agile because it fulfils the value preferences and principles of the manifesto is misleading. It may or may not be agile. Agility is not the procedural activity of following a certain 4+12 program. It is action in a state of flow, accomplishing things in an elegant way to contribute to specific values. For instance, agile teaching is not obediently following a teaching program, preferences, and principles, like an autocrat or a robot; it is teaching in a state of flow to assist students to become agile performers themselves. Likewise, agile leadership is not obediently following a specific program, preferences, and principles, like an autocrat or a robot; it is helping a team to develop agility in their manufacturing of quality value. The same applies to other relations, as, for instance, parenthood and other professions. The values and principles help to frame an environment for performance that is driven by agile cognition and free of autocratic and rigid control practices. Although the manifesto was written to improve the work of software development teams, it implies that IT-based control systems, as presently in use, do not operate in accordance with the 4+12 program of the *manifesto*. IT-based control systems are the antithesis of agility. They are rigid, they conflict with the principles of self-controlled teamwork, face-to-face communication, adaptation to changing conditions, the interventive approach with the recipient, as well as the adaptation to continuous transformation. The *Agile Manifesto*, on the other hand, outlines conditions that treat humans as subjects. It opposes procedures that treat people as objects to be manipulated.

Agile cognition

This analysis outlines a concept of cognitive agility as the way to succeed in handling the condition of continuous transformation, through creativity and collaboration, while downplaying the subject–object division between subjects in power and manipulated objects. There are various forms of cognition. Our focus is the process of conceptualization, that is, creating a suitable conceptual framework. Contrary to an agile cognition is a rigid and autocratic attitude. It takes a dogmatic stance to a given conceptual framework as the correct and right one that must be used. It assumes that the correct conceptual framework is being learned and trained through proper education and that after being learned, it can be used to run practice without major corrections later in life. Autocratic cognition takes the world for granted, presupposing that it is static and that the same phenomena continue to disappear and reappear. This reduces cognitive work to collect and analyze data based on the given conceptual framework, a lot which can be done by AI, and omits the conceptual work necessary to stay in touch with a world in transformation. Such attitudes to cognition create performance problems. Agile cognition is non-autocratic. A non-autocratic cognition assumes that no such correct framework exists, because different conceptual frameworks may be valid due to the complexity of the world. The complexity itself is a sign that even in a static world there are many uncovered possibilities that agile cognition can uncover through proper conceptualization. In a world in transformation however, known possibilities tend to disappear, while a range of new possibilities emerges. While autocratic cognition insists on the withering possibilities, agile cognition leads the actor to explore the emerging ones.

Agile actors are driven by values. They select goals according to their intrinsic values. Goals like fame, wealth, and influence are instrumental to generate power. However, instrumental values are not real values. Whether they are valuable depends solely on whether they are used to augment basic, intrinsic values. Thus, instrumental values may be cold, technical, and dangerous even when they serve intrinsic values. The agile actor is therefore driven by genuine intrinsic values. These are "warm" in the sense that they concern love and care for life (including one's own), that is, they include values such as friendliness, love, helpfulness, concern for people's well-being and support for people's endeavors and skills to perform, truthfulness, insight, reliability, and honesty. Agile actors aim at producing good quality. They are not fake. They do not pretend to do things that they don't do. They are accountable. When interacting they prefer to communicate face-to-face. To be driven by values differs from being driven by the desire to satisfy the norms. Norms express the conditions for acts and things to be good and socially acceptable.[2] Passing a norm (an exam) is a test for social acceptability, to be considered trustworthy and given responsibility. Then, by doing their best, the actor may further develop skills to perform at a higher level and become agile. The agile performance displays a form of advanced simplicity and beauty. It is responsive and forceful, and a state of flow. It is driven by a desire for good quality. Efficiency is for mass production, that is, automatization and IT. The difference between being a good agile performer who masters one's own profession but gets defeated by transformative disruption and being able to master transformational change itself while also mastering professional performance is the agile cognition, that is, the ability to adjust one's conceptual framework to the process of transformation. It enables an actor to continue to function. As transformation alters the conditions, they continue to perform in flow while conceptualizing and integrating transformation. They incorporate transformation in their perspective. They anticipate and prepare for it. During a lifetime, the transformation will be massive. Augmenting one's agile cognition is important. People do not need to be super-entrepreneurs to do well, but they need to make agile use of their cognitive abilities.

Agile frameworks

Abstraction and change

To organize actions, actors need a conceptual framework with which they can analyze their possibilities and their fit to their values. The framework must identify things and outline their interconnections and patterns for the actor to understand and analyze the effects of events and interventions. Given that everything always changes, one can question how it is possible that a conceptual framework can be used at different points in time. This basic question was expressed by Heraclitus with the dictum that one cannot swim in the same river twice. The reason being that the second time everything has changed – the river, the water, and the person are no longer the same. According to this argument, change dissolves the basis for any claim. Claims, concepts, and ideas have no resilience to change. Along the same line, one might argue that the current speed and rush of change might explain prevalent narratives such as post-truth, fake news, or even that concepts do not exist.

The problem is solved by concepts because they are based on abstraction. Abstraction opens a space where there can be variation and change and the thing still be the same. Concepts abstract from those variations and changes that are irrelevant for being an exemplar of the concept. Different concepts create different abstractions. For instance, human beings have varying colors and still they are human beings. The concept of a human being abstracts from most colors (and many other things) – except some colors like green or degrees of transparency. Such variabilities apply not only to general concepts of types of objects or properties, such as a human being; it also applies to concepts about specific entities such as a specific person, a city, and a river. Thus, there is an "abstract relation" between an actor's concepts and the world. To handle actions and relations the actors must conceptualize future events and act in an abstract manner so that they are able to observe if the specific occurrences match their conceptualization. The conceptual abstraction is specific to the type or specific phenomenon. Each concept creates a specific abstraction and thereby defines a different type of phenomenon or different individual. The abstraction outlines limits to the variations which are irrelevant to the type. The limit is a border.

It may be vague or sharp. If it is crossed, then the phenomenon is no longer an instance of the concept. If, for instance, the stream of water becomes too wide, it is no longer a river but a lake or an ocean. The abstraction outlines the range of change to which the concept is resilient.

The abstractions of concepts are interrelated to constitute specific models, patterns, and theories that match the structural relations in the world. The abstractions and their borders are formed to enable such patterns. They are cognitive constructs which enable the actor to analyze events and perform intentional acts, that is, to cope with change. The conceptual framework is the framework of these patterns. For a conceptual framework to function, the ability to identify phenomena and the patterns they are part of must fit so that the conceptual framework resonates with the world, that is, the possible expectations and actions it outlines must be able to be verified in practice. If, however, the actions function poorly, then there is dissonance between the conceptual framework and world. Each of the practices an actor participates in is organized by specific sub-conceptual framework. While each sub-conceptual framework must be internally coherent, the conceptual framework in its entirety may not be coherent, which makes it impossible for the actors to reflect their life consistently.

Thus, people can swim in the same river many times as long as the conceptual borders of the concepts – swimming, river, and people – are not crossed. For instance, the concept of the river is a wide flow of water running in a landscape, abstracting from the actual constant changes in shape and color and more. Although the river and the actor change, they are still the same river and the same actor. At some point, a border may be crossed – the river may dry out, it may disappear, or it may widen so that it becomes a lake or an ocean. The concepts of river, person, and swimming are all part of conceptual patterns. The river is in a landscape on Earth, a person is a special type of living being, and swimming is a special type of movement of a living being in a liquid, and humans can swim provided they are trained and not dressed too heavily. The Heraclitic question is not an unsolvable riddle, not even if everything changes, as long as the world resonates with the given conceptual framework. The stability of the resonance makes the conceptual framework resilient to the change.

However, in a world of continuous transformation, the problem of resilience to change is almost the opposite. While in a static world a resilient conceptual framework solves the problem, it is also this conceptual resilience that creates the problem. In a world of transformation, an unchanging conceptual framework is the recipe for actions to fail and systems to break down. In transformation, things are in the process of becoming something else and thereby they become outdated in the patterns of abstraction in use. In a static world, the actor–world, the actor's relations, and activities can be outlined once and for all by learning a resonant conceptual framework that reflects the social and natural conditions. When the actors have acquired such conceptual framework, then their learning is finished, and they are ready to function in society.

In a transforming world this is different. Here their cognitive endeavors must continue to form and reform their conceptual framework. It is never finished. It must always be in a process of change to enable the actor to continue to function. The actors need constant cognitive agility to adjust their conceptual framework to transforming conditions. The more agile their cognition is, the better is their conceptualization and thereby their conceptual framework and consequential performance. In a static world, the story of actors' cognition is like this: theyacquire their conceptual framework through learning and then use it as an actor. In the real changing world, this conceptual framework becomes fictive, which leads to failure, thus: the actors acquire their conceptual framework. They use it. It becomes dissonant with the changing world, and their activities become forced and ineffective. Their relations get brittle, and they get sidelined. On the other hand, the agile cognition of actors has a vivid story through the lifetime – conditions continuously transform, and resonance increases and decreases as they reform their conceptual framework and thereby open and enact new relations and possibilities. This story is a part of their self-narrative, about what they did and why. It is a story with plots, resolutions, and results. It is the story which shows the actors taking responsibility for their life. Transformation creates an additional problem. Each actor with agile cognition reconceptualizes transformation differently. This creates a problem of synchronization. The autocratic solution is to let the given conceptualization overrule the alternatives. To enforce this, systems of control are needed to prevent creative disturbances. This solution creates static organizations which develop dissonance in a world of transformation. Agile, non-autocratic organizations, on the other hand, develop direct communicative tools to synchronize the different conceptualizations – as indicated in the *Agile Manifesto*. Such synchronization integrates many ideas. This can generate synergy and develop new resonant perspectives. The possibility of synchronization is an opportunity with obvious potential for major advantages, provided leadership possesses an agile cognition that can augment the process of synchronization of the actors' conceptualizations.

Agile cognition is influenced by multiple factors, many of which are social. One factor is the complexity of the actor's concepts. Technical concepts are communicated as elements in a theory or model. In the individual cognition of the actor, the concept is likely to be more complex. If the actors know the subject well, then their concept is a whole habitus of ideas and theories about the phenomenon, one of which is the preferred one, which they mostly use in communication. A habitus-based concept that provides great understanding contains layers of possible interpretations – each involving various patterns – of the phenomenon. The habitus layers are interconnected in ways that enable the actor to explain the advantages of the preferred model. The richness of layers provides the actors with material to reflect alternative ways to define a concept and thus to reflect more agile than if they only possess a single-layered concept. A single-layer concept contains no reflective material. It is the result of simplistic learning and not supportive of agile cognition. Further, agile cognition involves the ability to calm the mind and concentrate. It senses the mood that indicates values, as well as the atmosphere that indicates new phenomena and possibilities. It combines values and possibilities in conceptualizations that create meaningful action. And its criterion for validity is its resonance, that actions realize the actor's values. To agile cognition, the conceptual framework is not only a toolbox for acting and understanding, it is also a toolbox for reflective analysis that may influence and change the conceptual framework itself. It contains methods for conceptualizing transformation and for communication that creates synergy by conceptual synchronization.

Creative cognition

The world is always more complex than a conceptual framework can accommodate. Thus, concepts are not only abstract but there are always different ways to conceptualize a situation. There is no a priori correct conceptualization. The actor has an unavoidable element of freedom of choice when conceptualizing. In cognition, their choices are guided by their understanding and intuition of what makes sense. It is not guided by their fear of deviating. They try to create a conceptualization that gives them understanding and leads to their values. Then they must wait for practice to demonstrate whether their solutions were valid. They must use their cognitive uncontrolled thinking to conceptualize the phenomena guided by their knowledge and their values. They scout for signs of emerging dissonances relevant to their values, and there are always many signs. Without agile cognition, they will lose track of their values. Agile cognition is a creative, value-driven, and explorative state. Explorers need cognitive skills, a methodology, to analyze the land that unveils before them. So does agile cognition require the use of cognitive skills, an epistemological and methodologic foundation to form resonant conceptual patterns. They need the skill to introduce divergent thinking relative to ongoing transformation and develop it into functioning patterns. There is a need for governance to cultivate the ability to identify relevant divergent ideas and conceptualize them (cf. Robinson, 2001).

> Actors have a dialogue[3] with themselves: They sit at their computer, thinking about something out of the ordinary that puzzles them. They are searching for information. Their search is guided by vague and weird questions trying to make sense of their observations that concern their values. Their questions are bold logical conjectures with which they try to make sense of their observation. When they get a promising idea, their fingers rush over the keyboard and objectivize the idea for them to see on the monitor. The idea came spontaneously as a response to their bold thinking. With a feeling of "aha," their fingers put it on the monitor.

> Then they look at their idea and evaluate it. It deviates from anything they know so far. Does it clarify the puzzle? It is as if they first discover their idea now. They enjoy the idea and find it. Then they start to question their idea and identify shortcomings. Their questions are logical. They are far from the questions that are formulated in any currently running practice. They are exploring the unknown and building conceptual roads and patterns where none yet exist. Their critical questions identify shortcomings of their idea. This creates new questions, and then supplementary ideas emerge to overcome the shortcomings, and they write them down. Out of their fingers come the ideas, and with the eyes they reflect and question them. The change between activities – question -> idea -> recognition -> criticism -> new question, etc. – continues. They are silently discussing with themselves. Soon many ideas have been put forward and analyzed. When there is no more question to be answered then the puzzle is solved, and they have a new pattern of concepts to cope with emerging phenomena.

To a person that enjoys creative work, recognizing a new idea is satisfying. The feeling of excitement regarding new ideas is rewarding and drives a positive creative loop that gives the person the motivation to disregard negative reactions from biases against divergent ideas. To a person that fears social criticism against divergent ideas, new ideas are not only exciting but they also cause anxiety, which often causes the creative process to stop. There is an untapped resource for innovative ideas, which is the task of agile teaching and leadership to activate.

The following illustrates cognitive acts and processes that typically are involved in agile cognition dialogues to develop new concepts.

1 *A question*: A question is an opening for something unknown to become known. Questions of agile cognition are questions concerning the concepts and their patterns, hinting at the existence of yet unknown phenomena and patterns. The starting point may be a feeling or observation that something is changing, that given conceptualizations do not function as expected, or similar. The actors feel that their conceptual framework does not provide them with appropriate understanding. They have an advanced sense of understanding which lead them to question their conceptualization. These questions differ from questions that call for information that is defined by their operative conceptual framework. Their questions open light rays into possible alternative conceptual patterns. They open the investigation of unknown territories and call for them to have the courage to use their cognitive freedom and analyze possible conceptual patterns that are not contained in the given conceptual framework. The actor aims at

new understanding. Their given conceptual framework understands that there is a question but delivers no answer and drives them therefore to develop the conceptual framework.

2   *Creating ideas:* The questions cause the actors to search for ideas that enable them to create conceptual patterns that give them a feeling of understanding. One cognitive activity is to ask a conceptual question, it is a different cognitive activity to create ideas – and especially ideas that answer the questions. The actors look for ideas in their head, on the Internet, by asking other people, by analyzing, and more. They even think while sleeping. They look in unlikely places and unlikely combinations of ideas. A person that is not using real time to look for unlikely ideas is not likely to find anything special. At some point, they may find an idea that solves some of the puzzles. They write it down and look at it. They feel that they understand something new. Actors get excited by their ideas. They are unique creations – the best and most advanced things that people can produce. It is hard work that demands skill and energy.

3   *Critical assessment:* Next cognitive process in an agile dialogue is a critical assessment of the idea. As they look at the idea, they reflect on its qualities, enjoy the new possibilities it opens, and the values it augments. And then they critically test the idea – is it coherent? Does it work? They analyse it and ask critical questions.

When they find shortcomings, then they formulate a new explorative question. They continue until they find no new questions that need to be answered. Then the dialogue is finished, and they have a new pattern of concepts involving new phenomena, new possibilities, and new ways to realize values.

Conceptual illusions

Agile cognition not only develops concepts. The value-driven cognition takes care that concepts are used in valid ways and that communication is not an exchange of words with little or no valid meaning. Such communication demonstrates no respect for people. A claim must be valid to be considered seriously. If it is not valid, then the question of its truth makes no sense, because then the claim only pretends to talk about the subject. But it is valid if the evidence for the claim reflects – that is, confirms or disproves – the meaning of the claim. If a concept is well-defined, then one can demonstrate its validity by analyzing whether the evidence reflects the meaning.

It is, however, a common question whether a claim is valid and really does analyze that which it pretends to analyze. When analyzing important but vague phenomena – like, for instance, agility, leadership, power, happiness, etc. – it is important to demonstrate the validity so as to avoid conceptual illusions which lead to misunderstanding and ineffective action. Thus, an analysis of such concepts is necessary. If people do not care about the clarity of their concepts, then their claims have no validity and do not mean anything – because one cannot know what they mean. This also applies to the concept of agility. There are various forms of conceptual illusions. A typical conceptual illusion is created when a concept is used as if it has an authoritative well-known meaning although it just is a vague idea. Another typical conceptual illusion is embodying inconsistencies in the way the concept is used. That a *word* is ambiguous is not a problem, if one keeps using it in the same meaning, and the context clarifies what that meaning is. But if a concept is used in incompatible ways in a communicative act, and if people are supposed to believe that it is used in one and the same meaning all the time, then a conceptual illusion is created. To avoid conceptual illusions, a cognitive culture in which people are aware of the clarity of the concepts and therefore point out unclarities and inconsistencies is necessary. With vague concepts, communicative practice gets lost in spin and illusion. One way to produce a conceptual illusion by inconsistency is by creating inconsistency between the *meaning* of the concept, that is, the literal or lexical meaning of the word that expresses the concept, and that which the concept in practice is used to *refer* to. One may, for instance, use a concept with a positive meaning to signify things that have nothing to do with that positive meaning. For example, the *meaning* of the concept "leader" may be explained as a person that is concerned with leading a group of people, guiding them to achieve certain goals. However, many people who are *referred* to as leaders do not do that, and still, they are called leaders. Some "leaders" only use formal control mechanisms without performing any leadership activities at all. Thus, there is an inconsistency between meaning and the reference. The word "leader" is used to *refer* to people in certain positions although what they do in this position does not match the *meaning* of the word. This inconsistency in the usage creates a conceptual illusion about leadership. Conceptual illusions penetrate into discussions and confuse societies.[4]

A skeptical perspective, which denies the possibility to distinguish between valid and invalid, implies that truth is lost. It implies that nothing people say can have a definitive meaning. No arguments and no reason can be real because arguments and reason all rely on valid use of concepts. Meaning would reduce to emotive reactions for or against something – and even that would become impossible, because the "something" must be specified by a concept.[5]

Action and agility

The focus on individuals in interaction in the *Agile Manifesto* leads first to consider the acting individual, the actor. The condition for being an actor is to master the conditions to act. Learning is learning to master these conditions. The difference between play and action is that the play only pretends to act. To analyze differences between pretending and acting, we analyze the cognitive conditions that a person must master to act. In a world of transformation, the problem of validity is especially important. When the meaning of concepts changes, then people need agile cognitive skills to control activities while changing the concepts. While the relation between expressed claims and expected action can be clarified in stable conditions, changing conditions make it easier to get away with scenic talk without committing oneself to any specific action but only pretending to do so (Paulsen, 2019). This makes it difficult to distinguish between valid communication and deceptive gaming by scenic illusions, which is a serious problem that is undermining democratic governance. The validity of decisions and claims involving future commitments is demonstrated by the attempts to fulfil some of the sufficient conditions for the expected activities. A claim that creates expectations for future activities is not valid if there is no attempt to realize the conditions for the activities.

The previous section concerned the abstract relation between actors and world in transformation that is created by their conceptual framework. It concluded that the validity of the conceptual frame, its resonance, is its ability to successfully guide the person in their activities to realize intended values. It is the basis of making the person into an actor in practice that produces something real and valuable and not just an actor making a show like on a scene. This section consequently analyzes conditions for acting and succeeding. It is this activity that is missing in the scenic pretense, and this activity is based on agile cognition, which pretense is unable to perform. Agile ambition is not just to satisfy a norm or the formal conditions but to optimize conditions for producing value. This section analyzes the conditions of action as the integration of four dimensions in the actor–world relational system. A resonant conceptual framework enables the actor to conceptualize ideas that integrate these dimensions. This enables them to control their activities and generate relations to structure their activities successfully. If the conditions for actions are not satisfied, then the actor must find a way to satisfy them or give up acting. It is a task of learning and leading to cultivate people's skills to organize and control these conditions. And because the conditions transform, the actors need special cognitive agility to re-establish integration and thereby their ability to act.

Integration

The condition for action to be performed and succeed is the integration of four dimensions in the actor–world relationship: values, facts, possibilities, and communication.[6] Actions need to be motivated by *values* that define the goal and commit the actor. Further, actors need a basis of *factual knowledge*, so that they know where they stand. They need to have *possibilities* that are real and not only speculative. This means that the possibilities must be factual, that is, grounded in facts such that they can be realized. Otherwise, they would not be relevant. Further, the possibilities must encompass the values so that they are factually possible and can be realized. With this integration of facts, possibilities, and values, an individual actor can, in principle, act and realize values. Their possibilities and acts are, however, insignificant without cooperation with other actors. To realize values and possibilities, cooperation is needed to get access to a basis with powerful possibilities as well as social values. Thus, it is also a condition that the factual possibilities and values are *communicated* and understood among participating actors. If these conditions are satisfied, then the actors are motivated and can produce the values and distribute them to value receivers through cooperation. Integration of these dimensions is a *sufficient* condition for human activity – building houses, performing a research project, or anything. If, on the other hand, possibilities are not factual, values are not within the range of the possibilities, or if the project is communicated poorly to the actors, then the value realization suffers. These dimensions are aspects of the actor's relations to the world. Facts, possibilities, values, and communication are neither entities nor properties. They are relational structures. Their integration must be reflected in the actor's conceptual framework for it to resonate. The facts are the actor's knowledge about the world, based on observational evidence. The possibilities link the factual situation of the actor to possible futures. The values are their personal motivations, their desires, and concerns – for others, themselves, and the conditions in the world. Communication is their relation to other actors and even to themselves. The integration of the dimensions enables actors to collaborate to influence future values. Reductivist conceptualizations on the other hand, which only focus on some of these dimensions, are dissonant and unable to guide actors. Integration means more than putting things together. Integration is an inherent connection – when the one is present then so is the other. Factual possibilities do not mean that there are facts and possibilities next to each other, but that the possibilities are in the facts. The possibility to make a call is inherent in the factually existing mobile in the actor's hand, not something next to it. The value of a good book is not something outside the book. The possibility to drink a cup of coffee is not something that exists outside the cup of coffee. Facts, possibilities, and values are integrated. If possibilities and values are integrated with the facts, then they are real, that is, they can be realized. Realization of values is the realization of possibilities that integrate the values. Finally, for people to understand each other and cooperate their communication must integrate the relevant facts, possibilities, and values. Thus, integration must involve communication – when one of the dimensions is not communicated, cooperation may fail. In a static world, a given conceptual framework encompasses the integration needed to organize the activities. Learning them is a one-time process and management and leadership only need to coordinate the activities. A world in transformation involves constantly changing conditions for action. This disintegrates the four dimensions. Thus, there is a constant need to create new integration. There is, however, no a priori way to integrate the dimensions. The actor is logically free to try anything – of course the better their knowledge of the preceding world, the better they can use conditions that are not yet changed, but as to the new emerging conditions, they need a strategy with which to explore the unknown, learning from every step on the way. Agile cognition is therefore important in all activities. The factual basis constantly changes, not only in quantity but also through the emergence of new types of phenomena and structures. A new factual basis must therefore constantly be conceptualized and integrated. The values change and must be reintegrated – the things that once were good are seen as less valuable when new values emerge. The horizon of possibilities develops and transforms immensely. Knowledge about possibilities almost explores with new knowledge and its many synergies. Agile cognition must constantly work to develop and integrate new possibilities. As communication transforms as new communicative systems are formed, thereby accelerating the synergetic transformative effects. Agile cognition is needed to integrate the many attempts to reconceptualize the conditions, thereby creating complex synergetic integration patterns. Transformations open great integrational possibilities, a field of unknown possibilities for actors with agile cognition to explore and populate with integrative structures that enable actors to contribute to the transformation.

Facts, values, and possibilities

Knowledge based on solid empirical evidence is knowledge about facts. Facts that are not known make no sense. Thus, facts as knowledge are relational structures between the knowing subject and the known phenomena. The difference between knowledge and facts is that knowledge refers to the knowing subject, while calling something a fact leaves it open for anybody to be the knowing subject. That something is a fact means that the knowledge is based on observational evidence using well-established concepts. In addition to factual knowledge, people create uncertain and hypothetical visions, beliefs, and narratives about the world. An actor needs a cognitive basis in the form of basic factual knowledge about who they are, what they are, where they are, what is around them, what their situation is, what their job is, etc. Without this knowledge, they cannot act. In addition, they need factual knowledge of more distant phenomena – that they are at a location on Earth, that they are a human being, and that there are many other types of phenomena, etc. These are the phenomena which the actors rely upon as factually true to perform their activities. Whether some specific factual knowledge is relevant to the actors depends on their situation. Thus, knowledge of their situation and the conditions for what they intend to do are conditions for their action. It is not just any factual knowledge that is relevant to the integration. They need factual knowledge about their situation. Facts are not things in the world. The world is not made of facts. Facts cannot be observed, things can. Facts can only be ascertained. For instance, a house can be seen, and it can be seen to be red. The fact that the house is red cannot be seen, it is nowhere, and has neither shape nor color because facts are relational structures, aspects of the actor–world relational complex. In a world of transformation, the nature of the actor's factual basis constantly changes, not only in quantity. To maintain conceptual framework resonance, it is not sufficient to update information in the form of facts, the conceptual basis for the information must change.

To function as an actor, it is not sufficient to have a collection of data. Not even the sum of all big data in the world enables a person to be an actor. Something other than a list of data and facts is needed: values, possibilities, and cooperative partners. They must be integrated with the facts. As with facts, values are not special entities nor are they properties. For something to be a value, it must be a value *to* someone, that is, it treats people and life as having intrinsic value. The value of something is its significance to something else – a person, a creature, or a piece of equipment – that makes something have value. Things are not values in themselves. Instrumental values of equipment and resources, etc. do not have value in themselves but only as instruments to intrinsic values. These are the values of life and well-being – that is, activity and happiness – of people and living beings. The intrinsic values are the intrinsic motivation in agile cognition. Instrumental values must support intrinsic values. All organization of activities serves the realization of values. Actors are value producers as well as value receivers. No fact, no possibility, and no communication are relevant without contributing to production and reception of values. Transformation influences the conditions and relations in which value production and distribution take place. Things lose their value and new things become valuable. Values cannot be produced and received as they were previously. Thus, the value drive of an agile activity involves agile cognition to maintain integration and thus the ability to act. The values that structure and drive the activities of a project are the intended end value, that is, the recipient's values. However, they are not the only values in a performance. All involved actors have intrinsic value that must be addressed.

Although most activities in the short term aim at instrumental values, an agile performance seeks the underlying intrinsic values. If activities are motivated by instrumental values only, then the contribution is not driven by the desire to do the best possible. However, people do want to do their best because it makes their life good – as lovers, parents, friends, and workers. People love to do their best. Not doing the best one can is wasting one's skills. The intrinsic commitment of actors gives them the perseverance in learning and satisfaction to develop agile performance (compare Ryan & Deci, 1988). Exclusive concern for instrumental values causes actors to lose touch with their intrinsic values and the feeling of meaning, and thus to face a life crisis. Then they need to rediscover their intrinsic values, for instance, by recognizing their emotional reactions to things. An agile actor must be sensitive to value signals. Although emotive reactions signal the values of a person, this does not mean that values *are* emotive reactions. Values are formed through experience and reflection including reflection of our emotive reactions. Reflections may conclude that something that people emotionally like is not a value – for instance, because it is unhealthy or dangerous. The reflections do influence our feelings and promote self-control.

> Metaphysical claims that values are transcendent and belong to another realm rules out people as agile actors, because then their values cannot be integrated in the practical world. Such a world might well still have systems of instrumental values, but they would be systems of dependencies that are without meaning.
>
> Positivism and the early language philosophy (Moore, 1903) have considered facts as void of empirical norms and values. To the young Wittgenstein (Wittgenstein, 1922) the world consists of facts, and ethics is outside the world. One argument for such a position is Hume's guillotine (Hume, 1739). Hume argues that there is an is-ought-gap because, it is logically impossible to reach a normative conclusion of the form "A ought to do B" from any set of factual premises of the form "X is Y." If this argument is valid, then there cannot exist any fact-norm integration, which would create problems for the fact-value integration.
>
> However, Hume's argument is based on syllogistic logic for simple categorical statements. It disregards the propositional logic that addresses complex statements. The following argument proves Hume to be mistaken: premise 1 "If person A participates in game G, then A ought to follow the rules of G". Premise 2: "A does participate in game G". Conclusion: "A ought to follow the rules of G." Premise 1 is a self-evident premise, explaining what it means to participate in a game. Premise 2 is an empirical premise. Both premises are of a factual character, and not normative. The conclusion is normative. The rule of inference is modus ponens. The inference is valid. One cannot participate in a game without being committed to the rules. Thus, obligatory values are integrative with facts.

Possibilities are also phenomena that are not perceptible. In the list of things in the world, there are stars and people and more, but there are no possibilities. For instance, on an actor's desk is a pot of water. The actor may drink it, boil it, water the flowers with it, and more. These are possibilities. They are not standing on the actor's table next to the pot of water. They are not to be seen anywhere. They are embedded in the pot of water. But if they become realized then they get an appearance – but then they are real and not possibilities anymore.[7] To analyze change, the category of possibility is necessary. It delimits the horizon of things that something can produce through a certain change, for example, through a certain action. The impossible is similarly something that a certain change cannot produce. Change is transition from possible to real and from real to impossible: something that is possible becomes real, and something that is real disappears into the unchangeable past where it is impossible to change or to recover it. Only people's knowledge of the past can be changed.

Since possibilities as such are not perceptible, knowledge of possibilities must be reflective constructs, created with the help of reflective tools such as concepts, imagination, logic, and mathematical systems and models. For each empirical concept, one can imagine an infinity of possibilities. For example, with the concept "apple," one can imagine all kinds and any number of apples anywhere. They are logical possibilities and exist only as abstract ideas. But if they are hungry for an apple, they are looking for places where it is likely to find them. They "move" from abstract imagination of logically possible apples to empirical search for real apples. And if they find an apple, it leaves their sphere of possibility. Possibilities are – like values – relational: they are possibilities for someone or something to do or perceive something. Abstract possibilities are automatically constructed by observers' conceptualization of their observation. The concepts that structure people's perception automatically invoke a horizon of alternative possibilities. The concept outlines what things can do and thus what possibilities there are belonging to the type of things, possibilities that are embedded in the abstraction that constitutes the concept. The level of possibilities actors can conceive depends on their knowledge and reflective skills. Some possibilities are factual because they are supported by empirical evidence – that is, they are integrated in the facts; others are speculative. There are various degrees in between speculative and factual possibilities, and possibilities that appear as speculative may be made factual by using agile cognition to develop methods to realize them. For factual possibilities to be relevant in a specific actor's integration, they need to be possibilities that the actor can enact. They need to be able by their actions to activate the antecedent conditions that trigger the realization of the possibilities.[8] Through innovative combinations of related factual possibilities, new technological causal chains are created to realize advanced goals and values.

Communication

The fourth dimension to be integrated is communication, which aims at establishing common understanding necessary for cooperation. The section first outlines the concept of understanding as the cognitive skills that enable the persons to act and cope with their situation. The agile perspective on understanding emphasizes the values – especially intrinsic values – that are used to lead and organize the string activities. This involves the narratives to outline plots of activities and events aiming at realizing values. Narratives create major synergy. And, since narratives are the basis, it leads to the focus on intrinsic values.

However, the ongoing process of transformations hollows out established understanding by disrupting established integrative patterns, sidelining the consequential actions. Thus, transformation demands reintegration, that is, agile cognition. To accomplish this agile communication must use dialogues to re-establish understanding and cooperation. The section finishes by analyzing the dialogue to create understanding as a double loop that integrates a loop around the topic based on transformational challenge and the understanding of the other person.

Understanding

> "How can you do that?" – "Because I *understand* how it works."
> "Why can't you do that?" – "Because I don't *understand* how it is done."

Understanding and action

The purpose of communication is to establish common understanding to enable cooperation. The meaning of communication is its consequences for action. To understand what communication means is to understand its consequences for subsequent actions. Subsequent actions may be subsequent communicative actions. But if it has no consequences or if the consequent actions only are repetitions of the utterance, then it has no meaning. This connection between utterance and consequential actions is the basis for validity. Various forms of gaming and spooky communication pretend to imply consequent actions only for later to deny these consequences. Communication unfolds in communicative patterns (language-games, Wittgenstein, 1953) of interacting actors. The meaning of the communicative patterns is that actors perform certain activities when specific conditions occur. Understanding the meaning comes down to knowing the implication for one's activities, and if it has no such implications, then it has no meaning. The activities may be practical, observational, calculative, or communicative. Understanding therefore generates specific expectations for people's activities. This inherent connection between communication and possible subsequent action determines the sincerity and validity of the communication.

It follows that to understand is not a passive contemplative state in which persons feel and contemplate their understanding. To understand is to know what and how to do (Wittgenstein 53). The feeling of an "aha," or "heureka!", when one suddenly understands, is not the understanding, but the excitement that one feels by believing that they have achieved understanding. Understanding is also not a single event. It is a state of mind, a flow, in which a person acts without needing to stop and reconsider what to do. It is a natural state in which persons have access to their field of knowledge. The agile actors act based on understanding which is created through the resonance of their conceptual framework. Their feeling that they understand is their way to perceive the resonance of their conceptual framework.

Actors may feel motivated to act spontaneously based on their feelings. However, when they act based on understanding, then they are not guided by blind feelings, beliefs, and somebody else's advice or command. Then they act based on the insight that their conceptualization gives them. If they understand, then they continue to act in a state of flow. If they encounter something they do not know, then they gather the knowledge, still being in flow; but if they encounter something they do not understand, then they need reflection to revise their conceptualization with ideas that re-establish integration.

Understanding and explanation

Understanding and explanation have been considered alternative paradigms – explanation being concerned with objective descriptions and causal mechanisms and understanding with a subjective state of mind. However, they are not alternative but complementary in ordinary usage. When persons understand something, then they are expected to be able to explain it. Their ability to give a comprehensible explanation is a test of their understanding. A good way to achieve proper understanding of something is to develop the skill to explain it. This training forces persons to improve their understanding by revealing their weaknesses. In this way, people also learn what it means to understand.

Understanding is not restricted to something conscious or something intentional. Understanding is not restricted to special intentional objects. Understanding is a sign that one knows, how it functions and therefore, how it relates to possible actions. One can understand physical mechanism as well as the development and behavior of living organisms including conscious and intentional beings, and one can understand the other as a person that has intrinsic value including intrinsic value to oneself. Understanding relates to desires, values, meaning, causes, conditions, and more that influence the forces of change that control time. Meaning and values are human signatures – they are not needed to understand physical processes. But depriving them from humans even in their communication is loss of humanity. In this way, the extended use of IT control systems endangers humanity. It involves a manipulation of language that weakens the human nature of communication. The principle of face-to-face communication of the *Agile Manifesto* is significant to uphold understanding and maintain a human character in work and living spaces.

Understanding and value

For communication to succeed in coordinating activities, mutual understanding is needed. An agile approach considers understanding differently than a more instrumental approach. Instrumentally, understanding is restricted to technical knowledge about the topic. If there are values involved, then they are treated as instrumental values. Even if the topic is basic, it is treated as instrumental – that is, in a disinterested way that is abstracting from what values mean to the participating actors. This cognitive separation of actor and value makes values instrumental and alien. It reduces the actors' value drive and thus the performance of the actor is reduced to a show because one cannot separate the intrinsic values of one's life from what one is doing. An agile approach reflects the significance of the values not only to an end receiver but also to colleagues and others. It treats actors as people, not as robots. They do not separate the values from their practice. Thus, to an agile actor, understanding of a topic is not only understanding its technicalities but also understanding what it means to people in praxis as well as in theory. Communication is not cold information into an objective and abstract sphere, which people must "understand." It enables people to understand what things mean to action and to each other. Agile understanding in this double sense is essential to make communication integrate values and make cooperation attractive. To reduce understanding to the technical meaning leads to a cold world, in which all values are instrumental, and no values are real. The agile value drive becomes fictive if the values they pursue are instrumental only.

Understanding things involves understanding the values it affects. Without understanding the value of things, one cannot understand. Since instrumental values depend on the value of something else which they affect, one cannot understand value without understanding their effect on the underlying intrinsic values that drive the actor, such as, for instance, the value of life, happiness, benevolences, or love – whatever they are. A basic value is, for instance, the value of truth. Without understanding being motivated by the concern for truth, one cannot not understand the meaning of any claim.

The value of truth emerges as one of the conditions for communication-based cooperation. It enables people to develop productive synergy in cooperation. And it makes the actors become unique individuals who have an irreplaceable value to each other. Irreplaceability is a sign of basic intrinsic value. When people meet, they are not irreplaceable to each other. But through development of synergetic relations created by interaction they become irreplaceable in the relation – whether in family, in work, in friendship, or in any other context. On the contrary, a negative effect of mass economy emerges, when people systematically are treated as replaceable units, as a piece of equipment – a replaceable member of a workforce or a class. This treats people in a manner that eliminates their unique individuality, and the possible relational synergy of agile cognition to which they could contribute is replaced with a standard program as if people are robots. Thus, the constitution of the individual as an irreplaceable value is a foundation of value and therefore a condition for understanding. Development of synergetic relations creates mutual understanding and trust (Liboriussen et al., 2022). Understanding leads to trust if it produces a synergetic relation. Trust presupposes ethics. The actors' commitment to the expectations created by the understanding of communication underscores the value load of the communication. This makes communication-based understanding a basis for social ethics. If actors do not feel committed to the actions implied by the narratives, then they are playing games to deceive and manipulate the other. If a communicator is trustworthy, then one can rely upon the expectations that are caused by communicator's narratives. The ethical reliability is the validity of the communicated claim (cf. the earlier discussion of Hume's guillotine). Participating in communication is committing oneself to be trustworthy and not to create expectations unless they are credible.[9] A culture of communicative deception is unproductive. The value commitment that drives agile cognition leads to avoidance of empty language-gaming. Instead, it focuses on creating a synergetic integration between the different insights of the actors. Relations between people who are unable to produce synergetic integration get uninteresting and brittle.

Narratives and synergy

The concepts that organize practices integrate the four dimensions to function. Practice is based on narratives that organize lines of actions involving actors, plots, and tools in various conditions to realize specific values to generate a live story. The narratives outline how the lines of actions and plots affect the realization of values. The effect of a specific action is limited by the narrow range of integrable possibilities. However, symbolic representation of actions enables people to combine actions in narrative storylines that create synergies which enables much greater possibilities and values to be realized. Thus, communication of shared narratives in which the different actors play different roles is the basis for effective organization of human actors.

Thus, there are two aspects of practical reason to be combined in a narrative: the validity of the specific action, that is, of the integration of factual possibilities and values that enables it, and the validity of the narrative storyline. The validity of the storyline depends on its consistency. The storyline itself as well as the underlying conditions of integration of the activities must be consistent. The communicated narrative storyline creates synergy by integrating how different actors consider integration in their cooperation. The holistic aspect of practical reason concerns the quality and validity of the narrative, while the detailed analytical aspects concern the quality and validity of the specific acts. The specific acts are tied to different professional roles, each involving specific concepts and criteria for integration. The overall narrative outlines plots involving a variety of professions to realize complex possibilities. The holistic reason analyzes the coherence of the narrative and develops conceptual topos (strategy plans, visions, missions, etc.) to guide the development of the narrative.

Transformation disrupts integration

In a static world, actors are familiar with the roles and activities of the operating narratives through education and training. Transformation on the other hand implies that narratives and integrative patterns are being outdated and disrupted and must be replaced by new ones. In a static world, the realization of possibilities involves a continuous process of marginal quantitative changes that result in qualitative transformations – for instance, trees become timber, timber becomes ships, houses, etc., or, soil and water become plants, plants become food that becomes an animal, etc. The transformation is indicated by the conceptual shift as, for instance, from "timber" to "house." The transformation is captured in the operating conceptual framework, which forms the basis for operating narratives. Thus, practice organizes activities as processes of transformation. These narratives and actions are not experienced as transformational but as normal because they already are conceptualized, integrated, and part of ordinary practice. Static societies are systems of repeated transforming activities. This repetition is the basis for the static character. Such society has no need for agile cognition.

Transformations that cause disruption and thus dissolve the static society are transformations that destroy the integration basis for existing practices. With this destruction, a given conceptual framework is no longer valid. It does not provide understanding; and the narratives it expresses are no longer effective. New abstractions, integrative conceptualizations, and narratives are needed. To create that agile cognition is needed. Agile cognition is the most important skill for sustainable practice under conditions of transformation. Reason itself must be agile. Thinking is not repetition of given ideas but production of new ideas to cope with the changing conditions. The brain is not supposed to rest. The narratives involve actions that realize different types of possibilities. Thus, the process of formulating a narrative presupposes high-level insight into the development of different fields. A good narrative is therefore a co-authorship (Nørreklit, 2011). Without co-authoring, the narrative becomes simplistic and prone to contain elements that are already overtaken. The role of teaching and leading changes from authoritative dictating the narrative to supporting and guiding in conducting co-authorship.

Agile communication

Under static conditions people can develop overlapping conceptual frameworks. They understand each other because they interpret situations similarly, they use similar patterns of integration and similar narratives.

Disruptive transformation on the other hand creates understanding problems. The shared conceptual framework loses validity, integration dissolves, and narratives lose relevance. In this situation, many actors use agile cognition to produce new ideas to understand things through creative cognition. A plurality of different conceptual frameworks emerges containing many new contributions.

This dissolves mutual understanding, and a problem of understanding emerges. When understanding between actors breaks down, then conversation and ordinary communication stop. Mutual understanding must be reestablished. An actor must not only understand the topics of this activities, he must also understand how other actors understand the topics. To bypass the understanding of the other is authoritarian, dissolves possible synergies, and creates simplistic performance. Actors need to understand how other actors understand the phenomena to cooperate and create synergy.

To establish new mutual understanding, actors engage in a creative dialogue with each other in which their agile cognition reaches out to understand and integrate the understanding of the other. In the dialogue, the actors perform a hermeneutic circle (Gadamer, 1975). They share and reflect their views on the topic to create a common perspective. This communication is a creative dialogue, in which the actors explain and reflect their ideas until a common understanding is achieved. When mutual understanding is established, the looping process of the dialogue is finished. A dialogue does not make people's different conceptual framework become identical. It enables them to develop sufficiently similar conceptual patterns to understand each other, cooperate, and inspire each other. It develops conceptual integration of their different perceptions to create the synergies upon which ultimately society is built. If all four dimensions are integrated, then activities can succeed.

The analysis of understanding so far is only concerned with the conceptualization of the topic, what one might call its objective aspects. Important to understanding is however the value which involves what it means to the actors. If it has the same meaning and represents the same values to the actors, this may not pose any problem, but often the difference in conceptualization is an expression of value differences. In this case, the actors cannot achieve a shared understanding without understanding what the topic means to the other and how this differs from what it means to the actors themselves. The problem is that understanding so far has been focused on understanding the topic and not on understanding and respecting people, specifically the other. There has been an implicit authoritarian approach that only one understanding is the right one. This approach makes dialogue impossible. It transforms the communication to a discussion that is a fight for having right. This destroys the agility of the communication. The agility is committed to basic value, which involves the value of the people with whom one communicates. Agile communication combines the understanding of the topic (conceptual integration of different actors' conceptualization) with understanding what the topic means to the other.

Double-loop understanding and co-authorship

Cooperation is based on combining a shared understanding of the topic of cooperation – that is, the relevant factual possibilities and values – with an understanding of the cooperating partners. This complex understanding is established by combining two loops in the dialogue: a loop to understand the topic and a loop to understand the other actor (cf. double-loop hermeneutics, Nørreklit, 2012). Both loops are important, and both are based on agile cognition.

The topic-loop

The process of producing a shared understanding of a topic is a dialogue, preferably face-to-face, that creates a communicative loop (hermeneutic circle) in which the participants take turns expressing their conceptualization of the topic and reflect that of the other. The understanding of the topic with which an actor enters the dialogue – actor's so-called pre-understanding – is gradually modified until they reach a common understanding in the form of a merging of their cognitive horizon. The presumption is that both actors are capable of contributing in order to enlighten the topic, and that a synthesis of their views produces a valuable synergy of insight, which is the goal of the topic-loop. The ability of creating synergetic topic-loops increases understanding and drives development.

The actor-loop

The attempts to reach common understanding may transform into a defensive discussion in which the actors want to convince the other that their interpretation of the topic is correct, and the other is mistaken. This either-or position excludes the possibility of a positive synergy of views and implies that they consider the other as having an inferior understanding. During the communication, signals may create anxiety or anger in one of the participants, which causes a distortion of the agile cognition and instead invokes a defensive posture. To avoid this problem, the actors need to understand each other, especially their pre-understanding of the topic and what it means to the actor. A pre-understanding of a topic is not only an understanding of the topic but very much an understanding of what the topic means to the actor, and how the actor must respond to maintain a good position. Thus, the pre-understanding is not only a cognitive lens with which to perceive the topic but a shield to protect the actor. If the actors' understanding of the topic is a defense against alternative interpretations that seem dangerous to them, then the actors are in a defensive mode and agile cognition sidelined. Then dialogue is replaced by defensive argumentation that tries to destroy the alternative views of the other instead of generating a synthesis with them.

> *A* and *B* discuss methodology. They disagree. *A* claims qualitative methods are best – they provide insight and understanding. *B* claims that they are subjective and not reliable – to obtain reliable knowledge, quantitative methods must be used. They debate for decades. They loop around the topic. They do not understand each other.
>
> Imagine they both start including an actor-loop in their communicative efforts. *B* finds out that *A* was bad in math at school – *A* was bullied by the teacher, but *A* was good in literature and psychology. *A* found out

> that B shined in math while insecure in literature and psychology. When they discover this about each other, their attitudes may change, because now they understand the other. The discussion can now transform into a dialogue. A still does not understand math, and B does not understand the qualitative approach. But they accept that the other has an important point of view. A is helping B to understand qualitative things. B is helping A with math. For years, they had not been interested in each other's subjective experiences, they did not consider it as important, and they did not like to display any weakness. Thus, they did not understand each other and were quarreling. But now they know that their previous opinions were subjectively biased and not an expression of agile cognition. Now they understand each other, synergy through cooperation and co-authorship can develop. In a proper understanding, both views are relevant.

To avoid such derailments of dialogues that should produce understanding, agile actors communicate so that they not only convey understanding of the topic but also of each other, especially what the topic means to each other. If actors do not understand what the topic means to the other, then they may trigger a defensive communication that blocks mutual understanding. Thus, it is a communicative task of the actors not only to communicate their interpretation of the topic but also why they interpret it in this way and what it means to them. Likewise, it is a communicative task of the actors to interpret not only what the other claims about the topic but also what the topic means to them. To do this, the actors invoke an actor-loop similarly to the topic-loop to develop understanding of the other. In the actor-loop, the actors signal interpretations of what the topic means to them and what they imagine it means to the other, and the interprets the reactions of the partners as signals to the adequacy of their interpretations. The purpose is to avoid anxiety, anger, or similar outcomes which can block agile cognition, and instead play positively into the values of the other. Thus, they form their communication to eliminate reasons for anxiety or anger and instead appeal to the values of the other.

The linking of the topic to its meaning and value to the actors is integral in the agile focus on values. One cannot consistently "theoretically" be value-driven while at the same time abstracting from the lived values in relation to partners and environment. Actors contributing to synergetic co-conceptualizations using their agile cognition are co-authors of the group's contribution to transformation. To participate, team members prepare and contribute their special integrative ideas concerning the common task and contribute to the synthesizing cognition in team meetings. Without prior personal development of ideas, meetings may become superficial brainstorms which reiterate already prevalent ideas.

The agile self

The *Agile Manifesto's* emphasis of self-organizing groups and individual actors highlights individuality, cooperation, and self-control. The person is an individual actor who is responsible to control one's own activities, contrary to being controlled by authoritarian top-down means. By self-control, we mean that actors control their activities based on a sense of who they are and want to be, their Self. We define the Self as a special form of relation, namely as relation, which relates to itself (compare Kierkegaard's definition of Self, Kierkegaard, 2012, pp. 129–130). The actors relate to the world based on who they are, and they relate to themselves. Thus, we consider the Self–World relations and the Self–Self relation.

An actor is not just a person; the actors are specific persons with a special identity which they cannot help but constantly enact in the way they live. This is the Self–World relationship. They experience that they have history, and that the history influences the kind of persons they are. They form a concept about themselves as a person acting in a certain way, a Self. From then on, they can form their values and influence who they want to be. Their activities become controlled by their intentions. Recognizing their history, they can evaluate what they are doing and what direction and relations in the world they want to realize. They can decide where and how to live, what to do, whom to relate to, etc. Thus, their Self–Self relation operates and influences their Self–World relationship, and they begin to form a life story that involves themselves as an actor. Now, their Self oversees their activities, endeavors, and relations. Since there is no a priori way to integrate the conditions of action, the Self is confronted with an open horizon of conceivable possibilities. The work to analyze which of them are both valuable and can become factually possible is the task of agile cognition. The ability of the Self to influence the actor's course of action depends on the commitment to agile cognition. The ability to maintain a certain control depends on the ability to conceptualize the disruptive transformation by enacting important values. If, for instance, the actors consider themselves in an authoritarian way, then this influences not only their behavior and relations but also their cognition. They lose flexibility and creativity, and transformation will create problems for them. The actors have an internal narrative about who they are. With agile cognition, they actively influence the narrative and lead it in the direction of their values in the stream of transformational changes.

The Self is a concept that relates to the Other as a complementary concept, as the agile actor in the *Manifesto* works in teams. Teams act as communities based on shared values and mutual understanding. Existing in interactive relations, each person is a Self that is interacting with another person that also is a Self, but another Self. Being another does not mean not being a Self, it means being another Self. A person cannot become a Self without interacting with another. The individuality of the Self is constituted in interaction with other Selves. In the beginning of the interaction, the actor is still replaceable. However, the continuing interaction creates a valuable uniqueness in which the actors become irreplaceable and thus of intrinsic value. The formation of selfhood is created by agile cognition through which persons constitute their individuality in relation. The task of the Self is to pursue values that create loving and ethical relations, the basis of happiness. The opposite of the Self, the Other, is another Self that tries to produce good values with others and thus depends on agile communication as any other Self. The other is no anti-Self. Demonizing the other as a creature with no concern for values is therefore demonizing oneself.

The agile Self is committed to maintaining and strengthening agile cognition, the commitment to values and the concern to maintain a live conceptual framework that resonates with and contributes to ongoing transformations by innovative integrative ideas. The abstractions create room top cope with changes and are also able to integrate ideas of cooperative partners. This leads to strong creative relations, intrinsic values, and healthy groups and communities.

The agile Self that is controlling the actor–world relations is the basis for agile control and leadership. It is the basis of self-control of any actor, and as an extension it is the basis of agile leadership of groups and communities. To lead a community or group a holistic perspective that combines actors and world is important in addition to the agile cognition. The power of agile leadership is its exemplary commitment to inspire the group to pursue intrinsic values and the skill created by agile cognition to envision how these values can be made factually possible. Leading by instrumental values will not do from an agile perspective. Its value commitment cannot be convincing, and "instrumental value" may mean anything, even the very opposite of valuable. For instance, many things have great destructive value, including many elements of leadership. This does not mean that they have great value but only that their instrumental value, that is, their effectiveness to destruct, is high. The power of agile leadership is its status as inspiring exemplar, its status as role model loved by the group and admired by the success its team creates. It serves intrinsic values and nourishes the development of agile cognition, creative relations, and community. Agile leadership does not need negative and threatening techniques to control people.

Autocratic leadership on the other hand does not lead by inspiration. It is no role model. It does not represent inspiration of the good but leads by the power to threaten and destroy. Its motive is fear. That is not able to lead by showing how the good values create a good life. To lead by aggressivity and threat is bad leadership. It may maintain power, but it creates little that is good. It is a waste of time and causes suffering.

In a time, when IT systems have enabled the creation of immense centralized control and hidden power, the danger of autocratic leadership is especially immanent, the symbolic effect of the *Agile Manifesto* aiming at mastering control of development of IT systems is symbolically inspiring.

Notes

1 Please always use a gender-neutral reading.
2 Cf. on the ethics of goodness, Nørreklit (2013, 2021).
3 Dialogue is used to refer to the interplay between complementary cognitive processes, not a conversation between two people. It may involve any number of people.
4 This challenges the Wittgensteinian theory that meaning *is* use, because a reference is a use, and it may be inconsistent with the meaning. If meaning was use, then there could be no misuse.
5 Many studies analyze severe dissolutions of the conceptual grip of reality: empty signifiers (Lévi-Strauss, 1987). defactualization (Arendt, 1972), simulacrum (Baudrillard, 1995), post-truth analysis (Keys, 2004) dissolving the basis of knowledge and recognition, and liquid thinking (Bauman, 2000), which combines these issues in the perception of the world as ongoing change. The present analysis aims at illuminating the skill of the agile actor to structure activities and realize values in a liquid world despite its Heraclitic nature.
6 Cf. Pragmatic Constructivism (e.g., Nørreklit 2011, 2012, 2017, 2020).
7 Ordinarily modal logic considers the factual as possible – if it was impossible, then it could not be a fact. In ordinary usage, it may however be a misleading understatement to call something that is known to be true, possible.
8 Zinkernagel (1962) coined the concept of action possibilities as an important element in the conditions of description.
9 In the Wittgenstein claim that the meaning of an expression is its use, the word "use" is here taken to refer to the activities it implies or gives rise to. Manipulative communication plays with misleading people concerning intended implications.

References

Arendt, Hannah. (1972). *Crises of the Republic: Lying in Politics, Civil Disobedience on Violence, Thoughts on Politics, and Revolution*. Houghton: Mifflin Harcourt.
Baudrillard, J. (1995). *Simulacra and Simulation*. Ann Arbor, MI: University of Michigan Press. ISBN: 0-472-06521-1.
Bauman, Zygmunt. (2000). *Liquid Modernity*. Cambridge: Polity Press, ISBN: 978-0-7456-2409-9
Beck, K., Grenning, J., Martin, R.C., Beedle, M., Highsmith, J., Mellor, S., Bennekum, A. van, Hunt, A., Schwaber, K., Cockburn, A., Jeffries, R., Sutherland, J., Cunningham, W., Kern, J., Thomas, D., Fowler, M., & Marick, B. (2001). Manifesto for agile software development. Agile Alliance. Retrieved from (2010) https://www.agilealliance.org
Buber, M. (1923). *Ich und Du*. Stuttgart: Reclam.
Csikszentmihalyi, Mihaly. (2014). *Flow and the Foundations of Positive Psychology: The Collected Works of Mihaly Csikszentmihalyi*. Dordrecht: Springer. ISBN: 978-94-017-9087-1
Gadamer, Hans-Georg. (1975). Hermeneutics and social science. *Cultural Hermeneutics*, 2(4): 307–316. https://doi.org/10.1177/019145377500200402.S2CID:144463701.
Hume, D. (1739). *A Treatise on Human Nature*. London: John Noon.
Keyes, Ralph. (2004). *The Post-Truth Era: Dishonesty and Deception in Contemporary Life*. New York: St. Martin's.
Kierkegaard, S. (2012) [1849]. *Sygdommen til Døden*. København: SK Forskningscenteret.
Iacocca Institute at Lehigh Universität in Bethlehem/Pennsylvania. (1991). "*Lehigh report*" – "*21st Century Manufacturing Enterprise Strategy: An Industry-led View*". Lehigh Univ. (1 Nov. 1991) ISBN-10: 0962486647, ISBN-13: 978-0962486647.
Lévi-Strauss, C. (1987) [1950]. *Introduction to Marcel Mauss*. Translated by Baker, Felicity. London: Routledge. ISBN: 9780710090669.

Liboriussen, J., Nørreklit, H., & Trenca, M. (2021). A learning method of trust building: beyond the performance management of artistic event. *Qualitative Research in Accounting and Management*, 18(4/5): 516–544.

Moore, G.E. (1903). *Principia Ethica*. Cambridge: Cambridge UP.

Nørreklit, L. (2011). Actors & reality: a conceptual framework on creative governance. In Jakobsen, M., Johanson, I-L., & Nørreklit, H. (Eds.), *An Actor's Approach to Management – Conceptual Framework and Company Practices*. Copenhagen: DJOEF, pp. 7–38.

Nørreklit, L. (2012). The double loop hermeneutics and emphatic aspects in social work. *Dialogue in Praxis. A Social Work International Journal*. @IUC Dubrovnik, 1–2: 159–165.

Nørreklit, L. (2013). Applied ethics and practice ontology. In Nykänen et al. (Eds.), *Theoretical and Applied Ethics*. Aalborg: Aalborg University Press, pp. 143–172.

Nørreklit, L. (2017). Paradigm of pragmatic constructivism. In Nørreklit, H. (Ed.), *A Philosophy of Management Accounting: A Pragmatic Constructivist Approach*. London: Routledge, pp. 21–94.

Nørreklit, L. (2020). A pragmatic constructivist perspective on language games. *Proceedings of Pragmatic Constructivism*, 10(1): 11–28.

Nørreklit, L. (2021). The language game of goodness. *Journal of Pragmatic Constructivism*, 11: 4–18. https://doi.org/10.7146/propracon.v10i1.119252

Paulsen, M. (2019). Understanding the Anthropocene world: contemporary difficulties. *Journal of Pragmatic Constructivism*, 9(2): 16–21.

Parsons, T. (1978). *Action Theory and Human Condition*. New York: Free Press.

Parsons, T., Bales, R., & Shils, E. (1953). *Working Papers of the Theory of Action*. Berlin: Free Press.

Robinson, K. (2011). *Out of our minds: learning to be creative*. Mankato, Minnesota: Capstone. ISBN: 1907312471.

Ryan, R., & Deci, E. (1988). The support of autonomy and the control of behavior. *Journal of Personality and Social Psychology*, 53(6): 1024–1037. https://doi.org/10.1037/0022-3514.53.6.1024

Vygotsky, L.S. (1978). *Mind in Society: The Development of Higher Psychological Processes*. Cambridge, MA: Harvard University.

Wittgenstein, L. (1922). *Tractatus Logico-Philosophicus*. London: Kegan Paul.

Wittgenstein, L. (1953). *Philosophical Investigations*. Oxford: Basil Blackwell.

Zinkernagel, P. (1962). *Conditions for Description*. London: Kegan Paul.

Chapter 3

Revisiting enabling formalizations of remote work

Learnings for short-term and long-term impacts

Teemu Laine, Tuomas Korhonen, and Natalia Niina Maria Saukkonen

Introduction

The chapter focuses on the possibilities of control and formalizations supporting people in organizations, especially in the context of digitalization, and more specifically in the context of the "new remote work" largely enabled by digitalization. As a point of departure, we believe that when digitalization comes into picture, which is the case in the remote work online, processes change at the micro level (Korhonen et al., 2020). The nature of different activities is changing all the time as well. Digitalization is one mega trend that influences how we live our lives. More specifically, a recent major change that has influenced many lives especially starting from the year 2020 is the shift to remote work settings and finding a balance between physical and remote work. If we intend to manage those activities that are now done online instead of physically in a "close, shared physical space" (Gray, 2014), it would be necessary to understand how the remote work setting influences actors' joint efforts to reach organizational goals (Errichello & Piarese, 2016).

Within this context, this chapter responses to the challenge of successfully organizing the new remote work, so that performance and employees' well-being are being supported and balanced. In response to this challenge, the chapter employs the concept of enabling formalization, which conveys the idea that management controls can support employees' work rather than restrict it. Adler and Borys (1996) discussed two types of bureaucracies, that are enabling and coercive, and concluded that there are four important characteristics in formalizations that lead to enabling type of support to the employees: global transparency, internal transparency, flexibility, and repair. The characteristics, presented by Adler and Borys (1996) have been transferred to the management control literature, with some modifications, refinements, and interpretations of those characteristics (Ahrens & Chapman, 2004; Jordan & Messner, 2012; Laine et al., 2020). In this chapter, we interpret the characteristics as follows:

First, *global transparency* means that the employee knows the characteristics of the business context. Then, building on this understanding, one can

DOI: 10.4324/9781003188728-4

understand and anticipate major trends and the organization's potential role in them. Second, *internal transparency* means that the employee knows how everything functions in the organization. Sometimes, it is the best insurance for the employee to know what the impact of one's work is, and actively work based on, discuss and share this understanding with others. Third, *flexibility* means that the employee can sometimes act outside the rules and routines. Perhaps, the employees are sometimes encouraged to think beyond the current procedures to attain the best possible result. Finally, fourth, *repair* means that the formalization encourages taking initiative and solving problems. To simplify, by following the example of Adler and Borys (1996), if the paper is stuck in the printer, it might not better to just leave it alone but react in one way or another that helps surmount this small problem.

The characteristics of enabling formalization and control are rather versatile and raise several questions. Essentially, it is about the perceptions of one employee and all the employees. Whether employees experience being supported or obligated by managers (who influence the employees in different ways) in their work determines whether control is enabling or coercive (Jordan & Messner, 2012; O'Grady, 2019). Indeed, the term control is not a synonym to surveillance. On the contrary, control consists of various managerial ways of aligning employees' interests with those of the organization, to motivate them to contribute to attainment of organizational objectives without coercion (Merchant & Van der Stede, 2007; Linneberg et al., 2021). The holistic framework of control includes administration of employees (e.g., the organizational structure and policies), long/short-term planning of business, budgeting of operations, personal incentive schemes, and even the organizational culture with shared values, identities, and symbols of success (Malmi & Brown, 2008). A formalization is a certain type of control: it is the "written rules, procedures, and instructions" for a specific operation or task (Adler & Borys, 1996, p. 62). In an organization, this definition of formalization works as a part of the holistic framework of control.

This chapter addresses the problem that there is not enough understanding about how controls and especially formalizations can support or restrict employees' performance in remote conditions (Errichello & Pianese, 2016). Therefore, it would be important to understand, what do the contextual characteristics of the remote setting mean from the viewpoint of enabling control (Brocklehurst, 2001; De Vaujany et al., 2021). Indeed, although the enabling formalizations and the wider perspectives of organizations controlling their members and activities have been already rather extensively examined (Adler & Borys, 1996; Ahrens & Chapman, 2004; Jordan & Messner, 2012; O'Grady, 2019; Laine et al., 2020), enabling formalizations are not well understood in the remote work setting (Bispe et al., 2019).

Figure 3.1 conveys a synthesizing idea of the research setting underlying this chapter. Different formalizations within the management control framework should support the perception of enabling control through enabling

How formalizations relate to control: While focusing on the concept enabling formalization, we will be able to understand *how formalizations* (i.e. written rules, procedures, and instructions) *function inside the holistic framework of control*, in the new remote work (e.g. administration of employees, long/short-term planning of business, budgeting, incentives, organizational culture).	Formalization Enabling *characteristics*: Internal transparency External transparency Flexibility Repair	Practice Values, meanings → actions	Impact Desired in the short & long term: Performance Business impact Well-being Sustainability

Figure 3.1 Characteristics, practice, and impact of enabling formalizations online.

characteristics, also in the remote settings. If this is the case, practice and actions could be driven by values and meanings and thus resulting in short-term and long-term performance, including well-being and sustainability among other possible impacts.

Within the broader research setting (Figure 3.1), as its research question, this chapter examines *how the new remote work affects the characteristics of enabling control and formalizations*.

The chapter provides a conceptual basis for responding to the question by examining the characteristics of enabling formalization, supplemented by three illustrations on the nature of those characteristics. The characteristics of the enabling formalizations are examined, first, at organizational level from the highly decentralized forerunner organizations and, second, at individual level regarding the processes of thesis supervision in education. As a third illustration, the chapter provides a metaphor of joint play between a parent and a child, where similar activities could be taken without the physical presence of the parent. This metaphor facilitates understanding that enabling control in the remote work setting might require thorough rethinking of what the intended outcome of action really is. The illustrations are based on the empirical experience and conceptual analyses of the authors during 2018–2021, although they do not represent any single organization or individual.

Altogether, we argue that considering well-being together with performance is the sustainable way of working remotely (and working in general). In the remote work setting as well, attaining the instrumental performance consequences is not enough, but activities require flexibility and versatility, to enable both short-term performance and long-term, sustainable learning, and thus performance. How organizations and managers can enable employees to deliver results effectively is critical always, but especially critical in the context of new remote work as the need to work from home has dramatically increased since the beginning of the COVID-19 pandemic.

The rest of the chapter is structured as follows. Next, we will discuss the nature of the new remote work as presented in the relatively recent literature.

After that, we will revisit the characteristics of enabling formalizations in the online settings. This conceptual analysis will be then reflected upon three illustrations as outlined earlier. The chapter ends with discussion, conclusions regarding enabling formalization in general and fostering learning in the "new remote work", in particular.

Understanding the "New remote work" and the characteristics of enabling formalizations online

What has changed in the new remote work?

To further specify the challenge of supporting people in the new remote work settings and outline our approach and contribution regarding it, we will first discuss the nature of the new remote work as presented in the relatively recent literature (What has changed in the new remote work) and more specifically the nature of remote work procedures (How procedures can be different in the new remote work?). After that, we will revisit the characteristics of enabling formalizations online (Developing enabling formalizations online).

Remote work has been possible already for a couple of decades, and it has become more common, and increasingly flexible due to the digitalization that has enabled conducting many work tasks, especially in expert work, without physical presence of the employees. Organizations that traditionally have adopted remote, online working practices have likely been characterized by informal controls (e.g., culture of flexibility, openness, and trust in work task completion, in Daniels et al., 2001). Such controls employees easily experience as being enabling. However, due to the COVID-19 pandemic, also organizations that have been using more formal controls (e.g., strict rules and processes) have had to shift to remote work. The central challenge is that how these organizations can support their employees? To answer this question, we need to learn from those companies that have already done well in shifting to remote work. However, also many other context specific considerations are required both at the organizational and individual levels.

Prior research on enabling formalizations does not address their specific characteristics in the new remote work context. The known characteristics of enabling formalization (Adler & Borys, 1996) can be conceptually connected to decentralized, remote work to elaborate upon the specific challenges that require thorough academic examination (O'Grady, 2019; Errichello & Demarco, 2020). In fact, the characteristics can be observed in current academic knowledge on controlling remote work (Errichello & Pianese, 2016). In particular, the current state-of-the-art knowledge is that flexibility of organization structure drives shifting to remote work (Lamond et al., 2002) and can serve as a facilitator of home-based working (Ollo-López et al., 2020). Remote work can lead to flexibility as well (Campbell & MacDonald, 2007), so there is a two-way relationship between remote work and flexibility.

But how is this flexibility enacted by managers' and employees' action and interaction? Internal transparency might be significantly hindered by being in contact with others only through remote connections, rather than with physical presence (Felstead et al., 2003). Yet, transparency to operations would be of utmost importance to survive in times of uncertainty, such as that caused by COVID-19 (Rikhardson et al., 2020), and thus transparency requires more detailed examination, as how it relates to actions that drive impacts. The same applies with global transparency, which is highly necessary for understanding what your peers and stakeholders are doing, to coordinate the joint efforts toward desired outcomes (Radtke & Widener, 2016) and to understand what is happening in the environment of your organization (Hall, 2010).

Transparency may also drive impact in remote work. Adaptation of managerial processes, that is, repairing them to fit to the current situation is central for an organization to make a shift to remote work as fluent as possible (Daniels et al., 2001; Siha & Monroe, 2006) and enacting decentralization (Lee & Edmondson, 2017; De Vaujany et al., 2021). However, no prior understanding exists on how control systems need to be repaired when moving to the new remote work, although research shows that some changes have taken place, for example, by mostly decreasing the amount of employee surveillance (Kovalainen et al., 2021).

Altogether, we define "new remote work" so that a significant part of work is done remotely and using information and communication technologies to a large extent. This means work that takes place outside office spaces or other cites of physical interaction with stakeholders such as colleagues, customers, managers, and subordinates. It is noteworthy that this chapter is not COVID-19 research *per se*, but it addresses new remote work both currently and in the long term. When a significant part of work (or even all work) is done remotely, organizing, division of work tasks, setting and following objectives, and contributing to financial performance can become increasingly difficult. The COVID-19 pandemic offers a highly interesting context to examine the constituents and practices of enabling formalization supporting employees' and organizations' performance under these new circumstances.

How procedures can be different in the new remote work?

A fundamental problem regarding the shift online is that it can be surprisingly difficult for practitioners (managers, employees, and other stakeholders) to understand which parts of work (i.e., processes, activities, and individual tasks) can be shifted to the electronic mode, and if, how and under which circumstances (Korhonen et al., 2020). The reason is that from a distance, many work tasks may appear much simpler than they really are when examined from close range.

To start solving this problem, we cannot stay at the level of organizational controls and formalizations. Instead, we need to delve deeper into practice to understand the relationship between the enabling formalization and impact within practice, as in Figure 3.1, from close range, within an actor's operational context (their facts, possibilities, values, and communication, for example, in Nørreklit, 2017). Our standpoint is that in making decisions and taking actions, different actors' (i.e., employees', managers', and other stakeholders') values, preferences, and perspectives need to be balanced in order to enable long-term, sustainable impacts (Saukkonen et al., 2018).

In all, as further illustrated in this chapter, we need to understand the impact of remote work on people and their practices, and the consequent (business) impacts of those activities (De Jong et al., 2014). In practice, one needs to be careful in changing the division of tasks between employees and digital tools to maintain or to further develop the value and impact of the activities under development (Korhonen et al., 2020).

Developing enabling formalizations online

The characteristics of enabling formalizations (Adler & Borys, 1996; Jordan & Messner, 2012; Errichello & Pianese, 2016) provide a sound starting point for assessing new remote work and online practices as well. The intention of an organization to continue working according to those characteristics is reasonable and potentially valuable for learning and positive impacts. However, as the remote work settings, especially due to the COVID-19 pandemic, have emerged rather rapidly, there could be a temptation to increase monitoring and mechanistic controls in order to keep up the sense of control in the new settings, though some research points the otherwise (cf. Kovalainen et al., 2021). Still, *no control* does not mean enabling control. Therefore, instead of establishing mechanistic controls for the sake of crisis management, or in response to the perceived lack of control, an organization should critically examine its practices in the new settings and find ways to ensure and further develop its enabling formalizations.

In practice, the online settings provide clear possibilities to critically examine each of the characteristics of the enabling formalizations, thus reflecting the challenges faced by many organizations that have rushed to the new remote work:

- *Repair* may take place in the online settings individually and in isolation, if new processes and divisions of tasks have not been articulated. There is then a greater chance that repair efforts are taken case by case, which may cause sub-optimization and, remarkably, learning from each other is limited.
- *Flexibility* may naturally be increased in the online remote work and thus some people may take advantage of the situation. Positive flexibility would mean organizing of work and developing the practice independently on the time and space. Negative flexibility would mean reduced integrity and

lack of self-discipline in carrying out the needed tasks, which results in lower or negative impacts.
- *Local transparency* may clearly be challenged, when the employees do not informally meet and discuss with each other. In the online settings, there seem to be more information sharing meetings, which, in turn, increase the overall burden of the calendars and thus restrict possibilities to rethink and learn. Furthermore, if informal meetings become fewer, one needs to find ways to discuss the wider potential of individuals and teams as a learning enabler.
- Regarding *global transparency*, online settings enable documentation and even recording of many new activities. This might help in local transparency building as well. However, despite the increased amount of digitalized data on the activities, the "big picture" may not be understood by anyone anymore, but fragmentation of the knowledge may increase.

Altogether, given the challenges presented earlier, the new ways of working need to be critically examined and decided. Once the COVID-19 pandemic allows the organizations to escape the "survival mode" (flee or fight) or preferably before that, there is a need to revisit and discuss the organizational values and assess, if the organizational practice remains in line with them also in the new settings. Enabling formalizations may be built in the new settings also, if the practice is built on the values, not necessarily continuously compared to previous practices. This mindset acted upon in the organizations constitutes the development and desirably agile learning activities in the online settings also in the long term.

Illustrations

The chapter provides three illustrations on the potential benefits and pitfalls of the new remote work, from the perspective of enabling formalizations in practice. The illustrations provide different viewpoints to the challenge of supporting employees in the new remote work, and thus they form together a rich account to respond to the challenge. The illustrations are structured from the more generic (organizations) to the more particular (individual) perspectives. The first empirical illustration (Learning from the forerunner organizations: values and meanings drive action at the organizational level) deals with the lessons learned from forerunner organizations that have, already for some time, provided flexibility for the employees to work remotely. Those companies seek for other ways to support the well-being and performance of the employees. However, as the organization level does not unveil all the fundamentals related to the enabling formalizations that are essentially related to the subjective interpretations of the people involved, we delve deeper into the individual level. Second, we illustrate the processes of thesis supervision, where the authors have been involved with during the new remote work (An empirical illustration:

how student supervision and instruction remain enabled for the individuals in the remote work setting). After that, as a third, more conceptual illustration, we illustrate a metaphor of joint play between a parent and a child, essentially also at the individual level, to discuss how enabling control in the remote work setting might require thorough rethinking of what the intended outcome of action really is, in order not to lose the value basis of the activities (A conceptual illustration: How we can miss the point when changing processes?).

Learning from the forerunner organizations: values and meanings drive action at the organizational level

The employment of the characteristics of the enabling formalizations do not result in short-term and long-term impacts in a straightforward manner (cf. Figure 3.1). The desired benefits, such as good individual performance and employee well-being, become eventually realized though the actions made in practice. The practitioners and their actions become the essential link between enabling formalization and impact. Such a link has been identified and acted upon in forerunner technology organizations that the authors of the chapter have been observing while collaborating with them (2018–2021). The lessons learned from those contexts provide useful information about the enabling formalizations more broadly.

It is noteworthy that in an enabling setting, like in those forerunner organizations, the created procedures and instructions leave space for the practitioners to act based on their values, judgments, and interpretations of meaningful work. This helps sustain practitioners' motivation toward the work, which is a topical goal for organizations. Achieving a value-driven and functioning practice (Nørreklit, 2017) is becoming increasingly relevant, as employees long for purpose, meaning, and value alignment in their work. Flexible possibilities for remote work are rather natural choices for organizations that in general leave space to act for their employees. In all, there are organizations that have been flexible in their remote work arrangements already for several years, while investing in employee well-being at the same time.

Indeed, examining the forerunners allow us to identify functioning practices which can be further developed and transferred to other organizations. Altogether, the identified forerunner practices can support employees in realizing personal values in everyday work. We have made the following observations:

- Control systems in the forerunner organizations are based on the assumption that people's knowledge and capabilities are recognized, realized, developed, and thus they add value to all the parties involved.
- Organizations promote employee judgment over formal guidelines. They give responsibility and autonomy to people, employees are encouraged to make decisions, even investments for better results. Trust leads into commitment.

- Empowerment helps in using one's full potential. Once the wider potential can be used, performance and profitability will follow.
- Organizations emphasize a comprehensive view on meaningful life and well-being, rather than acknowledging only career achievements.
- Organizations emphasize project outcomes rather than project budgets, encouraging to keep promises to the client.

In sum, enabling good work performance in remote work requires courage to allow and support activities beyond the current indicators and strict rules. Trusting employee judgment on relevant actions may not fit to the mechanistic view on controls and formalizations. However, it can pay back in the forms of employee commitment and sense of meaningful work. For management, relaxing and loosening the formal controls may require stepping out from the comfort zone to make the difference. In other words, adding mechanistic monitoring in the new remote settings moves practitioner's attention from the work itself to reacting on the increased monitoring requirements. While keeping up the sense of control, organizations simultaneously challenge their employees' possibilities to align their personal values and reasoning to everyday work.

Of course, organizations and individuals within are not homogenous. Organizations have had different starting points in complexity, stability, and routinization when entering the remote settings. Therefore, the constituents of the enabling formalizations in the online settings deserve further attention and examination, also with the access to the day-to-day practice. Essentially, learning from the forerunner organizations does not mean merely copying organizational level principles and "enabling formalizations" accordingly. Instead, we need to better understand the individual level values, perceptions, and interpretations. The remaining illustrations operate therefore at the individuals' level.

An empirical illustration: how student supervision and instruction remain enabled for the individuals in the remote work setting

The authors of this chapter are involved in dozens of thesis supervision processes annually, ranging from BSc theses to MSc and PhD theses. Similarly to the course teaching also, these processes were shifted online during 2020. As student supervision stands for a formalization, somewhat similar to formally supervising expert work in companies, we provide our experience on interacting with students in the remote setting, with the characteristics of enabling formalizations in mind.

The first observation about thesis supervision is that many students were supervised partially online already before 2020. Especially, when it comes to MSc and PhD students, working outside the university while doing their theses, online tools were conveniently used already before. Indeed, also in the companies, there were flexible remote work settings before 2020 and the dramatic change in 2020 was of different scale and scope for different organizations and people.

In the context the authors are involved in, BSc theses follow a more uniform process within either autumn or spring semester, whereas MSc and PhD students work more autonomously and take more initiative for getting the supervision. However, there are issues of transparency in both cases. For example, as observed by the authors, the supervisors do not get to know the students that easily, as informal *ad hoc* meeting is rather difficult without meeting at the campus. As a result, the global transparency on, for example, the availability of relevant thesis positions in companies and the sense of the overall progress of the thesis processes are not easily maintained. Nor is a more informal, personal connection with students so easily attained, as it might seem that the supervisor is controlling progress rather than being there for the student. At least, it might be more difficult for the supervisor to become confident that they have given the students an experience of "being there" for them. Moreover, in the online setup, it might be more difficult to make sure, if there are any concerns among the students, for example, as one cannot interpret the body language of the student if the cameras are off (e.g., looking heavily stressed).

Also, regarding the local transparency, for example, the progress of a single thesis and related issues is not that easily discussed, if the students do not use cameras in the meetings, especially regarding BSc theses with more uniform processes for the student group. The similar issue may take place also in MSc and PhD thesis supervision, especially if the meetings are limited to the strict agenda, without the possibility to raise problems or informal concerns of the students. In response, it would be very important for the supervisor to pay extra attention to make sure that the students are also feeling good about their theses, preferably by using their own wording about the situation.

While the transparency issue requires attention in thesis supervision, also the flexibility and repair seem to hold important characteristics in the online supervision processes. Earlier, the students initiated supervision meetings in a given time, in a given place at the campus. Now, the hurdle of contacting via online tools and initiating shorter *ad hoc* meetings seems to have lowered, thus increasing the flexibility of the supervision process. For example, it might be easier for the student to send an email or chat message to the supervisor.

At the same time, some repair efforts have taken place. It is the responsibility of the supervisor to guide the students toward an autonomous, professional project management regarding the thesis. Therefore, it is not necessarily desired to develop highly flexible processes with remarkably short response time for any issue by the supervisor. Also, when shifting the processes online, some information exchange could easily be shifted to commercial, not necessarily that secure online tools and using those has been restricted in the university policies.

Whether students feel supported or obligated by the thesis supervision determinates its enabling or coercive role. To further illustrate how supervision can remain enabled in remote settings, we can use the formalization of "supervision plan," which is agreed upon by the student and the supervision in the beginning of the thesis process. The plan is one example of recently introduced formalizations to MSc thesis supervision. In practice, the plan is a form that requires announcing examiners and expected completion date for the thesis. The form asks the students to describe their commitment, expectations toward the supervisor, and qualitative goals for the thesis. Similarly, the supervisors must state their commitment and expectations toward the student. After the form is filled, attached guidelines instruct the student to submit the plan to faculty's Student Services. In physical settings, the student and the supervisor would most likely meet and sign the form together using pen and paper. Such event could encourage the student and the supervisor to discuss on the expectations and goals related to the thesis journey. In remote settings, the digital version of the form adds flexibility to the process. The parties do not need to meet in an agreed time and place to print, fill, and sign the plan. Email exchange, online meetings, and electronic signatures can be utilized to arrange the form submission.

If enabling formalization takes place, the valuable discussion on commitment and expectations happens also remotely in connection with the thesis supervision plan. Both parties reserve enough time for this interaction to cover the important topics stated in the form. Here the form can empower students to ask rather personal questions from the supervisor, as commitment and expectations are easily neglected topics when rushing to the substance matters of the thesis. However, rushing to concrete outputs and task fulfilment may also risk the enabling potential of the form. The discussion around the form may narrow down to two exchanged emails that fulfil the task of form submission. In this case, the thesis supervision plan shrinks to a coercive role of a certain rule in the remote settings.

Overall, based on the experience of the authors, the thesis supervision has been rather efficient and effective also in the new remote work conditions. This is supported by the number of graduated students in 2020–2021. However, regarding the characteristics of enabling formalization, the findings suggest that extra attention needs to be paid on the thesis supervision processes to observe possible challenges and to understand the overall circumstances, where individual thesis workers are in. There is a pitfall of proceeding with the sense of efficiency and the focus on the outputs at each stage of the process, which could result in neglecting the personal situation of the student(s) involved in the process.

A conceptual illustration: How we can miss the point when changing processes?

For understanding even more profoundly why the digital setting matters, we use the metaphor of rope-skipping as a form of play that can be changed, as many other activities, with the help of new technologies. Indeed, let us consider a child playing. The child might be alone or with others in this play. If the child is playing alone, they do not interact with others, whereas if they are playing together with others, they are involved in some kind of interaction. The others might be friends or family, either adults or other children.

One possible setting is that the child is playing with their parents. Let us consider this situation. The child is playing with their parents and let us imagine that they are on a beach, skipping rope. The parent is swinging the rope as the child is jumping over it. The other end of the rope is tied on a tree. Both are seemingly happy: they are smiling and laughing. A warm breeze of summer wind accompanies their afternoon outdoors.

The child's heart rate is up as they have been playing rope-skipping for some time already. After a while, the parent and the child decide that it is time to eat some picnic on a blanket that they brought with them. They open the picnic basket and take out sandwiches. The parent knew that the child would love tomato, so that is naturally included.

Let us then consider the imagined situation from a theoretical point of view. The joint play has brought the child with their parent onto the beach. They have had a vision that they would be doing something specific on the beach, that is, they would be skipping rope and eating some delicacies from the picnic basket, on a blanket. In order to achieve this vision, they needed to prepare the trip to the beach by finding a suitable time to go, a way to transport themselves there, and obtain and pack the items they need for the play and the picnic: at least the rope, the blanket, and the picnic basket with tomato sandwiches.

What do they then gain from this joint play? For example, they might "fuse" together in the joint activity of play; so they might become attached to each other (Gray, 2014, p. 44). Their rope-skipping play might involve "high excitement," "movement," "exaggerated expressions," "creativity," and "body contact or close, shared physical space," that might contribute to increasing the two-way attachment between the child and the parent (ibid.). Moreover, the rope-skipping play together at the beach might be good exercise and thus healthy. Certainly, it involves breathing fresh summer air since it takes place at a beach, that is, it is outside, which is also healthy. One could say that, for the child, it is a "good" way to spend one's free time outside the hours at school or daycare; and also, a good way to spend the free time outside hours at work or other chores, for the parent. They both gain something from the joint play. Maybe they did not set targets for their play beforehand since it could have made the play feel instrumental. They just wanted to spend some time together and they selected going to the beach as their activity. The play was not instrumental – it was just play.

Let us then consider a different kind of situation, now a more hypothetical one. Let us say that the parents cannot attend the rope-skipping now, because they have become too busy. Luckily, they have earned so well that they have afforded a rope-skippers' swinging machine (of course such a machine might exist somewhere but, in this case, we just use this machine as a hypothetical, imaginary, what-if idea). This imaginary machine has a lever, that is powered by a battery, and that can swing the rope as many minutes or hours as the child wishes, without any fatigue. The battery can also be charged during the night so the play can continue without pause, if needed. The machine is portable too, and therefore the child can easily carry it in their picnic basket. So, the child goes to the beach, again, in this alternative setting without the parent, but with the fine rope-skippers' swinging machine. The child ties the other end of the rope to a tree found at the beach; the other end is tied to the dedicated lever on the side of the swinging machine. The child starts the machine, which very gently and precisely swings the rope, allowing the child to inhale the healthy outdoor air, get the heart rate up, and have some time outside their daily responsibilities (such as the school or daycare). A warm breeze of summer wind accompanies also this afternoon.

After a while, the child decides to have picnic. It's the sandwich time – though there is no tomato in the sandwich this time.

The idea of a child with a rope-swinging machine, on the beach, sounds absurd. It just does not *feel* right. *But why is this so?* Why cannot it be a nice thing to spend your afternoon on the beach with a machine that allows you to do some exercise, movement included. It is good to have fresh air too. And the summer breeze does not depend on the company you are on the beach with. What is *different* in the two settings is that they allow different approaches to the concept of *attachment*. In the first example, the attachment between the child and the parent comes to a large extent from their togetherness at the beach (cf. Gray, 2014). In the latter setting, the attachment comes from the parent's kind thought to replace themselves with a machine (because they are so busy themselves and wish the best for their children). It is better than nothing, one could say! However, the question why the latter situation feels somehow wrong is not as easy to answer as one might imagine. Approaching such an emotional situation with analytical logic would require high skills in children's psychology – not everyone has those skills.

Somehow the nature of play is different when the two settings are compared. In the first setting, the play itself was maybe something that allowed something else to happen (e.g., fusing the parent and the child) but it has value itself as well. It was done for the sake of play and togetherness. Just being together is different than playing together. In contrast, in the latter situation, play is possibly *hollower*. The play is there because it was seen so necessary that it requires a machine to facilitate it. Skipping the rope must be done. The rope needs to be skipped. The rope needs skipping. Is this what the child needs as well?

New remote work has rapidly changed the conditions and formalizations affecting many people in organizations. The scope of the changes regarding many activities is similar to the metaphor of replacing parents by a machine in the rope-skipping. Some of the consequences of these changes have been desired and intentional, such as increased flexibility in work activities, but some of them have caused lack of human interaction, shared physical space and many implicit, yet extremely relevant impacts such us performance based on informal interaction and broader well-being impacts. No one would want parents to be replaced with machines of narrower possibilities. Similarly, in the long term, one needs to pay attention to the explicit and implicit consequences of the new remote work, to maintain, revisit, and extend the perception of enabling formalizations.

Discussion and conclusions

Findings on the characteristics of enabling formalizations in the new remote work

As the central challenge underlying the chapter, there has not been enough understanding about how controls and especially formalizations can support or restrict employees' performance in remote conditions. The chapter has employed the concept of enabling formalization, which conveyed the idea that management controls can support employees' work rather than restrict it, also in the context of the new remote work. The chapter has provided a conceptual basis for the examination, further reflected by illustrations on different organizational and individual level settings.

As a general observation, we argue that the characteristics of enabling formalization (Adler & Borys, 1996; Jordan & Messner, 2012) provide a useful starting point for analyzing management practice also regarding the new remote work (Errichello & Pianese, 2016). However, regarding the effects of the new remote work on the enabling formalizations online, we cannot remain at the organizational level, but need to address the microstructures that are not easily seen with a quick look at action (Masquefa et al., 2017) and, essentially, acknowledge the people as the most crucial link between the formalization and impact (Nørreklit, 2017). If we miss or do not understand the value basis of the people involved, any control may be perceived as coercive. Furthermore, if we just try to reenact the physical work setting online (Brocklehurst, 2001), controls might become coercive after all, if some fundamentals of the activities have changed in the new remote work.

The illustrations of the chapter provide more specific lessons for establishing and developing enabling formalizations in the new remote work. First, observations from the forerunner organizations suggest that we do not have to give up our values in the remote work either. We can find ways to make controls and formalizations function in an enabling manner in the remote work setting. If people are given flexibility to act, as is the case in highly decentralized organizations (O'Grady, 2019), the values and meanings are more easily observable, and the controls are perceived as more enabling. This finding poses the challenge to any organization: How to provide the feeling of meaningful work when working primarily via electronic ways of communication?

Second, observations from the thesis supervision highlighted the importance of individual level interaction also in the new remote work. Even though the supervision processes have functioned rather well, concerns regarding the transparency to individual challenges emerged. A thesis is a grand aim for an individual and thus comparable to some projects taken by expert workers in other organizations. A remarkable challenge for such settings was observed: How can one have experience of becoming supported and important while working in a significant project in the new remote work? The availability of such support may help solving short-term challenges – and is important for long-term development of individuals in their career.

Third, the short-term and long-term impacts of the new remote work were further examined with the help of the metaphor of automating the rope-skipping of a child. Indeed, the last illustration shows that nevertheless, we can lose something central even though we try to do everything as well as possible, when we shift to more automated remote work setting. Meeting short-term objectives should not be overemphasized, as undesired side effects take place. Furthermore, the value basis of any action, employed implicitly and explicitly in raising the children, supervising the students, and working in the organizations provide a profound starting point for any practice now and in the future. Therefore, developing the new remote work in line with the characteristics of enabling formalization is one important guideline for avoiding fundamental mistakes.

This chapter has discussed the characteristics of enabling formalizations in the remote work mode that has remarkably expanded during and after the COVID-19 pandemic settings. The chapter suggests that these characteristics, transparency, flexibility, and repair, hold important perspectives to assess and develop remote work settings as well. Furthermore, as illustrated in this chapter, the advantage of those characteristics is that they do not require a certain type of control, practice, or action, but more readily they serve as principles of approaching given practices. In other words, functioning practices in the remote work should not imitate functioning practices in the offices but enabling formalizations need to be designed and implemented case by case.

One of the starting points of the remote work settings is the empowerment of the people. After examining and illustrating the enabling formalizations, the chapter suggests the following principles to be enacted in the new remote work, in order to enable functioning practice and performance both at the individual and the organizational levels:

- Make sure that everyone understands and is able to observe the rationale of performance in the organization.
- Make sure that everyone is supported and dares to be oneself and use one's capabilities and potential at work.
- Make sure that there are avenues and mechanisms to think and act beyond the current boundaries and performance indicators.

Altogether, success and performance are based on understanding, courage, and empowerment and thus thinking and acting accordingly. Essentially, further research is needed in order to better understand the constituents of success and performance in the new remote work, in different organizational contexts.

Further research agenda and concluding remarks

As discussed earlier, the characteristics of enabling formalization and, essentially, the empowerment of the people involved seem to provide a fruitful starting point for management also in the new remote work. However, further research is needed to learn from and transfer existing functioning practices and empirical observations to other contexts. In-depth, qualitative inquiry would be needed in order to understand how the forerunners have shifted to the remote work mode and managed to create enabling formalizations. Therefore, field data collected among organizations before, during, and after changing their formalizations online could enable better understanding about the practical implications of the enabling formalizations online. Such analysis, naturally, would require both archival data from organizations (such as interviews and observations), and collecting new field data. Engaged research (Van de Ven & Johnson, 2006) among forerunner technology organizations as well as many other types of organizations is encouraged to ensure a detailed, relevant knowledge about the antecedents and characteristics of enabling formalizations online, and to enable the transfer of best practices of enabling formalizations online to other contexts.

Finally, enabling formalizations are essentially about learning from the organizational context and interactions, and developing the practice accordingly. Developing the understanding about enabling formalizations is not only an academic exercise. Instead, once such better understandings have been achieved, educators can transfer the learnings to students, that is, those people who will formulate the future workforce. Similarly, it is important to support those already in the working life by possible link between the academia, professional training, and business networks and the public and the third sector. Essentially, agile learning should take place at all levels in a continuous manner.

Acknowledgments

We would like to express our gratitude to Business Finland [NewBI5 project] and the case companies for funding and supporting the research that yielded this chapter.

References

Adler, P.S., & Borys, B. (1996). Two types of bureaucracy: Enabling and coercive. *Administrative Science Quarterly*, 61–89.

Ahrens, T., & Chapman, C.S. (2004). Accounting for flexibility and efficiency: a field study of management control systems in a restaurant chain. *Contemporary Accounting Research*, 21(2): 271–301.

Bisbe, J., Kruis, A.M., & Madini, P. (2019). Coercive, enabling, diagnostic, and interactive control: Untangling the threads of their connections. *Journal of Accounting Literature*, 43: 124–144.

Brocklehurst, M. (2001). Power, identity and new technology homework: implications for new forms' of organizing. *Organization Studies*, 22(3): 445–466.

Campbell, J., & McDonald, C. (2007). Defining a conceptual framework for telework research. *ACIS 2007 Proceedings*, 120.

Daniels, K., Lamond, D., & Standen, P. (2001). Teleworking: frameworks for organizational research. *Journal of Management Studies*, 38(8): 1151–1185.

De Jong, B.A., Bijlsma-Frankema, K.M., & Cardinal, L.B. (2014). Stronger than the sum of its parts? The performance implications of peer control combinations in teams. *Organization Science*, 25(6): 1703–1721.

De Vaujany, F.X., Munro I., Nama, Y., & Holt, R. (2021). Control and surveillance in work practice: cultivating paradox in 'new' modes of organizing. *Organization Studies*, 42(5): 675–695.

Errichiello, L., & Demarco, D. (2020). From social distancing to virtual connections. *TeMA-Journal of Land Use, Mobility and Environment*, 151–164.

Errichiello, L., & Pianese, T. (2016). Organizational control in the context of remote work arrangements: a conceptual framework. In *Performance Measurement and Management Control: Contemporary Issues*. Bingley: Emerald Group Publishing Limited.

Felstead, A., Jewson, N., & Walters, S. (2003). Managerial control of employees working at home. *British Journal of Industrial Relations*, 41(2): 241–264.

Gray, D.D. (2014). *Attaching Through Love, Hugs and Play: Simple Strategies to Help Build Connections with Your Child*. London: Jessica Kingsley Publishers.

Hall, M. (2010). Accounting information and managerial work. *Accounting, Organizations and Society*, 35(3): 301–315.

Jordan, S., & Messner, M. (2012). Enabling control and the problem of incomplete performance indicators. *Accounting, Organizations and Society*, 37(8): 544–564.

Korhonen, T., Selos, E., Laine, T., & Suomala, P. (2020). Exploring the programmability of management accounting work for increasing automation: an interventionist case study. *Accounting, Auditing & Accountability Journal*, 34(2): 253–280.

Kovalainen, A., Poutanen, S., & Arvonen, J. (2021). *Covid-19, luottamus ja digitalisaatio. Tutkimus etätyöstä ja sen järjestymisestä Suomessa keväällä ja syksyllä 2020* [in Finnish]. Turun yliopisto. Retrieved from http://urn.fi/URN. ISBN: 978-951-29-8421-3.

Laine, T., Korhonen, T., & Suomala, P. (2020). The dynamics of repairing multi-project control practice: a project governance viewpoint. *International Journal of Project Management*, 38(7): 405–418.

Lamond, D., Daniels, K., & Standen, P. (2002). Teleworking and virtual organisations: the human impact. *The New Workplace: A Guide to the Human Impact of Modern Working Practices*, 197–218.

Lee, M.Y., & Edmondson, A.C. (2017). Self-managing organizations: exploring the limits of less-hierarchical organizing. *Research in Organizational Behavior*, 37: 35–58.

Linneberg, M.S., Trenca, M., & Noerreklit, H. (2021). Institutional work through empathic engagement. *European Management Journal*, 39(1): 46–56.

Malmi, T., & Brown, D.A. (2008). Management control systems as a package – opportunities, challenges and research directions. *Management Accounting Research*, *19*(4): 287–300.

Masquefa, B., Gallhofer, S., & Haslam, J. (2017). Developing appreciation of micro-organizational processes of accounting change and indicating pathways to more 'enabling accounting' in a micro-organizational domain of research and development. *Critical Perspectives on Accounting*, 44: 59–82.

Merchant, K.A., & Van der Stede, W.A. (2007). *Management Control Systems: Performance Measurement, Evaluation and Incentives*. Harlow, England: Pearson Education.

Nørreklit, H. (Ed.). (2017). *A Philosophy of Management Accounting: A Pragmatic Constructivist Approach*. New York: Taylor & Francis.

O'Grady, W. (2019). Enabling control in a radically decentralized organization. *Qualitative Research in Accounting & Management*, 16(2): 224–251.

Ollo-López, A., Goñi-Legaz, S., & Erro-Garcés, A. (2020). Home-based telework: usefulness and facilitators. *International Journal of Manpower*, 42(4): 644–660.

Radtke, R.R., & Widener, S.K. (2016). The complex world of control: integration of ethics and uses of control. In *Performance Measurement and Management Control: Contemporary Issues*. Bingley: Emerald Group Publishing Limited.

Rikhardsson, P., Wendt, S., Arnardóttir, A.A., & Sigurjónsson, T.O. (2020). Is more really better? Performance measure variety and environmental uncertainty. *International Journal of Productivity and Performance Management*, 70(6): 1446–1469.

Saukkonen, N., Laine, T., & Suomala, P. (2018). Utilizing management accounting information for decision-making: limitations stemming from the process structure and the actors involved. *Qualitative Research in Accounting and Management*, 15(2): 181–205.

Siha, S.M., & Monroe, R.W. (2006). Telecommuting's past and future: a literature review and research agenda. *Business Process Management Journal*, 12(4): 455–482.

Van de Ven, A.H., & Johnson, P.E. (2006). Knowledge for theory and practice. *Academy of Management Review*, 31(4): 802–821.

Chapter 4

Digital technologies, management, and big data
A way to a "living" or a "dead" (school) life?

Finn Wiedemann, Dion Rüsselbæk Hansen, and Michael Paulsen

Introduction

Data is produced, collected, and shared more than ever by means of digital technologies. The growing desire for big data seems endless and unstoppable. We are encouraged to rely on data to the point that our lives and bodies are governed and regulated by it. We bestow our belief in (numeric) data. We trust it and think that it can help us make the "right" decisions and predict whether something will occur or not – especially if we have access to enough data. The logic for this? *The more, the better.*

On the one hand, digital technologies and big data may have the potential for constructing spaces in which Bildung and democratic processes can thrive and be supported. We understand Bildung as being related to the cultivation of subjectivity through a curious and self-reflective attitude toward different social, cultural, and natural phenomena (Rüsselbæk Hansen & Toft, 2020; Nielsen, 2005; Paulsen, 2022c).

With a Bildung perspective, data can, for example, be used to widen horizons that can make it possible for us to transcend the ways in which we understand ourselves, others, and the reality we are formed by as well as we contribute to the forming of (Rüsselbæk Hansen & Phelan, 2019; Tække & Paulsen, 2022). That said, within such a perspective data may help us to expose, the "secret" patterns and perhaps obscure forms of systemic and structural violence that we might unconsciously contribute to (re)producing on a daily basis; this might deny participation to particular groups in democratic processes as well as the privilege of being seen and heard as political subjects (Žižek, 2009). Put differently, it will be problematic to dismiss big data, as it can enrich our understanding of complex matters – for example, climate change, virtual capitalism, imperialistic exploitation, and asymmetries in wealth and power – and how such issues are entangled in ways that we might not be aware of. Still, the term raises a lot of questions: What does big data mean? Who has the power to define this? Which data is taken into consideration, and based on what decisions it is considered? What forms of data are valued, and what forms are left out?

DOI: 10.4324/9781003188728-5

On the other hand, though, different forms of digital technologies and rationalities have been used to support techno-bureaucratic forms of regulation and the installation of pseudo-market spaces that colonize life in general and school life in particular, which does not always support democratic participation and complicated conversations.

What goes on in schools today is highly regulated by a techno-bureaucratic logic and decisions made by politicians, policymakers, leaders, and (perhaps some) teachers, which often rely on market actors, digital devices, platforms, and social media; these entities, they promise, can *improve* learning results, increase teaching efficacy, and raise standards of education. A lot of the digital technologies and devices that are being introduced and used in school are not questioned and problematized. It is worthy to bear in mind that it has become important for politicians and policymakers to measure and compare schools and teachers, so the public (for example, parents and students particularly) can choose which schools and teachers they want to invest in. That is one of the reasons school leaders and teachers are using a considerable amount of time on digital technologies to produce the "right" visible data that can create a good impression of them in the eyes of others thereby strengthening their standing in the competition. These increasing expectations on teachers and school leaders to use data can be understood as part of a long positivistic and mechanical tradition of educational discourse inspired by Anglo-Saxon thinking and research, which plays an even larger part now in educational policy and science than it did in the past (Williamson, 2017).

In this chapter, we reflect on the possibilities and difficulties that come with digitalization and big data and how we, in a liberal-democratic way, can respond to these phenomena within and beyond the educational field by discussing the following questions: What promises are attached to digitalization and big data? How do digital management technologies and big data regulate and structure our society in general and the work with democracy and Bildung in schools in particular? What does it mean to be identified and understood by means of digital technologies? What underlying knowledge regime(s) supports big data, and with what consequences does it do so for democratic and Bildung processes in school? To deal with these questions, we develop three perspectives on big data, inviting the reader into a pluralistic democratic dialogue.

The first perspective focuses on biopolitics and what promises are attached to digitalization and big data. Further, the second perspective focuses more closely on the life of the school and how the application of big data alters this life. The third and last perspective returns to a broader scope and links big data tech to the Anthropocene, Earth forgetfulness, and the current environmental problems.

Together, the three perspectives points in the direction of changing our expectations of big data, applying it more democratically, if that can be possible at all, and developing more "life-friendly" technology in the future. As we see it, these perspectives could contribute to developing more of a living rather than a "dead" school.

Perspective one: biopolitics and promises attached to big data

There are many reasons the society in general and schools in particular have been – and still are – being digitalized and datafied. As Hacking (1991) argues, the increased "fetishism for numbers" (p. 192) supports the belief that the world can be counted, calculated, and formulated in numeric ways. Digitalization and big data usher in a lot of promises, which can sometimes be cruel – for example, if they hinder what they are supposed to deliver (Berlant, 2011). That said, new knowledge and other forms of insights can be generated, for example, on educational life, classroom activities, and students' well-being, feelings, moods, and learning results as well as on how their socio-economic background might support or hinder their success. The formula seems to be that the more data that can be produced and digitalized, the better it is; this is because it can be used "to facilitate greater control and thus intervene more effectively in social affairs" (Mau, 2019, p. 3). But again, what kind of data is produced is not irrelevant. Additionally, more data does not necessarily lead to more knowledge but can instead generate huge information that we cannot handle and understand. The point is that more information can lead to lesser knowledge and insight. Nevertheless, big data is based on the powerful assumption that claims that if we have enough data, which we never have because we can always generate more, it can help us calculate, explain, and make complex matters visible – for instance, our behavioral patterns, inner thoughts, and emotional conditions (Rüsselbæk Hansen, 2020). Furthermore, big data is being used as an attempt to regulate and predict our behavior in instrumental and antidemocratic ways now more than ever (Zuboff, 2019). However, abstract mechanistic models and calculations based on huge amounts of data *cannot*, in concrete detail, map how subjects react, interact, think, and feel in real-time situations. Something is always "left out," because it cannot be conceptualized and/or transferred into, for example, (digital) symbolic data. Yet, we have not given up regulating and governing humans by means of big data. This is because the failures we have been confronted with, in this regard, are typically perceived as only a bump on the road that can be overcome by more and precise abstract big data. However, producing precise and reliable data is not an easy task. One of the problems that the contemporary COVID-19 situation has taught us is how algorithms and statistics, for example, have been built on data that comes from unknown sources and that is mislabeled. It highlights a relevant problem called "Frankenstein data sets, which are spliced together from multiple sources and can contain duplicates. This means that some tools end up being tested on the same data they were trained on, making them appear more accurate than they are" (Heaven, 2021, p. 2). It is noteworthy that data comes in many forms (as qualitative and quantitative), can be produced with different purposes, and are always serving particular interests. Still, there is, as Mau (2019, p. 11) argues, a growing tendency to *translate* qualitative into quantitative data. This means that the social world is often conceptualized in numeric ways so that diagnostic models can be developed and correlations can be formulated, for example, between input interventions and output results. It is difficult to deny that many of us find digital technologies very useful and important in our daily lives, and it has also become very difficult to live a social life without digital technologies and the quantitative data that they generate for us or allow us to have access to.

But that does not mean that we should uncritically accept digitalization and big data as "a necessity" – that is, as something that we should be enslaved by and cannot resist. Instead, we must continue to question why we should rely on digital technologies and data and discuss whether they can support, for example, Bildung and democratic matters in education. In truth, digital technologies are not just tools that can be used in neutral ways, and data is not just composed of signifiers that mirror the reality (Rorty, 1979; Žižek, 2008). In other words, it must not be used blindly as a way of promoting "the good school life." On the contrary, if it is not used wisely or if it cannot be problematized, discussed, and even suspended from time to time, it can hinder a school life that supports political engagement (and democracy) and critical self-cultivation (Bildung) and thereby the students' intellectual, sensible, and emotional flourishing (Toft & Rüsselbæk Hansen, 2017).

That said, there is a close link between the production of data by means of digital technologies and the ways in which life is managed in schools and Foucault's concept of "biopolitics" (2003). With this concept comes a paradox, which Ajana (2019) describes in this way: "whereby the same techniques that are designed to enhance life can also lead to exposing some people to death" (p. 464). For example, they can be used to enable "democratic deaths" that are realized through exclusions, marginalization, and classification or categorization regimes denying the subject "to take or have part" and participate as a political subject within a given socio-symbolic order (Rancière, 2004), because one might be recognized and reduced to "pure data" and not perceived as a human subject, which is much more than what can be conceptualized via data. We must not forget here how our biological state can be affected by symbolic data. Consider, for example, how people can feel that they are perfectly fit and healthy before they check their smart watches but can feel the opposite in a split second when they check their data on their smart watches, which might illustrate that they are not perfectly fit and healthy. *No matter what they feel*!

Let us take another example, which relates to the medical field. Here, we can experience how a data-based discourse that values objective knowledge has the potential to de-subjectivize the subject (the patient) by reducing one "to an object of research, of diagnosis and treatment" (Žižek, 2004, p. 506) based on data on one's health condition. Still, what often disturbs and problematizes the promises that are attached to such objective data-driven discourse is how the subject is never just an "object of research." One might act as "a worried hystericized subject, obsessed with anxiety, addressing the doctor as his Master and asking for reassurance from him/her" (p. 506) based on the data the doctor has access to about the subject's life and health situation. Conversely, the subject can also re-subjectivize oneself by resisting the process of diagnosis and be understood by means of the data that the doctor relies on, because one might find them "wrong" and not "desirable." In schools, though, such re-subjectivizing processes are not easy to support. Because today's students want to be evaluated and measured; they constantly ask for feedback: "How was my performance? Where am I standing? Please, evaluate me." In other words, students want to "be observed and evaluated" (Simons & Masschelein, 2008, p. 201) and thereby datafied. This mirrors a general belief in data and its ability to reveal an "objective truth" about our lives. Regarding this, Ajana's (2017) arguments flow as follows:

> By laying claim to the idea that identity can "objectively" be determined through the body, biometrics has given the body unprecedented significance over the mind, casting it as a source of "instant truth". This is encapsulated in the expression "the body does not lie", an expression that became the marketing slogan of the biometrics industry. (p. 5)

Critical considerations

Following Agamben (2008), we need to be critical about the biopolitical and data-based relation that has been installed between the citizens and the state and – we may add – between schools and students. What we according to Agamben must notice in this case is that the relation between, for example, the citizens and the state "no longer has to do with free and active participation in the public sphere, but instead concerns the routine inscription and registration of the most private and most incommunicable element of subjectivity – the biopolitical life of the body" (p. 202). Humanity and living subjects have "become a dangerous class" (p. 202), which must be controlled and be put under surveillance. From an American educational context, Lewis (2006) has, for example, described how a biopolitical school regime *includes* students' life as a political concern, while it, at the same time, *excludes* their life from the political sphere. Through zero-tolerance laws, politicians seek to bring safety back to schools by means of punishment and nondemocratic exclusion procedures. That means that zero-tolerance laws have produced atmospheres of terror that have "collapsed educational life into bare life" (p. 169). Indeed, it has collapsed into a life without political rights and where, for example, some of the students are reduced to biological bodies that must be politicized and monitored by means of digital data. This tendency is not new but reinforced in ways that we have not witnessed before. It is as if we are doing our very best to eliminate all forms of risk, under this consideration, in schools. And the best way to do this is through biopolitics and by means of big data about students' bodies and minds. As Agamben (2021) argues, the desire for security, order, and health (in all its various forms) has installed a date-driven "new paradigm of biosecurity – a paradigm in the name of which all other needs must be scarified" (p. 57).

Perspective two: big data and school life in a Danish context

Since the 1980s, digitalization has been a high-rated political goal in Denmark. Denmark's political goal has been that it should be at the forefront of the era of digitalization. Only in a few other places in the world has the excitement for digitization been higher (Balslev, 2020; Bernsen, 2019; Forskningsinformeret, 1994). This tendency goes hand in hand with the tendency toward increased datafication. As a matter of fact, the two tendencies support and stimulate each other. Digitalization refers to educational entities and activities that were analog earlier but are digitalized now – for example, learning materials, teaching, and evaluations of students' behavior and performances. On the other hand, datafication refers to information about learning and education achieved through surveys or machine learning that is translated into digital data (Williamson, 2017). For example, student absenteeism, behavior, and activities. The digital data are the basis for databases, tables, graphs, and different forms of visualizations. Through the combination of datafication and digitalization, our basic understanding of time has changed. Not only are we able to uncover activities and experiences from the past through digital surveys but we can also interact directly with the present as we know it from our interaction with social media platforms such as Facebook and Google.

New trends

Internationally, the measurement and monitoring of issues concerning education have dramatically raised the level support received by transnational organizations, such as EU and OECD. PISA measurements and tests, which countries and governments are using for benchmarking and as the basis of national educational reforms, are a well-known example of this. On a national level, test and measurements of the students' performances and transitions are made *regularly*. On a local level, municipalities or every single school or class collect data about students' learning and well-being *continuously*. In an attempt to promote and institutionalize the use of data on different levels, a "data warehouse" has been established. Here, schools and municipalities can shop for data about education-oriented issues, which they can use for decision-making and launching initiatives for the development of schools.

Background

The first PISA test was conducted in 2003 in Denmark. At almost the same time, an international report revealed that Denmark had a weak culture of evaluation. The problem was, according to the report, that it was not possible to compare schools and their performances (Ekholm et al., 2004). In 2006, in connection with a new school reform, the municipalities began to act on a more systematic ground to produce data about school matters and made it visible for the public. The production and use of data were further intensified in 2014 with another new school reform. With this reform, an extended culture focusing on measurement and accountability emerged, which is well known in the Anglo-Saxon world. The tendency toward the extended use of data and measurement can be interpreted as a "victory" by Anglo-Saxons and an empirical data-oriented educational culture, which puts the traditional Bildung-like and a democratic culture aside in education (Moss et al., 2020).

Advantages and disadvantages

The described development might offer new possibilities for school development but also creates several problems. At best, datafication does provide the school with new insights. For example, data has challenged the national myth that the Danish school system was world leading. At the single-school level and on several occasions, data has contributed to creating increased focus on pedagogical and content-oriented challenges that were otherwise invisible. For example, one of these challenges is that specific groups of pupils performed worse than expected. The increased use of data does offer new perspectives when it comes to illuminating problems and challenges that were difficult to grasp earlier on. The challenge, though, is to avoid only having *confidence in* and *desire for* specific forms of data in a naïve and unconditional way – often quantitative and algorithm-based forms. At worst, qualitative or narrative knowledge, for example, based on personal and social experiences can be downgraded or even neglected when it comes to decision-making and school development. Using data in schools and education might be relevant if it is used wisely. But if data becomes *an end itself*, it might reduce complicated and democratic conversations about school life. The problem will occur when teachers and leaders are not able to make content-oriented pedagogical choices and decisions based on their professionalism, experiences, and judgment. A further problem will be when their context-sensitive knowledge about singular students' situations and challenges is perceived as useless and without value, because they are not based on numeric data. Put differently, the risk will be great when only the numbers count while the contexts and subjects (teachers and leaders), who have specific experiences and insights about them, are excluded. Indeed, experts, policymakers, and politicians often claim that they have objective and value-free knowledge about specific school contexts based on quantitative data. But it is not the case!

The school as a democratic community

While dealing with data, three current educational positions can be found: (1) a reform-oriented and optimistic position, which claims that data can be used to reform schools and educational systems; (2) a critical position, which argues that the use of data is about power and control; and (3) a pragmatic position, which emphasizes democratic conversations about data when it comes to decision-making. Here, quantitative data might be helpful, but it cannot stand alone or overrule all other perspectives (Wiedemann, 2020, 2021).

We must insist that the school is a democratic community, as influential researchers such as John Dewey (2011) and Gert Biesta (2010) have claimed. When analyzing from a pragmatic position, one might ask if the use of digital media and datafication creates spaces in which "good" thinking habits and democracy can be developed and supported (Dewey, 2011). If we only use symbolic data and surveys stored in databases as the "data warehouse" when we identify issues and patterns and make decisions, it can prevent us from directly creating experiences with the world. Dewey (2011) would probably not deny the use of data and digital systems but would ask what they can offer us. It is worthy to bear in mind that digital technologies are based on different ideas of learning and pedagogics (Balslev, 2020; Selwyn, 2017). Very often, the ideas stem from individualistic behavior and cognitive theories, which are incompatible with those put forth by Dewey, who has a social, interactionist, and experimental understanding of learning and pedagogy. Working with datafication can promote an understanding of knowledge, where knowledge is seen as objective and numeric. This stands in contradiction to a narrative or qualitative notion of knowledge, which is more subjective and based on experiences and dialogue. The development of democratic habits includes involvement in social contexts where it is possible to practice democracy and obtain concrete bodily, sensual, and social experiences with different forms of democracy. The personal and individualistic learning, which can be a result of working with data and digital media, does not necessarily create the space for students' experiences with social and democratic matters, which can contribute to the development of democratic habits and relations. There is a risk perceived over digital life separating us, instead of bringing us together, even if the digital media also have a potential to create communities and new forms of social life. Data must be understood and discussed in the perspective of its ability to contribute to the ongoing complicated conversation about the (educational) world we live and take part in. Perhaps, a pragmatic and a context-sensitive position may offer a way of dealing with some of the many new possibilities and challenges that come with datafication and digitalization.

Perspective three: the Anthropocene, big data, and future life

Big data, datafication, algorithmic machine learning, and artificial intelligence are not *only* discursive and ideological phenomena. They are also real, in a more extended sense, and generate real effects, including those that are material and physical (and psychic as well). They are components of a new kind of digital machine, which could be called "big data machines" (which can also be linked to other machines giving rise to further possibilities, risks, and effects) (Tække & Paulsen, 2022). The core function of big data machines is producing and storing huge and complex digital data sets (Paulsen & Tække, 2020). For example, they are efficient in completing the following tasks, among others:

- Collecting, storing, and analyzing data about the weather; making weather forecasts
- Collecting, storing, and analyzing data on how people translate words and sentences from one language to another; suggest how a given word or sentence should be translated
- Collecting, storing, and analyzing data about people's traits and behaviors; predicting who someone is from videos or photos and where this person is at a given time; connecting this information with an autonomous death drone that finds and kills them
- Collecting, storing, and analyzing data about a student's behavior; suggesting appropriate learning tasks, punishments, and rewards for them

Yet, big data machines can be developed, used, modified, and responded to in different ways (Paulsen, 2020). This means that they, in their specificities, always build on ideologies, values, and world views – or in short, cultural patterns (Tække & Paulsen, 2022). To understand the new machines and what they do, we therefore need to both understand how they basically work and how they can be modified and responded to in different ways. Furthermore, to understand this, we must also grasp the cultural and social frameworks that they, as technical phenomena, are embedded in. Not forget, how they are reshaped by them as well as how they contribute to shaping them (Tække & Paulsen, 2022).

The desire to turn the world into objects that can be manipulated

In broad terms, we would propose that behind the development and use of big data machines lie a desire and world view, in which everything is seen as objects that can be manipulated (Paulsen, 2022). Without such a basic framework, it would not make sense to invent, develop, and use big data machines to monitor and control parts of the world (Caputo, 2018). If instead the world was seen first and foremost as consisting of unique and, therefore by definition, unpredictable singular subjects, it would be more likely to invent and shape technology that could be used to make dialogues possible (and not technology that could monitor and control behavior, assuming that the world is, in principle, predicable and something that could and should be calculated, controlled, and manipulated) (Paulsen, 2022d).

Now, one could further argue that the prioritization and valorization of "the controlling world view" is part of and the main reason behind the fact that we are now living in an *Anthropocene age* (Paulsen, 2019). Thus, the Anthropocene signifies the epoch we are now living in, here on Earth, in which human activities have greater impact on the whole life-critical zone through technology slightly below and above the surface of the Earth than anything else, giving rise to climate instability, mass extinction, global warming, decreasing biodiversity, pollution, stress, breakdowns of ecological systems, and much more, including perhaps also uncontrollable domino effects and unforeseen further consequences (Paulsen et al., 2022).

Earth forgetfulness

Ironically, numerous negative effects like these are linked to our subjective desire to control the world understood only as a vessel for objects and resources that can be manipulated (and therefore to not seeing the world as inhabited by unique singular subjects with intrinsic values). Thus, it is a part of what Heidegger called the forgetfulness of being (*Seinsverlassenheit*) or what could also be called *Earth forgetfulness* (Paulsen & Nørreklit, 2022).[1] Yet, it is not only an arbitrary discursive construction to treat everything and everyone as objects that can be calculated and manipulated. The point is that this is possible because it "it works," because the world we live in virtually consists (in some cases) of something that can be calculated and manipulated.

Thus, throughout the Holocene, which constitutes approximately the last 11,500 years – especially considering the late Holocene – human subjects have developed monocultural agriculture, cities, science, calculation, bureaucratization, capitalism, and resource management, including human resource management. This is arguably *because* the world *is* formed in such a way that this is possible – and that also has some advantages (increased human control over different cultural and natural matters, for instance).

Thus, it has been possible, for example, to construct large pig farms (rather, *factories!*), where living beings are treated exclusively as objects that can be manipulated, controlled, and optimized for meat production, *as if* they were not creatures at all. Similarly, for example, at the university in which this article's authors work, the students are named (by the managers of the university) "the stock" ["bestand" in Danish]. In other words, the students are seen as objects that can be manipulated, controlled, and optimized in order to secure the university's earnings and profitability. Such examples illustrate the same basic *Earth forgetfulness* (Paulsen, 2022d).

Digging out the forgotten – the meaning and capacity of life

Nevertheless, this does not exhaust what the "world is" in its capacity and virtuality. The price for "the control development" has been Earth forgetfulness: Forgetting, in our sociocultural–technological practices, that the world is not only a pile of resources and objects but also *a place* where unique singular subjects live with intrinsic values, caring for each other. It is, thus, a world of love, carefulness, enjoyment, and dialogue (Paulsen & Nørreklit, 2022). Of course, we know these *love aspects of life* form our own lives and life forms, but the point is that these aspects have been increasingly neglected in the sociocultural–technological practices we had constructed in the (late) Holocene, which has led to this Anthropocene situation we now inhabit, where the big data machines are just the last "shot at the trunk" of the Earth forgetting way of being present in the world.

A critique of big data machines must, therefore, question not only the ideological discourse of big data and its mere technical aspects but also the whole world understanding, which is grounding and immanent in our language, technologies, sociocultural practices, and reflections on them (Caputo, 2018). Further, we must ask what is forgotten in this world understanding – not accidentally but by "necessity" – and what might be of value and possess "virtual capacities" (Bryant, 2014) to de-territorialize and create "a new Earth" (Paulsen, 2022). As examples, we can consider the act of reshaping, modifying, and responding to our technologies, including big data machines, in alternative directions (than continuing the monitor-and-control-everything path in its different modalities and mix of state control and market capitalism) (Paulsen et al., 2022). This will demand new imaginations, new stories to tell, and new kinds of technological development inventing and modifying small dialogue machines that are more rhizomatic and transversal in nature (Braidotti, 2013) as well as call for the transformation of our sociocultural practices and institutions.

Toward dialogical life-friendly small data machines

A first step in this direction could be to make sense of a more *dialogical* and *zoëlogical* (i.e., life-centered) world understanding (Paulsen, 2022b). Then, one could begin to experiment with how alternative stories, practices, technologies, and institutions can be developed around such an outlook. This might seem very fragile, marginal, peripheral, and almost infinitely small compared to the gross development of big data machines and the "society of control" (Deleuze, 2006), but because of its vitality and capacity to generate life value, it might also *light a fire* that may turn out to spread faster and more extensively than we can imagine (Paulsen, 2022). Thus, instead of continuing the late Holocene line of technological development, concerning the improvement of communication devices only adapted to human bodies and for human subjects (the Internet, for instance) *and* technologies that increase the transformation of "everything" into objects that can be manipulated (i.e., resources), we should *look out for* and *begin to* develop, educationally approve, and apply more life-friendly technologies (small data machines) that can help create complicated interspecies democratic dialogues between the living beings of Earth. Perhaps, this can open a post-Anthropocene future of better coexistence and common life.[2]

Notes

1 One might object that current big data machines can create unique "profiles" for each singular subject, and that they can monitor, analyze, and say something unique about them. Yet, this is only based on past behavior and does not take into account of singular subjects' unique capacity for creativity, their essential unpredictability, and their personal and social life. At least this is not so if these machines are developed only to monitor and control. If they instead are transformed into small dialogical machines, it might turn them into instruments that can mediate dialogical unfoldment and complicated democratic engagements (Paulsen, 2022).
2 To mention just one example of such new small data machines, we think that the different kinds of technically mediated collaborations paid heed to by Donna Haraway (2016) – for instance, "The Pigeon Blog team of human beings, pigeons and electronic technologies" (p. 23) – is exemplary.

References

Agamben, G. (2008). No to biopolitical tattooing. *Communication and Critical/Cultural Studies*. London, 5(2): 201–202.

Agamben, G. (2021). *Where Are We Now? The Epidemic as Politics*. London: Rowman & Littlefield.

Ajana, B. (2017). Digital health and the biopolitics of the quantified self. *Digital Health*, 3: 1–18.

Ajana, B. (2019). Digital biopolitics, humanitarianism and the datafication of refugees. In Cox, E. et al. (Eds.), *Refugee ImaginariesResearch Across the Humanities*. Edinburgh University Press, pp. 463–479.

Balslev, J. (2020). *Evidence of a potential. The political arguments for digitizing education 1983–2015*. Doctoral dissertation, Roskilde University. https://jesperbalslev.dk/evidence-of-a-potential-ph-d-thesis/

Berlant, L. (2011). *Cruel optimism*. Duke University Press.

Bernsen, M. (2019). *Denmark disruptet. Tro, håb og techgiganter* [Denmark disrupted. Belief, hope and tech giants]. Gyldendal.

Biesta, G. (2010). *Good Education in an Age of Measurement: Ethics, Politics, Democracy*. Boulder, CO: Paradigm Publishers.

Braidotti, R. (2013). *The Posthuman*. Polity Press.

Bryant, L. (2014). *Onto-Cartography – An ontology of Machines and Media*. Edinburgh University Press.

Caputo, J.D. (2018). *Hermeneutics. Facts and Interpretation in the Age of Information*. Pelican Books.

Deleuze, G. (2006). *Forhandlinger 1972–1990* [Negotiations 1972-1990]. Copenhagen: Det lille forlag.

Dewey, J. (2011). *Democracy and Education*. Simon & Brown.

Ekholm M. et al. (2004). OECD-rapport om grundskolen i Danmark – 2004 [Rapport about the primary school in Denmark]. Uddannelsesstyrelsens temahæfte, 5. Retrieved from http://static.uvm.dk/publikationer/2004/oecd/oecd.pdf

Forskningsinformeret (1994). Info-samfundet år 2000: Rapport fra udvalget om informationssamfundet år 2000 [The information society 2000].

Foucault, M. (2003). *Society must be defended: lectures at the Collège de France, 1975-1976*. New York: Picador.

Hacking, I. (1991). How should we do the history of statistics? In Burchill, G. et al. (Eds.), *The Foucault Effect*. The University of Chicago Press, pp. 181–195.

Haraway, D. (2016). *Staying with the Trouble-Making Kin in the Chthulucene*. Duke University Press.

Heaven, W.D. (2021, July 30). Hundreds of AI tools have been built to catch covid. None of them helped. *MIT Technology Review*. Retrieved from https://www.technologyreview.com/2021/07/30/1030329/machine-learning-ai-failed-covid-hospital-diagnosis-pandemic/

Lewis, T. (2006). The school as an exceptional space: Rethinking education from the perspective of the biopedagogical. *Educational Theory*, 56(2): 159–176.

Mau, S. (2019). *The Metric Society: On the Quantification of the Social*. Polity Press.

Moss, L. et al. (2020). *Re-Centering the Critical Potential of Nordic School Leadership Research. Fundamental, But Often Forgotten Perspectives*. Springer.

Nielsen, H. (2005). Totalizing aesthetics? Aesthetic theory and the aestheticization of everyday life. *Nordisk Estetisk Tidskrift*, 17(32): 60–75.

Paulsen, M. (2019). Understanding the Anthropocene world: contemporary difficulties. *Journal of Pragmatic Constructivism*, 9(2): 16–21. https://www.propracon.com/article/view/117568

Paulsen, M. (2020). The good, the bad and the ugly: How different teachers will construe digitalization differently. In Kergel, D. et al. (Eds.), *Communication and Learning in an Age of Digital Transformation*. Routledge, pp. 152–170. https://doi.org/10.4324/9780429430114-14

Paulsen, M. (2022). The plateau of learning in the Anthropocene: how to relate differently to the earth. In Kergel, D. (Ed.), *Learning in the Digital Age: A Transdisciplinary Approach for Theory and Practice*. Springer, pp. 63–86.

Paulsen, M. (2022b). From late Holocene to early Anthropocene educational thinking: Humanism revisited. In Pedersen, K.B. et al. (Eds.), *Rethinking Education in Light of Global Challenges: Scandinavian Perspectives on Culture, Society and the Anthropocene*. Routledge, pp. 204–219. https://doi.org/10.4324/9781003217213-16

Paulsen, M. (2022c). Bildung & technology: historical and systematic relationships. In Kergel, D. et al. (Eds.), *Bildung in the Digital Age: Exploring Bildung through Digital Media in Education*. Routledge, pp. 7–24.

Paulsen, M. (2022d). From onto-sympathy and ecological awareness to ethico-sympathy and zoölogical interaction, embodied beings, and pedagogy in an Anthropocene age. *Futures of Education, Culture and Nature – Learning to Become (FECUN)*, 224–139.

Paulsen, M., & Tække, J. (2020). Acting with and against big data in school and society: the big democratic questions of big data. *The Journal of Communication and Media Studies*, 5(3): 15–31. https://doi.org/10.18848/2470-9247/CGP/v05i03/15-31

Paulsen, M., & Nørreklit, L. (2022). To love and be loved in return: towards a post-Anthropocene pedagogy and humanity. In Paulsen, M. et al. (Eds.), *Pedagogy in the Anthropocene: Re-Wilding Education for a New Earth*. Palgrave Macmillan.

Paulsen, M. et al. (Eds.) (2022). *Pedagogy in the Anthropocene: Re-Wilding Education for a New Earth*. Palgrave Macmillan.

Rancière, J. (2004). *The Politics of Aesthetics: The Distribution of the Sensible*. Continuum.

Rorty, R. (1979). *Philosophy and the Mirror of Nature*. Princeton University Press.

Rüsselbæk Hansen, D. (2020). Digital technologies, big data and ideological (neoliberal) fantasies: threats to democratic efforts in education? *Obra Digital*, 19: 15–28.

Rüsselbæk Hansen, D., & Phelan, A.M. (2019). Taste for democracy: a critique of the mechanical paradigm in education. *Research in Education*, 103(1): 34–48.

Rüsselbæk Hansen, D., & Toft, H. (2020). Play, Bildung and democracy: aesthetic matters in education. *International Journal of Play*, 9(2): 255–267.

Selwyn, N. (2017). *Education and Technology*. Continuum International Publishing Group.

Simons, M., & Masschelein, J. (2008). 'It makes us believe that it is about our freedom': notes on the irony of the learning apparatus. In Smeyers, P., & Depaepe, M. (Eds.), *Educational Research: The Educationalization of Social Problems*. Springer, pp. 191–204. https://doi.org/10.1007/978-1-4020-9724-9.

Toft, H., & Rüsselbæk Hansen, D. (2017). *Ustyrlighedens paradoks: Demokratisk (ud)dannelse til debat* [The Uncontrollable Paradox – Democratic Education for Debate]. Aarhus, Klim.

Tække, J., & Paulsen, M. (2022). *A new perspective on education in the digital age: teaching, media and Bildung*. London: Bloomsbury Academic. https://doi.org/10.5040/9781350175426

Wiedemann, F. (2020). The struggle or data – a ghost goes through the world. In Moss, L. et al. (Eds.), *Re-Centering the Critical Potential of Nordic School Leadership Research. Fundamental, But Often Forgotten Perspectives*. Springer, pp. 129–144.

Wiedemann, F. (2021). *Hvor kommer lyset fra. Data i uddannelse og ledelse* [Where does the light come from? Data in Education and Management]. Odense: University Press of Southern Denmark.

Williamson, B. (2017). *Big Data in Education*. Sage Publications.

Žižek, S. (2004). From politics to biopolitics . . . and back. *The South Atlantic Quarterly*, 103(2/3): 501–521.

Žižek, S. (2008). *The Sublime Object of Ideology*. London: Verso.

Žižek, S. (2009). *Violence: Six Sideways Reflections*. Profile Books.

Zuboff, S. (2019). *The Age of Surveillance Capitalism: The Fight for the Future at the New Frontier of Power*. Profile Books.

Chapter 5

Paranoiac versus agile management of universities

Lennart Nørreklit, Lisa Jack, and Hanne Nørreklit

Introduction

Facilitated by information technology, governance models are progressively observed around the use of performance measurement of all kinds of organizational activities including public institutions (O'Neil, 2016). Obviously, many of the systems now in place in public institutions are designed to combat governance problems of favoritism and prejudice that always have been a challenge. The increased collection and calculation of (big) data might provide a more solid knowledge foundation for making the organizational managers and employees more accountable (Messner, 2009). Paradoxically, however, it is argued that we live in a post-truth era where references to facts and logos appear to be displaced and fictional, with a scant regard for truth (D'Ancona, 2016; Keyes, 2004). The post-truth elements might influence not only the media and political culture but also the culture of management and professions.

Specifically, with the aim of increasing accountability in higher education, we have observed how much of the new public management is now dominated by performance measures, targets, journal rankings, league table placing, income generation figures, student survey scores, and other attempts to capture "excellence." Based on Readings' (1996) prescient *"The University in Ruins,"* Barcan (2013: 68) comments that "Content, he famously declared, is being supplanted by the notion of 'excellence'. He sees excellence as an 'integrating principle' rather than an ideology per se, for it 'has no content to call its own'. Rather, it is a 'unit of currency within a closed field' – a set of measures that assume that there is a 'single standard . . . in terms of which universities can be judged', irrespective of content." In the context of Higher Institutions, there are those that report psychosis among both managers and the managed (Bloch, 2016; Craig et al., 2014; Barcan, 2013). In particular Craig et al. (2014) identify the university within an audit culture dominated by numerical governance as having a psychotic, or paranoid schizoid identity implying a split between the university and the institutional environment. Thus, the governance model that at the surface level is looking as lucid appears less reflective and exhibit indicators of emotional appeal, impoverished logic, and an overreliance on

DOI: 10.4324/9781003188728-6

calculations of performance indicators. Translated into spreadsheets for management and cascaded through the strategic to the day-to-day operations of the university, managers may become paranoid[1] about being seen to create this nebulous "excellent" university and the managed struggle to meet numeric "targets" that demonstrate the attainment of such excellence. The figures have the appearance of being factual, but long-established research in the accounting field alerts us to the illusory nature of such figures and their use by the powerful as ammunition. In such a paranoiac culture, time is spent by managers and co-workers on feelings that people are going to harm or criticize you (Cambridge dictionary definition), rather than in being creative and reflective, perhaps. Consequently, the mind might be deluded by narratives of whether one's perceptions of own identity and that of others can in fact be relied upon.

This chapter is concerned about exploring the nature of the paradox that our governance models increase use of information technology in the production and use of data seems to facilitate a psychotic governance culture. A psychotic can flourish in a post-truth era, where the differences between lying and telling the truth, and between the value of logical reasoning and emotional appeal, are blurred and even lost and where an unhealthy relativism prevails over facts and evidence (D'Ancona, 2016). But, what makes the change into a psychotic culture possible and what leadership is possible for the organizational managers to use in the control of the employees in such a culture? This chapter focuses on the evidence that individual managers in universities can develop paranoid behaviors as a mode of leadership.

Universities are relevant to investigate not only because they, similar to most other public institutions in Western societies, are subject to new public management but also because they play a unique role in that they are the institutions that provide the foundation for a scientific basis where a scientific basis, the secularization, separates from issues of belief, habit, and tradition. If they are unable to fulfil this role then the whole project of enlightenment and knowledge-based society has lost its institutional foundation. Even worse: then the institutional foundations may promote deception and make beliefs of a totally irrational character. That humans are not purely rational beings has been scientifically demonstrated – but science tries to provide instruments with which to understand the irrational elements. But if science itself is an irrational element in the sense mentioned earlier, then society is based on superstition and make-belief, and the basis for reasonable critique and improvement of social power is lost. In such post-truth situation, there is no ethics. One cannot claim that one action is good and another is bad without accepting that others make the opposite claim.

To understand this situation, we start with the notion of language-games that constitute the social factory that must function pragmatically. We have looked for developments that influence the functioning of language in communication.[2] Here, the relatively new control function of scripted language in information technology with its hidden definitions and hidden agendas of control stands out. The more one looks at what is happening, the clearer it becomes that this is something that interferes with and inhibits the social factory by taking control over the concepts and language of the social, increasingly undermining self-controlling individuals on all levels.

We reveal that in an organizational context with conflicting values prevailing narratives of both managers and the managed are paranoiac in ways that were less evident in the past, and this can be linked to these widespread changes in the language of control into the digital language embedded in information technology thus contributing to a post-truth culture. More specifically, the chapter argues that "management by dashboards, Excel spreadsheet, and template" epitomizes digital scripts. Such scripts are given formal status but their content is abstract. Managers in thrall to the digital language of control presented by IT use it to create operational paths that crowd out professional cognitive habitus. The narrative culture changes to one in which convincing logos is replaced by simplistic paranoiac narrations dominate. One example of this is when managers look for culprits and circulate only bad reports of those identified – although there is rarely any credible pragmatic evidence to support the reasons for the attack. Overall, an extensive use of digital scripts as control tools paves the way for the construction of a post-truth state of a paranoiac culture and the establishment of paranoiac targets as a way to exert power and leadership. Even so there is a palpable change in university workplace narratives, the governance problems of favoritism and prejudice have not been solved by the extended use of control systems dominated by the digital founded scripts. To counter the formalistic digital ruling and paranoiac leadership culture, governance system should be changed to reinstall objectives and performance management that are substance related, purposes focused and based on genuine high-level research habitus. In the first section of the chapter, we explain the methodology used. The following section provides theoretical frame of managing a pragmatic functioning social factory and of digital and paranoia management. Subsequently, we illustrate the theoretical framework in examples of corporate university practices. In the final section, we conclude on the problems of digital management of the corporate university and outline the change in governance needed to overcome some of these problems to create an agile university.

Methodological analysis

The methodology that we have developed considers the language-game as life-form philosophy. This follows Wittgenstein's later ideas as a basis of production of meaning and social practice. To understand the concept of a social factory that manufactures functioning practice, we draw on Wittgenstein's later work (1953) that conceives practice as a life form organized around language-games and on pragmatic constructivism to outline what is required to create functioning practice (L. Nørreklit, 2017a, 2017b). Emphasizing the cognitive complexity embedded in the live language-games of capable practices, we use the term a habitus-based language-game. Accordingly, we borrow Bourdieu's (1990) notion of habitus but without using his theoretical meaning and apparatus. Subsequently, to analyze the effects of the comprehensive use of information technology (IT) in social control, we identify the language scripting characteristics of IT systems. The language of IT encapsulates an analytical idea of meaning derived from logical positivism. This is further guided by a form of digital language close to that found in the philosophy of language of Wittgenstein's earlier work, Tractatus Logico-Philosophicus (1921). By contrasting this philosophy of language with that of life-form as language-game, we are able to explain not only the increase in social control by numbers but also totally contrary tendencies such as an apparent decline of rhetoric logos, excessive use of pathos, tendencies to post-truth, and more. We reflect upon whether the managers' actions in such a post-truth culture might become one of floating or executing power. In view of that, we conceptualize the language-games of paranoiac management. Additionally, we illustrate our theoretical framework by studies of contemporary management as experienced by employees in some organizational units of public-funded European University. We look at both publicly accessible narratives and interviews of university researchers. The interviews were shaped in the form of dialogues focusing on how researchers in business and social science studies experience university management. The researchers' micro-stories provide a basis for conceptualizing the management approach as paranoiac. Our study puts forward a conceptual model for understanding the recent development into a paranoiac discourse. The depiction is created in a form that makes it possible for anyone interested to trial in another context. A description of the theoretical and empirical context provides the reader with knowledge of the sites to which the methodologies are applied. In this way, a pre-understanding is provided of whether it is reasonable for the reader to assume that generalization can, and cannot, be extended to another setting. In the conclusion, we concentrate the issues and outline how overcoming the present situation of formalistic and paranoiac ruling by replacing the limitations of present moderate-level centralistic governance by using high-level competence leadership to install agile research based on scientific substance and purpose and supporting this by an active purpose-based network organization to stakeholders.

Habitus-based language-games versus digital language

Language-game and habitus

According to the older Wittgenstein (1953), human life form and practice are unfolding in language-games. A language-game is a story in which narration mixes with other forms of action that are regulated by the various narrations and underlying narratives. Hence language-games produce social and physical realities. They produce a story in which people develop social characters as well as knowledge and skills that enable practices to construct material and human relations and make actions to produce performance. Accordingly, the language-game makes up the social factory that is to produce intentional results and hence to function pragmatically. The story always produces memories through which knowledge accumulates and skills become more and more complex and advanced. The complexity of cognition is expressed by the notion of conceptual habitus. We use the concept "habitus" to emphasize that the live language-game produces a cognition and understanding which is many layered, constantly developing and thus very different from the simplistic or one-dimensional definitions of concepts in theories as well as in performance measurements. Concepts are understood and delimited by understanding their function in the reality construction of the practice or life form. Definitions that delimit the extension of a concept do not produce the understanding but *presuppose* an understanding of the concept (Nørreklit L, 2011, 2017a, 2017b). Practices accumulate our knowledge and add details, aspects, and layers of all possible kinds of insight. Concepts become richer and "thicker" in usage and reflection. A growing cognitive habitus provides abilities to advanced understanding, high-level structuration and thereby to optimize performance in the complexity of situations of real life. The richness of conceptual and other cognitive habitus is a condition for professional cooperation, work, problem-solving, and development of first-class solutions.

Management narration through logos

The language-game of a social factory growing cognitive habitus is free to develop as the participants act on their own initiative. They are agents in the sense that they take care of the life form of people concerned, but their interaction is not a manipulation of each other. When the participants develop their cognitive habitus, the communicative interaction is governed by facts and argumentation. Also, it is important that the narratives are ethical. Ethics is an aspect of social behavior that aims at transforming social interaction to something that is beneficial for the members of society. It promotes actorship as a world of creative co-actorship which promotes construction of social conditions favoring human values and rejects activities that are detrimental to human co-actorship. Obviously, this presupposes general conditions of truth so that people can know and understand each other and achieve realistic estimates whether their activities creative the desired conditions. Without a condition of truth, no co-actorship based on common and coordinated intentions can be constructed.

According to Aristotle (367 BC–322 BC), actors have the following three rhetorical means to obtain approval to their narration: ethos, logos, and pathos. Ethos is the authority, trustworthiness, and power of the narrator. Pathos is the feelings that the narration produces in the receiver, the audience. Logos is the quality of the argument and analysis, which in practice is the feasibility of the knowledge of the situation and how things function. In a knowledge society, logos is supposedly most important. It is a basis for judging and controlling ethos and pathos, avoiding favoritism and prejudice. Without logos, we operate in a post-truth situation. If our rhetoric loses its logos, then our language-games do not produce advanced cognitive habitus to handle the complexities of our situation – because then they are socially useless. Instead they produce authority-pathos-driven communication, that is, opportunistic behavior driven by emotional states such as fear and stress. In a truth situation, leadership is primarily based on logos to develop knowledge and structures that lead to professional competitive performance. Logos presupposes a culture and mindset of ataraxia. Due to the individuality of the cognitive habitus of employees and due to the use of complementary professions, the role of leadership is not simply to dictate their narrative to the employees. Their task is to produce a narrative that enables employees to work at the best of their capacities. To achieve this, they must be involved in the narration, which means that leadership primarily is to orchestrate the narration process – in which they also should participate. A leadership that makes the narrative all by itself is not able to involve the special capacities and motivations of the employees and leads therefore to underperformance. However, if for some reason, the logos becomes insignificant then the integration of the professional knowledge habitus becomes insignificant too, and hence performance may decline or become mediocre. If logos is sidelined, then leadership methods are based purely on ethos and pathos.

Pragmatic reality constructs

It is the language-games that produce the social stories, but we only know the story through the narration of it. It is told in different ways, depending on who tells the story. It may even appear as different stories. These differences are the stuff that conflicts are made of. The only way to analyze which – if any or all – story is trustworthy or truthful is by studying the evidence, if any. But no matter how much we know about "the" story, it is only an abstraction. Nevertheless, it may be more or less true. We argue that although there is no absolute evidence of a story, one can approach the truthfulness of it through the pragmatic truth of the narration. More specific, the narration of language-games is the basis of organizing actions and events, and of structuring cooperation in accordance with desires, knowledge, and skills. The relational structure between actors and their world constitutes their (co-)construction of reality. In some activities, it functions well and produces results, but not so in other activities. In view of that, we use pragmatic criteria to uncover the differences between realistic constructs and illusionary ones. The pragmatic perspective of truth implies that a narrative is trustworthy if it facilitates actions that can fulfil the pro-active true expectations of outcome thus leading to performance.

The pragmatics of narration is the vehicle of successful reality construction. Without this pragmatics, the world of narration is a world of translation only. Action, succeeding, suffering, construction, and failing would be narratives only, there would be no story to be told "behind" the narrative. Thus, it is through the production of narratives that a communication can produce a pragmatic practice and thus develop structured reality in which we can distinguish story and fiction, truthfulness and lies, correctness and error by analyzing the truth gap, that is, the difference between pro-active truth and pragmatic truth (Nørrekli et al., 2007). Thus, a cognitive process (a logos) is being installed that aims at controlling the outcome of actions by reducing the truth gap.

Scripts and dialectics

Verbal expressions and body language communicate their message in a short period of time. They are expressed as they appear, and having once appeared they are already gone. Their expression only lingers in the impressions and memories they produced. Scripts, on the other hand, continue to exist and continue to emit their message as long as they are not destroyed, and are perceivable by somebody who understands their language. Scripts may include tattoos and bodily decorations that signal who you are. It is, however, their ability to endure to exist that separately from the drawings in sand. Enduring scripts on stones, clay, papyrus, and paper produce a message existing independent of a visible messenger. The message of a script is especially powerful because it is enduring. It continues to radiate from its medium. This endurance has made it especially influential as a basis of the social factory. Furthermore, the endurance of scripts has created an ability to focus on important topics, and thus support reflection and develop deeper analysis of important topics. Thus, specialized professional knowledge could be developed and be transmitted through learning. Scripts eventually enabled construction of larger social structures, organizations, cultures, and states. Most scripting is a written presentation of the verbal communication and thus relates to the same underlying conceptual habitus. The use of symbolic forms to produce models and theories is, however, a different form of scripting. It creates sharpness and clarity that enable measurement and calculation, but it eliminates the habitual conceptual complexity.

The symbolic scripts have a special life embedded in human life forms, which they strongly influence. Similar to the absorption of mitochondria by the cells of living organisms, the scripts create new power and energy to organized human life. They influence the language-games to contain messages common to large communities, and they enable development of scientific and professional practices that are impossible without them. In a learned society, they are the common reference points for professional users who have varying complex habitual concepts about the common topics that are represented symbolically. And, it is the independent judgment of the professionals, based on their cognitive habitus, to decide whether the scripted representations are to be believed or whether they should be met with skepticism. Without adequate cognitive habitus, one cannot really understand and use the theories. Thus, the symbolic scripts are common reference points and kind of backbones in the live language-games among scientists and professionals. Scientist and professional users have very complex habitual concepts about the things that are narrated by the scripts that are comparatively simplistic as expressed in simple statements or formulas. Thus, the scripts can function through their interplay with habitual concept formations of the professionals as mediated by academic language-games. Still, it is the live language-game that rules, and it produces the scripts that present the results. Compared to the conceptual habitus, scripts are generally more reductivist in meaning. Especially in theoretical and symbolic languages. Reductionist scripting enables precision, calculation, and control and is thus the basis of a wide range of applicability's augmenting controllability and the production of complex constructs. The interaction between the simplistic symbolic abstractions and the complex cognitive habitus is a dialectic engine driving the development of science. In this dialectics, man makes herself – not a God or higher authority – the master of the symbolic scripts. This epistemological dialectic is a condition for pragmatic truth, the relation between narrative and story, the advancement of conceptual and other cognitive habitus. Losing it means losing the cognitive habitus. This would bring us to the post-truth situation. The world would reduce to impressions. The use of logos and with it structuration and performance would decline.

Digital language

Ordinary language under attack by language puritanism

The language of narratives and narration that creates cognitive conceptual habitus has been under attack. Specifically, the ambition of logical positivism was to replace the logically fuzzy and imprecise language of everyday narration, with a precise and clear unitary language suitable for handling scientific knowledge. The formalization of logic by Frege (1879) and Whitehead and Russell (1910–1913) was the breakthrough in formal logic that constituted the framework for such language. To this formalism, logical positivism added a theory of meaning, the so-called verification theory of meaning, according to which the meaning of a concept, "C," was defined as the set of observations that would verify the existence of a thing or phenomenon of type C. The meaning of the corresponding word, "C," would therefore be a logical function of a set of simple and precise observational statements. One occasional participant in logical positivist meetings was the young Wittgenstein. His early work, *Tractus Logico-Philosophicus (1921)*, analyzes the meaning of a statement by translating it to the symbolic unitary language. In it, complex meanings are to be expressed as a function of basic observational statements called elementary (atomic) sentences

(1921) that are assembled logically to constitute the whole meaning. Wittgenstein envisioned a language demonstrating a world of logical structures that can be projected (translated) in all kinds of language and other phenomena. They illustrate the idea with the logical structure of a piece of music which exists in many forms, in the sound waves that affect our ears and in the vibrations of our eardrums when we hear the music. It exists symbolically in the printed score that is used by the orchestra as well as in the digital structure of the recorded files as well as in the electromagnetic fluctuations controlling the loudspeaker that plays the music, etc. All these phenomena mirror each other because they have the same or at least a rather similar logical structure. Thus, we live in a world of phenomena that are translated into other phenomena by transforming the logical structure into different media.

According to the young Wittgenstein, each elementary shows its own logic. Therefore, they do not need to be demonstrated in an axiomatic system. True and false are basic values concerning the relation between proposition and world. An elementary sentence is true if its logical structure is mirrored in the world. Otherwise, it is false. Accordingly, Wittgenstein's unitary language is operating with a two-valued logic and hence digital in nature. The phenomena that are referred to in the unitary language are logically simple – such as a note and a sound – and referred to by logical names. Since these are quantifiable, the unitary language is quantitative. Although the project to replace ordinary language with a symbolic digital language through translation was eventually given up as impossible and replaced by the philosophy of live language (Wittgenstein, 1953), it was nevertheless realized in the development of IT during the following century. IT is based on a language, which expresses digital logical structures. Many concepts of professional interest and interest of control have been translated to this (these) digital language, implying that the sentences of the system are shaped quantitatively. Each profession has computer operations embedding their major concepts, facilitating analysis, calculations, and operations.

Digital language crowding out conceptual habitus and ethics

IT systems are greatly beneficial if they do not infringe on the epistemological dialectic and harm the social factory. But, if we replace the language used for narration in language-games with such *language puritanism*, the cognitive habitus through which knowledge develops would be eliminated and the social factory would be seriously damaged. The knowledge of the professionals is full of complexities and nuances that cannot be grasped within the two-value logic of the elementary sentences. Applied on such complexities, the true/false value of the elementary sentences and the algorithm calculating the outcome might be highly questionable (O'Neil, 2016). Also, human insights and argumentation would lose its power because it could not add anything to the concepts that they not already have. There is no epistemological dialectics for concepts to unfold in. Also, as there would be no real way to bridge different human interpretations and insights, it would make it difficult if not impossible for people to understand each other. Finally, it should be noted that Wittgenstein (1921) himself draws the inevitable conclusion from his theory of facts and meaning that the subject, meaning, ethics, etc. must be outside the world:

> The subject does not belong to the world: rather, it is a limit of the world. (5.632) . . . All propositions are of equal value (6.4) The sense of the world must lie outside the world. In the world everything is as it is and happens as it does happen. In it there is no value – and if there were, it would be of no value. If there is a value which is of value, it must lie outside all happening and being-so. For all happening and being-so is accidental. What makes it non-accidental cannot lie in the world, for otherwise this would again be accidental. It must lie outside the world (6.41). Hence also there can be no ethical propositions. Propositions cannot express anything higher.
>
> (6.42)

We witness that in the digital/Tractatus-based language, value and the world of facts are separated. Since the purpose of management is the production of value and since facts and truth are the bases of practical reason it follows that a managerial discourse is in a post-truth condition when the language is an IT/Tractatus-based language only. Such post-truth situation implies that there is no reason on why an action is good and another is bad and hence it becomes arbitrary. Eliminating the cognitive approach in post-truth leaves ethics with an eventually possible emotivism in which ethical reasoning just is forms of attempts to manipulate and influence the emotions of the others. Power wins – ethics does not exist. Overall, when the IT scripting changes from being a tool to support professionals' cognitive habitus to become a tool that controls professionals, it sidelines the cognitive habitus and stops the epistemological dialectic. Hence, there is an infringing on professional work, frustrating the professionals. The digital language takes logos out of the managerial discourse because the concepts and structures are predefined in a script outside the reach and control of professionals.

Chamber of delusion

The result of an undermining of the epistemological dialectic is a life in a world of Chinese rooms. Thus, the philosopher John Searle (1980) outlines a world of delusion in his thought experiment called "the Chinese room." Here is a world controlled by symbolic communication. Imagine that a person is locked in a room. Assume they only speak English. There are neither windows nor doors. There is however an inbox and an outbox plus a dictionary expressing rules for translating symbols from – say – one system or language to another. These persons cannot touch nor see the outside world with or about which they are to communicate. They communicate by receiving messages in their inbox and translate them according to their rulebook and deliver the translation in the outbox. When they receive a paper with string of symbols – that are unknown to them – then they look up the symbols in the dictionary and use it to "translate" them to a different string of symbols which they then put in the outbox, without knowing what any of the symbols may refer to. Outside the room, may be two people with different languages communicate through their translations. They know what the messages are about although the translator doesn't. The Chinese chamber is like the von Neuman architecture scheme of a computer: There is an input device and an output device. In the chamber, then there is a memory and a central processing controlling a calculation of the responses. And then there is one writing the message and one receiving and reading the message. They know what things are about, the computer doesn't. Similar constructions are organizational units where people collect and process (big) data – without really relating the data to the pragmatics of the surrounding world, or where they make theoretical analysis without pragmatic access to practice.

Digital language shaping paranoiac management action

When logos is excluded in the managerial communication, only ethos and pathos are left and hence it opens the space for a post-truth culture, with a scant regard for truth (D'Ancona, 2016; Keyes, 2004). It implies that management will be dominated by delusion, and it would become impossible for management to create a successful reality construction. But how and what leadership is possible – if any – in such a sit where logos breaks down? One type of management action might be paranoid schizoid in nature implying a detachment between management and employees and hence managers float and lose control of the employees' actions. They see the digital language of control as a matter of legitimation of their position to the environment (Meyer and Rowan, 1977), but leave it to the cognitive habitus of the employees to find a solution. However, given the institutional power of the digital language it might be difficult to escape in a hierarchical organizational structure. There the targets of the digital language might be powerful ammunition for the superiors to win the political struggles with subordinates about non-shared values (Broadbent and Laughlin, 2005). In view of that another type of management action might be that in defence of the reality loss of the digital language, ongoing emotional management agitation might overrule the interpretations and insights of operational employees of rather obvious facts and evidence. Management might then reinterpret everything as a confirmation of a specific paranoiac axiom involving a delusion of persecution.

In paranoiac argumentation, the ruling narrations and choice of language are dominated by impoverished logic, arguments using authority and emotional appeal. Additionally, one sees a process concerned with establishing the following paranoiac axiom: looking for a culprit. The basic paranoiac culprit claim is an axiom because there is no reason behind the claim. We call it paranoia because it (re) interprets evidence so that it always cooperates the basic paranoiac claim. All rules of evidence are then bent and bowed so that all evidence seem to support the paranoiac axiom – although to non-pathological people with elementary knowledge, it is obvious that this way of interpreting the evidence is distorted and unrealistic. A pathological paranoia distorts and destroys cognition, logos, and the sound judgment of an independent mind. It does so not so much by denying the existence of phenomena but by distorting their relations. The focal point of finding a culprit makes the paranoiac argumentation different from more unfocused psychotic types of language where arguments are floating in nature (Craig et al., 2014).

Empirics: digital and paranoid university management

In recent decades, the corporate university has replaced a profession-driven governance system that had developed over centuries in most public-funded Western universities. The corporate university is subjected to the governance principles of New Public Management (Craig et al., 2014). A board composed of people from universities and public and private sector organizations has the authority to appoint the university management. The relation between the university management and the funding ministries are governed by rules and contracts including quantitative measures. The university is organized as a top-down hierarchy implying that there is trickle-down effect, where externally evoked quantitative objectives that are targeted at an entire institution are translated into measurable objectives that are deployed further down in the organizational structures within the various departments, research groups, and eventually on the individual researcher.

Digital management

University management by Excel spreadsheet

In recent years, we witness, the discovery that IT is an exceptional instrument for hierarchical control of the conceptual habitus has created impetus to implement IT systems in any sector all over society. Specifically, at universities, we see that IT, first in the form of Excel spreadsheets and templates, and more recently in the form of dashboards, have come to dominate the ministry's governance of universities. For instance, the resource allocation of funding among universities and the performance evaluation of the university management, the minister of education and research uses quantitative output measures. Thus, most university revenue is directly linked to the activity of produced student output units and efficiency in student throughput time. Also, the allocation of research funding among universities is to a large degree based on the calculation of publication points earned according to a journal-ranking list. Increasingly, the quality of the study programs is driven by standards and criteria formulated by external agents rather than academics' knowledge and judgment. These dashboards, Excel spreadsheets, and templates also dominate the management approach within the university. Thus, dominating tools for management control of employees are teaching workload models, journal ranking lists, student satisfaction surveys, annual planning cycles, employee conversation templates, course description templates, etc. The following utterance by a former member of a management team exhibits calculative economic mindset of the management team aiming at installing what we term *management by Excel spreadsheet*:

> we were considering putting all work tasks into a weighted norm-system, i.e. prices on different types of research, teaching, dissemination then make a great metric . . . There was a heavy economist toolkit way of thinking around the table . . . And our department management has human characteristics where he's probably closer to an Excel sheet than most.

Embedded in the Excel spreadsheet and the templates is the binary digital language of computers, where answers to a set of elementary sentences are a matter of true or false statements. For instance, the quantitative output measures of journal ranking list is based on a set of elementary sentences where publications belong to category I, II, III, or IV that can be on one and zero, representing whether it should be counted for or not. Aiming to put all activities into a weighted workload model such as they were advocating is a quite extreme version of Excel spreadsheet management. Yet the formulae and calculations in an Excel spreadsheet can be read and analyzed if one chooses and one has an unlocked version of the spreadsheet. Some literacy in equations and logic enable the reader to reconstruct the purpose of the equations, and to audit them. However, in more institutions, large-scale digital education management platforms are being used to collect data on staff and students, reporting back through pre-programmed key performance indicators, graphical images, and alert systems presented on a dashboard. While a function could be used to expose the programming beneath the images on the screen, many managers may not be able to follow the logic in the programming. Hence, the simplification of presentation by graphics, which can be monitored constantly, is a further reduction of language and amplifies issues relating to the diminished recognition of professional judgment.

There are a growing number of studies around "personalized learning analytics for students" both from the viewpoint of academics and administrators, and from the student viewpoint (see, for example, Roberts et al., 2017). However, we are more concerned here with what McCoy and Rosenbaum (2019) identify as "Decision Support System Data Dashboards," designed to help managers make institutional decisions. They uncover unintended consequences in the form of shadow practices, arising from implementations of systems that fail to seek the input from professional academics in the design phase of the system.

They also identify that there is little work so far on such systems and observe the following (2019, 370): As these systems begin to proliferate throughout HEI, attention must be given to how their user-facing dashboards influence decision-making practices and behavior. While there are cited benefits of DSS dashboards, the underlying algorithms, data selection and analyses, and visual representations of the data are often indiscernible to users, yet these technical and analytical processes are designed to produce and support specific user interactions and practices (Williamson, 2016). Like McCoy and Rosenbaum (2019, p. 372), we are trying to understand "the interplay between use and the complex socio-technical nature of these systems." Overall, we witness that the description of many complex practice activities such as teaching, and research are written into dichotomous elementary sentences and hence into digital statements that can be counted. As the departments have many different specialties that are to be managed within one organizational unit, the use of the unitary digital language implies that the qualities of the various professional fields can be made into standard comparable units measured by the same measurement norm. However, the ideal of the elementary sentence projecting and objective phenomenon out there is questionable, which is further explained in the following section.

Dashboards and Excel spreadsheet taking power over the conceptual habitus

Interviewees observed that the production and use of numbers put into the Excel spreadsheet is not based on open and sound argumentation among colleagues but rather on hidden agendas. In an experience relayed by a former member of a management team, decision-making is not driven solely from ideas of the management but through hidden lobbyism where people with special self-interests influence the managers' decisions. As there is distributed access to management, we see that the management decisions are more closely attached to some individuals than to others. One employee felt that the journal ranking lists give higher preference quantitative research while excluding much conceptual and qualitative research. Some high-ranked journals within some professional-based fields have been taken over by mathematicians, statisticians, or sociologists, who do not have any intention of relating to the conceptual habitus of practice in the profession. Also, highly recognized journals within a small field of research are excluded, because their impact factor is not deemed to be sufficiently high (Archambault & Larivière, 2009, p. 639). Although the ranking tables might have a bias toward research less relevant in relation to teaching for practice, they govern the recruitment process and influence researchers' behavior toward certain directions. This can be seen as an example of how professional comment from academics on the quality of work in their field is discarded in favor of more reductive metrics that can be incorporated more easily in an Excel spreadsheet for the purposes of comparison. Another instance of crowding out specialist insight came in relation to teaching evaluation where a program leader felt pressured to exclude professional considerations and certain notions of quality. They argue that one should listen to the students, but academics should define the content and the academic level of the courses. They think that management will agree in principle, but in their everyday talk what dominates are the performance measures. The program leader expressed this thinking as follows:

> Can we get our student income, can we get our student finishing bonus, can we have some evaluations that show that students have learned what they need from day one and all that kind of thing?

Again, meetings with managers around teaching initiatives appear to many non-managers to take form of a pseudo-debate governed by a hidden agenda. Often what comes out of the meeting doesn't look like what is agreed upon but something else.

Overall, we observe that the Excel spreadsheet numbers and dashboard visualizations are taking over professional knowledge and argumentation. The production and use of numbers seem to be driven by a hidden reasoning that involve self-interest and is executed by hierarchical power. Professional habitus are supplanted by power and control habitus that are concerned without maneuvering the habitus of employees and other "adversaries." Overall, there is a breakdown in logos in relation to the production and use of the numbers. To employees, the flexibility in the rules controlling the language can be simply perceived as deceiving and cheating and demonstrates that the leadership is aiming to make itself unaccountable. In this case, there is a distrust in management reasoning and ethics expressed by academics.

Chamber of delusions

The digital language implies that the management detach themselves from core problems experienced by the employees at the operational level. "Only the number of articles published to increase the number of stars in the rankings" might count when promoting or recruiting employees. Jérôme Barthélemy). The system significantly impairs the use of professional judgment. Accordingly, important decisions tend to be outsourced to bodies external to the particular university context, who do not know or care about the university and its stakeholders. It implies that some university units come to not to care about the research content of the teachers they recruit. As there is a bias in the journal rankings, some fields are advanced while others are hindered (Archambault & Larivière, 2009, p. 639). Journal listings privilege quantitative research as shown by the observation that high-ranked journals are dominated by quantitative research appear to exemplify this position (Merchant, 2010; Nørreklit et al., 2019). Also, embedded in such management approach is a systematic crowding out of some relevant and professional knowledge areas and of teaching. As one employee pointed out, some teaching programs seem to be the losers in the decision-making process:

> Again and again in connection with recruitment, we see the question in relation to the people employed . . . what the hell are we going to make them do? And finally, when we have some applications with competences where we have something to make them do then they don't fit into the department.

Problems integrating research and teaching arise because of a split between two types of managers governed by different Excel spreadsheets. The managers of teaching do not have authority in terms of recruitment, while managers of research and recruitment are far less knowledgeable about what goes on in the educational area. The conflict is shown by the fact that disagreements among the managers of teaching and research often arise at meetings. However, in public they lay down the conflict, which creates uncertainty at operational levels about the conditions for construction of their practices. Navigating in such a field is as mentioned by one employee: "as if one walks around in a minefield in the dark." The recruitment policy implies that it is impossible for the program leader to develop teaching programs highly relevant for practice: "We have some ideas . . . but we lack people that can teach the courses. . . . It is always the next best solutions we come up with." We see that the development of an advanced conceptual habitus is under-discouraged. But management does not appear to regard the lack of staff with relevant qualifications as a problem. One reason, according to the leader of the teaching program, is that the employees have to make the teaching function. Hence, management does not hear about or experience that it is a problem. But it puts a lot of pressure on the employees:

> All the colleagues I have within my field teach too much. And if you get sick or is on leave, have a kid or quit, then there is a House of cards that collapses. And then we have to get it to work again in one way or another.

"Makes things work" can be said to be the conceptual habitus at the operational level. Overall, the management approach contributes to a research-teaching-practice gap, but the management detaches themselves from this. We witness a management chamber of delusion. Here there is a world controlled by symbolic numbers. The managers are locked in a closed chamber. They only speak the language of Excel spreadsheet. The Excel spreadsheet provides the managers inbox. It has a dictionary expressing rules for translating the language of professionals to the symbolic language of numbers. The managers cannot touch nor see the professionals' practice situation. The managers communicate with the professionals by receiving messages in their inbox and translate them according to their flexible rulebook and deliver the translation into action in the outbox to the professionals. Outside the room there are people with different languages who have to take action based on the communication through the manager's translations. They know what the messages are about and implies although the managers don't. Ironically, politicians and organizations call for applicable research and teaching relevant for practice. Accordingly, we find a management view apparently dominated by systematic delusions. They do not appear concerned about the pragmatic implications of their management approach for practice. And politicians and organizations cannot see what is going on, as the numbers of Excel spreadsheets also dilute the institutional environment (Craig et al., 2014).

Paranoiac management action

Despite the chamber of illusion, the managers now and then meet with the problems and arguments of the professionals. We find that the managers' narrations and choice of language in this interaction tend to use insubstantial argumentation and systematic intimidation of culprit and hence establishing the paranoiac axiom. In the following, we illustrate the paranoiac argumentation of the university managers.

Managers meeting conceptual habitus with insubstantial argumentation

One interviewee points out that managers, when interacting with professional academics, sometimes tend provide poorly structured argumentation. Managers are alleged to suppress arguments requiring professional and specialist knowledge. For instance, older scholars might be accused of being management-resistant and not keeping up with times:

> We are accused of being grudging and nostalgic people, who have not kept up with the current areas and do not understand today's rules – We just want to go back to the old days of nepotism, at home research and general idleness.

Also, a dominating argument used by managers is that academics in the department do research across a broad spectrum of fields and consequently, anybody can teach any part of the curriculum at the BA level. Similarly, one manager claims, "I can judge all applications at the PhD, assistant, and associate professorship level within all the department areas of disciplines." When a committee with no specific knowledge within the discipline recruited a person with poor qualifications, the department manager said that this could also happen to a committee with knowledge within the field. This leads to a strange form of argument that posits that if all people, including those within a field, are liable to error failure then it does not matter whether you know something or not. It demonstrates a lack of ability to tell the difference between truth and falsehood, that is, insubstantial argumentation, characteristic of a post-truth environment (D'Ancona, 2016). Similarly, a case of lack of respect for field specific knowledge came across in a situation where a young researcher was invited to give a paper and a job interview to two managers. Neither of the managers knew anything about the field. Therefore, an academic within the field did some lobbying to make the management agree to get a competent specialist reviewer attend the interview. The applicants gave a substantial presentation, but did not get the job with the argument from the manager of research unit that they had not enough "edge." Instead, they appointed one outside the teaching area of the department, but close to the research network of the management. Professional detailed insight into the matter is not used for decision-making, because the management does not have the prerequisites for recognizing and using it. By the same token, managers might become aggressive and use absolutistic ruling techniques. For instance, two employees had been called for warning meeting with their managers regarding teaching capacity within their academic field. They explained that they did not have the surplus capacity themselves to teach the course, and that on the whole the department had a shortage of people with qualifications in the field. They hoped that the manager could help finding some who could teach the course. After the meeting, they send e-mail to the managers and ask for their conclusion to the meeting. The answer was as follows: I concluded that you are not willing to teach the course. Since professionals have a strong culture, the implementation of language puritanism inevitably involves conflict. In these cases, we see how managers use nonvalid and unsound argumentation and consider professional fields as being broadly open to interpretation by nonspecialists. This contributes to a sense of outrage but also paranoia. Furthermore, the patronizing and undermining of the argumentation of professional academics can be incorporated into allegations against them when culprits are being sought.

University management by systematic intimidation of culprit

The university managers' paranoiac axiom is somewhat hidden because managerial decisions are made behind closed doors. But although the specific culprit maybe hidden, it should be noted that embedded in a language-game governed by language puritanism, conceptual habitus is defined as bad, while the numbers signify the right or good. The scholars with publication in top-ranked journals are ranked above the teaching scholars in the organizational hierarchy. For instance, in France, some scholars publishing in top-ranked journals are "living like a mercenary star who goes from one international conference to another . . . and avoiding teaching" (Barthélemy, Le Monde 28 Octobre 2018, translated from French). In the UK, the adjective "REF-able" dominates university discourse. The term means that one has enough publications of sufficient quality within the REF period (five to six years) to be included in the department's submission to the REF. However, this might not be sufficient, because the publications should have three or four stars in order to be "internationally excellent". The REF has become naturalized in the rhetoric of what academic success is understood to mean. Moreover, the journal guide is conflated with decisions about which papers to submit to the REF, despite the fact that journal rankings are not used in the assessments of individual papers. This constitutes a form of symbolic violence that can unduly influence management decisions. The Guardian newspaper has reported a widespread culture of bullying at UK universities:

> Research staff who had fallen out of favour would routinely be denigrated behind their backs, and her boss responded with explosive anger to scientific setbacks and made comments seemingly designed to humiliate. "She'd ask the impossible and get really angry when you said no. Too much was never enough," she said. "People would be in tears." . . . The head of department was aware of the problem but had an attitude of "just take it on the chin and get on with it."
>
> (The Guardian, 2018)

Interviews also revealed that managers apply a sinking warship language-game in response to an issue raised by an employee affected by a management decision: "Oh no, it was not you we wanted to *strike*." Another example is the comments of two managers in relation to a couple of academics' problematic behavior in relation to teaching: "I can hit him through the teaching norm system" and "we have made the new norm system so we can get him now." In general, the experience is that when someone is found to be in bad standing, then a new administrative rule is applied to challenge the conceptual habitus of academics. Similarly, management communication is heavily laced by straw man arguments of unprofessional behavior by an employee as, for instance, "now you should be careful not to show opportunistic behavior." The management argumentation is clearly dominated by paranoiac axioms: they are looking for a culprit. Drawing on the Excel spreadsheet or dashboard, leaders have a tool for fighting and subduing their professionals' cognitive habitus – their own "army" – rather than helping them to perform. Also, some academics can find themselves in bad-standing with the management if they are critical toward the management strategy: "I've come in bad-standing . . . Because I have said something . . . I've said it to them a few times too many" (employee). More specifically, a very successful academic had pointed out organizational problems in some areas of the university and made constructive suggestions to enable a more pedagogic and practice-relevant direction to be adopted. Reportedly, the reaction from management was to exclude academics from various university support services. The example they chose to give was that in conjunction with a top-ranked consultancy company, they were going to launch some pretty big, very business relevant research at a conference with many highly influential politicians and businesspeople. They informed the Communications Department about the event and asked whether they were coming. It should be of interest for the university as the top management repeatedly in their newsletters claim that they will move closer to business. Nevertheless, the message from the communication department was that "they have no resources to do this." The employee's conclusion on the event was "I very strongly believe that they are trying to make sure we are sidelined." Regardless of the strength of these allegations, the employee felt that management was actively looking for ways to criticize or harm them and their team.

Similarly, we were told that academic arguments are crowded out in the interaction between management and academic staff by bullying. One stated management aim is to implement common teaching methods and courses in all the educational programs. The program leader has raised substantial arguments against a method being useful for students of leader's area of specialty. But the leader was met with what can be construed as bullying:

> I noticed a pressure and then when the material for the next meeting came out they wrote that the method course is for "(almost) all programs" where you put "almost" in brackets . . . my criticism is communicated in a way that I perceive as laughing at me. I ignore it in the context, but when I go home after coming from a meeting then I am thinking 'damn, why should something which . . . is a serious, professional, fundamental point be made fun of?'

Some months later, the course was implemented as management required a top-down decree overruling the conceptual habitus of academics.

Finally, a manager might intimidate the individual employees directly to put them "in their place." For instance, one employee expressed a criticism of the journal ranking lists at a department meeting. Then, at their yearly employee appraisal, the manager gave them a reprimand because they had said too much, and this reprimand closed down the debate. The employees were criticized for the position that they took in an anonymous, unclear manner. The manager claimed to be passing on a criticism made by another person. After the meeting, the employee felt puzzled and uncomfortable:

> you sit back just wondering how can we understand this . . . What are the norms here? . . . I've experience several of the subliminal ways in which they go after their man . . . Not my professional assessment but that there is something wrong with me personally.

Other interviews also report being taken to task by managers over anonymous allegations about their social behavior, rather than matters being resolved more openly and professionally.

We see in the quotes that managers, through hostile actions, turn those academics that raise fair critique into enemies. Such allegations against sensible arguments from the surrounding world are characteristics of paranoid delusions. Overall, the paranoiac culture thrives when it reaches the stage where people are afraid to take a reflective and independent reasoned stance, because such a stand puts one in danger.

Discussion: paranoiac versus agile governance

Paranoiac management by digital technology

The article has examined some implications of using IT as an exceptional instrument for the new public management of the professionals and their conceptual habitus. IT is an efficient instrument wherever it can be used. As a general instrument, IT is neutral – beyond any value and meaning – and therefore a neutral non-biased technology for communication, calculation, information, and much more. These features make it flexible and often usable in agile projects where it also facilitates high-level conceptualizations and theoretical developments. Thus, developers produce IT technologies for all kinds of purposes – good as well as bad – including the purpose of performance management. Also, in that regard, it is effective but at the present, it is often used to enforce detrimental forms of performance management. However, the analysis demonstrates that management by digital technology interferes with and inhibits the social factory of researchers by taking control over the concepts and language of the social. The control software uses a reductive language based on one-dimensional definition that expresses simplified concepts based on the developers' limited level of knowledge of the field they are interpreting in their efforts of "translation." This comprehensive digital form of control involves control over the language and the meaning of words. Making such definitions becomes the basis of control of research processes, disables the abilities of high-level habitual cognition of researchers to function and enable production of theoretically interesting results. The researchers lose their control over the meaning of their language and hence they cannot develop concepts and theories. We witness that IT is used to produce infinite amounts of administrative reporting about the performance of the university scholars, which are used by management to exercise rigid and autocratic governance of researchers. Such governance approach eliminates agility in leadership of research and education and influences innovative high-level research performance negatively.

More specific, the low-level IT conceptualization, that in principle measures something irrelevant, provides space for governing bodies to produce fictional results by changing the rules of language – that is, by changing the criteria and definitions. Increasingly, governing bodies have autocratic power to define the rules of the language-games even though their knowledge about the work is not on the professional level of their employees. The systems of IT-based formal performance criteria have been introduced to ease managerial control using enforced self-regulation mechanism to keep employees stressed and busy. Employees are always forced to compete against each other in a way where some of them must lose. Additionally, management enforces isolation, stress, and fear by enforcing paranoiac principles. It is the formal nature of the performance criteria, which generates post-truth situations because formal criteria have no real conceptual content and are consequently not in a meaningful relation to advanced – university level – research performance, which involves development of conceptualization and theoretical work. A consequence is that conceptual criteria are replaced by paranoiac principles of control. Although they give the impression of producing control, they produce stress, fear, and nonsense.

The formal nature of criteria enables the paranoiac process because the formality means that the substance, the real content, and thus the real purpose of the performance are fictive. It is a number (e.g., be number 1) or a formal reward (excellence). Real performance on the other hand needs a purpose related to conceptualized and recognized values. A performance can only be a contribution to any such purpose. All goals need to be formulated in relation to a purpose. The formal criteria of performance are, however, not tied to any research purpose. A purpose must be conceptualized, it cannot only be a number in a ranking, number of articles, number of references, etc. It must be the contributions the research articles make. Formal criteria pollute research by inspiring to manipulate and produce alliances to generate the numbers instead of inspiring to producing results with a purpose. Neither employees, managers, nor society know the purpose of the formal numbers. The only obvious purpose is the ability to brag, but the purpose of social institutions is not to brag.

It is no surprise that when managers with low knowledge in a special field control high-level knowledge researcher,[3] then they cannot formulate and enforce genuine performance goals. They may create the impression that their paranoiac leadership is agile, but this is an illusion. The only thing agile about low-knowledge leadership is that it may be agile in dismantling high-level of knowledge to maintain control. Agile leadership presupposes advanced cognitive habitus that enables them to function in a high-level language-game in order to set up the various steps or incremental sprints and lead them in the direction that produces cognitive development – that is, research – and not reproduction of low-level knowledge proving trivialities almost on pair with ordinary professional reports written in any practice. IT control systems function as a protective layer which enables management to "control" just about anything – except agile research development or agile development of educational activities.

The agile university beyond the paranoia

We suggest that the focus on agility can be used to overcome the paranoiac rule, minimize favoritism and prejudice, by installing a high-level, dynamic, and purpose-based research management at the university. To implement agility in research and higher education, a high level of conceptualization – an advanced cognitive habitus – in leadership of research and high-level education is needed. In the agile university, the research and education activities are led by high-level habitus-based competence and insight with a view to addresses essential research-oriented social purposes. Accordingly, the governance structure of universities must be changed. The hierarchical structure of the corporate university governance has to go. We emphasize two structures in the governance of the agile university: i) a network management to facilitate a formulation of purposes and ii) a high-level research and education management to facilitate agile research and education in accordance with the purpose. The network management analyzes the university's purpose and service to society. The service is to be conceptualized and communicated in a much richer language inside the university as well as outside. The purpose and goals of the activities must be clearly and meaningfully formulated by the managers of research and educational activities. As the purposes and goals serve social values, the formulation must be carried out in interactions and negotiations with external stakeholders. Formalistic goals with no social meaning must be avoided. This should ensure that they are formulated, and their achievement monitored, according to a research-based understanding of social needs. The final decision of the university's purposes and goals is with the management of research and education because they have extensive insight in the meaningfulness of the objectives and whether it is factual possible to realize them. Accordingly, the university needs to be able to set up a network management system that conveys the purposes and goals of university activities by externalizing them outward and the interests of the external stakeholders by reporting them inward. The network should negotiate the purposes and goals of the university. IT should create a sound and productive relationship between the purposes of research activities and the external stakeholders' requests. The role of the current members of boards and university leaders should therefore shift from controlling researchers to supporting the formation of the network's necessary agile management of the various research and training activities.

Research and teaching activities must be led by leaders that possess the competences of advanced university researcher in the specific field, so that they are able to communicate with the researchers in a competent, inspiring, and meaningful way. This leadership is to help the research projects achieve high-level research goals in contrast to average reporting that managers with a narrow research experience and limited understanding how research functions can support. In addition, leaders should comply with principles of agility to play an active role in the research team. Agility in research and education is enforced through a continuous stream of short-term incremental project steps whose progress, in turn, is monitored and enforced through a learning process that observes the difference between pro-active expectations and pragmatic realization (Nørreklit, 2017). In view of this, it is important to develop some new conceptual frameworks for the performance management of university activities that meet basic criteria of conceptual qualities such as abstract and criterion-based meaning and exemplars. These criteria are developed, justified, and criticized by researchers. The present formal criteria should be sidelined in research evaluation or be redefined to match the research substance, its purpose, and the status and progress. IT performance measurement systems should be developed and made an informative tool that openly reflects the work of all researchers with their special projects, resources, and purposes. In this way, it may – eventually – be transformed to support agile research management. When research is led by high-level knowledge and principles of agility, then there is no need for paranoiac control, which therefore is replaced by advanced evaluation related to the research area and thus the function this research serves. This implies that the role of IT in control is transformed to an auxiliary instrument to qualified leadership. Formal low-level rule through IT-controlled conceptualization is replaced by substantial high-level research and purpose-based rule, which involves more advanced artificial intelligence.

The agile university promises much better performance in respect to relevance, quality, and efficiency. It is a more motivating workplace, where researchers communicate on small- and high-level issues, and where ideas are produced and tested continuously. It is a place where favoritism and prejudice have difficult times and paranoiac leadership has no chance. Further, it is a place where IT-based performance systems become much more advanced, more open, more directed toward being informative, and useful to researchers.

Generalization and further research

Although our findings focus on a few members of staff in European Universities, the narratives and stories of delusions are found in other institutions, in other developed countries, and international politics (Barcan, 2013; Craig et al., 2014). The issues are found across disciplines. Other forms of management narratives may be possible, and for Barcan (2013) there is a hope that "rather than striving to be the one who embodies it all, we should rather celebrate the fact that between us, as a collegiate, we have the bases covered." It means, however, creative construction of a communication in which the story has a different driving narrative to the paranoia induced when managers rely on themselves to act as arbitrators of all activity and needs. However, our analysis gives reason to have major concerns. The IT system provides technological power that can exercise control to an extent, that it in detail can prescribe, what the employees must do, while managers might invoke motivational action in the employees though emotional pressure as, for instance, formulating unrealistic and ambiguous motivational targets, and linking punishment and rewards to the degree of achievement. Additionally, the power of managers is reenforced by the fear that the paranoia process produces. This is exacerbated when the culprit has been found and established in the mind of people as the chosen culprit (the paranoiac axiom). From that time, evidence is put forward that supposedly confirms that this is a culprit, even where the evidence is allegedly unreliable. Somebody trying to be fair and defend the culprit or point out their good sides find suspicions turned on themselves as one with the culprit. The uneasiness in living under the expectation of attack adds to the fear within the paranoiac culture and motivates people to adapt rather than to become victimized. Furthermore, language only functions if people can trust what the words mean. As soon as there is a remote control of the meaning of words and this remote control always is busy manipulating the meaning, then researchers' conceptual habitus are sidelined. What appears as logos is most likely a part of the paranoia culture and not trustworthy as logos any longer. Thereby our findings match the conclusions by Wittgenstein (1921) in the *Tractatus* and described earlier that the subject, meaning, ethics, etc. must be outside the world. We appear to have reached such a post-truth condition state, where rational thought and ethics are without value.

We need further research on the effect of such simplistic, yet powerful instrumental language-game and how to act against such development. In particular, it seems fruitful to investigate the possibilities of withdrawing from a paranoia culture. We seem to be trapped in the language-game of paranoia, but a new type of language-games might make us able to transgress the paranoia culture.

Notes

1 Paranoia is a psychosis that includes a specific dominating claim involving a systematized delusion of persecution toward oneself despite strong evidence against it (Merriam-Webster, 2017). An ongoing emotional agitation against someone or something overrules ordinary interpretation of evidence and reinterprets everything as a confirmation of the specific paranoid claim.
2 A language-game is in our usage any communicative interaction ranging from communication to coordinate organized activities, to express fantasies and play or simply to engage in conversation.
3 We define high-level knowledge researchers as researchers with substantial research experience well beyond the PhD level and familiar with the workings and needs of projects of research groups. In contrast, average and moderate level refers to a knowledge level below high level.

References

Archambault, É., & Larivière, V. (2009). History of the journal impact factor: Contingencies and consequences. *Scientometrics*, 79: 635–649. https://doi.org/10.1007/s11192-007-2036-x

Aristotle. (367 BC-322 BC). *The Art of Rhetoric (τέχνη ῥητορική)*, translated by Lawson, H. London: Penguin (1991).

Barcan, R. (2013). *Academic Life and Labour in the New University: Hope and Other Choices*. Abingdon: Routledge.

Barthélemy, Jérôme (2018). Le Monde, Paris. 28 Octobre.

Bloch, C. (2016). *Passion and Paranoia: Emotions and the Culture of Emotion in Academia*. London: Routledge.

Bourdieu, P. (1990). *The Logic of Practice*. London: Polity Press.
Broadbent, J., & Laughlin, R. (2005). Organisational and accounting change: theoretical and empirical reflections and thoughts on a future research agenda. *Journal of Accounting & Organizational Change*, 1(1): 7–25.
Cambridge Dictionary. (2017). Retrieved from http://dictionary.cambridge.org
Craig, R., Amernic, J., & Tourish, D. (2014). Perverse audit culture and accountability of the modern public university. *Financial Accountability & Management*, 30(1): 1–24
D'Ancona, M. (2016). *Post-Truth: The New War on Truth and How to Fight Back*. London: Ebury Press.
Frege, G. (1879). *Begriffsschrift, eine der arithmetischen nachgebildete Formelsprache des reinen Denkens*. Halle: Nebert.
Keyes, R. (2004). *The Post-Truth Era: Dishonesty and Deception in Contemporary Life*. London: St. Martin's Press.
McCoy, C., & Rosenbaum, H. (2019). Uncovering unintended and shadow practices of users of decision support system dashboards in higher education institutions, *Journal of the Association for Information Science and Technology*, 70(4): 370–384.
Merchant, K.A. (2010). Paradigms in accounting research: a view from North America. *Management Accounting Research*, 21(2): 116–120.
Merriam-Webster Dictionary. (2017). Retrieved from https://www.merriam-webster.com/dictionary/dictionary
Messner, M. (2009). The limits of accountability. *Accounting, Organizations and Society*, 34(8): 918–938.
Meyer J., & Rowan, B. (1977). Institutionalized organizations: formal structure of myth and ceremony. *American Journal of Sociology*, 83.
Nørreklit, H., Nørreklit, L., & Mitchell, F. (2007). Theoretical conditions for validity in accounting performance measurement. In Neely, A. (Ed.), *Business Performance Measurement – Frameworks and Methodologies*. Cambridge: Cambridge University Press, pp. 179–217.
Nørreklit, L. (2011). Actors and reality: a conceptual framework for creative governance. In Jakobsen, M., Johanson, I.-L., & Nørreklit, H. (Eds.), *An Actor's Approach to Management: Conceptual Framework and Company Practices*. Copenhagen: DJOEF, pp. 7–37.
Nørreklit, L. (2017a). Paradigm of pragmatic constructivism. In Nørreklit, H. (Ed.), *A Philosophy of Management Accounting: A Pragmatic Constructivist Approach*. London: Routledge, pp. 21–94.
Nørreklit, L. (2017b). Paranoia and control. A narrative about the social factory. In Hepp, R.D., Kergel, D., & Riesinger, R. (Eds.), *Social Vulnerability. Hyperprecarization and Social Structural Transformations in European Societies*. Springer. Wiesbaden (Forthcoming).
Nørreklit, L., Jack, L., & Nørreklit, H. (2019). Moving towards digital governance of university scholars: instigating a post-truth university culture. *Journal of Management and Governance*, 23(4): 869–899.
O'Neil, K. (2016). *Weapons of Math Destruction*. New York: Crown Random House.
Readings, B. (1996). *The University in Ruins*. Boston, MA: Harvard University Press.
Roberts, L.D., Howell, J.A., & Seaman, K. (2017). Give me a customizable dashboard: personalized learning analytics dashboards in higher education. *Technology, Knowledge and Learning*, 22(3): 317–333.
Searle, J. (1980). Minds, brains and programs. *Behavioral and Brain Sciences*, 3(3): 417–457.
The Guardian. (2018). Retrieved from https://www.theguardian.com/education/2018/sep/28/academics-uk-universities-accused-bullying-students-colleagues

Williamson, B. (2016). Digital education governance: Data visualization, predictive analytics, and 'real-time' policy instruments, *Journal of Education Policy*, 31(2): 123–141.

Wittgenstein, L. (1921). Tractatus logico-philosophicus. In Pears, D.F., & McGuinnes, B.F. (Eds.), *Annalen der Naturphilosophie*, English translation. Routledge & Kegan Paul, London and Henley (1961).

Wittgenstein, L. (1953). *Philosophical Investigations*, translated by Anscombe, G.E.M. Oxford: Basil Blackwell.

Part 2

Learning and management in the digital age

Chapter 6

From agile management to agile-orientated teaching and learning
A heuristic analysis

David Kergel and Birte Heidkamp-Kergel

Dialog as a principle of digital communication – or: on the way to the digital age

The digital age offers a decentralized communication infrastructure. From a genealogical point of view, the Internet can be seen as both:

- a collaborative learning and management project: There is no particular person who invented the Internet as such. In the development process that gave birth to the Internet, the collaborative exchange of knowledge and collaborative construction were the actual "pacemaker." Spontaneous ideas such as the invention of e-mail in 1987 were generated and changed the communication culture permanently.
- a challenge for management: Elaborate management strategies were required to link the various networks that emerged from the late 1970s onward.

For example, a standardized protocol was needed to connect the multiple networks to establish the Internet as a network of networks. This happened in 1983 when the TCP/IP protocol was introduced (this protocol defined how data packets were resolved and sent to the receiver). The TCP/IP protocol is paradigmatic because the Internet as a network of networks is the result of collaborative learning and management process.

As a communications infrastructure, the Internet community between the 1960s and 1990s can be seen as both: a community of practice and a learning community. However, before its commercialization in the 1990s, the Internet was primarily a platform for researchers. One of the main activities within the first years of the Internet was a decentralized and democratic exchange of ideas. The Open Culture projects such as Open Software or Open Educational Resources and the WWW designed by Berner Lee are still symbols of the collaborative dimension of shared learning with and via the Internet (cf. in more detail Kergel, 2018).

The Internet is both forum and result of a collaborative management process leading toward the digital age. To unfold this thesis, a definition of the guiding

DOI: 10.4324/9781003188728-8

term "digital age" seems relevant. Looking at the literature on this topic, almost everyone seems to agree that we are living in a digital age. However, this fact cannot hide the fact that there seems to be a lack of a definition of the characteristics of the digital age. Such a definition provides the epistemological basis for discourses around media education, learning, and management in the digital age.

Features of the digital age

To define the digital age, a first step can focus on how information is conveyed through digital media. Such an approach has its origins in media theoretical reflections: Information is not simply given but conveyed/transferred via the media. However, there is no sharp distinction between the media on the one hand and the mediated information on the other. The media structure defines the information with, or McLuhan's words, "The media is the message." A feature of digital communication, or the way a piece of information is transmitted through digital media, is what can be called dialogic "de-location" (Han, 2005). The Internet enables the instantaneous transmission of information. By comparison, the book culture of the so-called Guttenberg Galaxy disseminated information written on paper in geographic and cultural domains previously untouched by textualized, objectified knowledge. With the book culture, an objectified standardization of language and the scientific system took place – for example, the citation system. The use of literature and sources affects book culture in the subsystem of science (Heidkamp & Kergel, 2016).

With the electronic age, which replaced the Gutenberg galaxy, the first processes of de-location emerged. For example, postal workers played chess over the telegraph: they met over the telegraph line, which transmitted the information needed to play chess – the chessboard was thus de-located.

In the next step of telecommunication development, the telephone removed and delocalized our voices. A little later, the television brought images from all over the world directly into our living rooms. One effect of this de-location and de-removal was the acceleration of globalization of economy, culture, and protest movements. Among other things, television influenced the 1968 movement as the first global protest movement: Images of victims of the Vietnam War politicized people in Germany, France, and America. The communication structures of the electronic age were – at least in its macrostructure – not characterized by a dialogic infrastructure. Thus, Baudrillard points out that television, as the primary medium of the electronic age, is a mass medium. It is a mass medium because television transmits information to many recipients. In his "Requiem of the Media," published in 1972 in the aftermath of the 1968 movement, Baudrillard analyzed television and radio as undemocratic mass media of the electronic age:

> The mass media are anti-mediatory and intransitive. They fabricate non-communication – this is what characterizes them, if one agrees to define

communication as an exchange, as a reciprocal space of a speech and a response, and thus of a responsibility (not a psychological or moral responsibility, but a personal, mutual correlation in exchange).

(Baudrillard, 1986, p. 280)

Instead of sending information to a mass of recipients, a de-democratic communication is defined by exchanging information. Thus, Baudrillard speaks of "communication as exchange." Here, the dialogue comes into play: The information needs a response. The interplay of utterance and answer is, according to Baudrillard, the basic prerequisite for communication. And according to Baudrillard, communication is, in turn, the precondition for democratic interaction. From this point of view, the book of the Gutenberg galaxy and the television of the electronic age do not enable democratic communication.

With digital media, the unidirectional orientation of mass media is being abandoned, and they are becoming increasingly dialogic. To justify this, an analytical look at dialogue as a communication practice seems to be valid. What Baudrillard calls communication is usually thematized in terms of "dialogic communication." Referring to the Greek origins of the term dialogue, "dia" means both a distance and a process:

- Distance can be seen as the distance between the interlocutors.
- As a communicative process, the interlocutors exchange points of view.
- Within this exchange process, the interlocutors move and thus reduce the distance between each other.
- In this movement process, a new, shared understanding of a phenomenon is built up.

From the point of view of media theory, digital media can be defined as enabling dialogic communication. Digital media overcome the book's unidirectional structure as the Gutenberg galaxy's leading medium and the unidirectionality of television as the leading medium of the electronic age. Thus, the digital age is characterized by a redefinition/deconstruction of mass media. This redefinition corresponds to Baudrillard's requirements for media that should enable (dialogic) communication. The digital age is defined by a media lifeworld whose communicative structure can be dialogic.

Dating the digital age

In addition to this conceptual analysis, the question arises about when the digital age began. Is there a year in which the digital age began?

Even if such a dating determination represents little more than a heuristic approach to systematizing historical processes, it is possible to define 2002/2003 as the beginning of the digital age. The term Web 2.0, which was introduced into the discourse by Tim O'Reilly, is symbolically influential: Web 2.0 tools like wikis need users as producers of content. Thus, the receiver who answers the message becomes the sender. Without the interactive dialogic dynamic, Web 2.0 tools like WhatsApp or social networking sites like Instagram would not unfold their potential. Individuals can become part of a collective and collaborative process of knowledge construction via the Web 2.0-based digital lifeworld – for example, via wikis like Wikipedia. At least the discourse about Web 2.0 started in 2003, and this discourse also created a new way of thinking about communication. In the field of e-learning or digitally supported teaching and learning, a dialogically oriented concept of e-learning 2.0 became established (see Heidkamp & Kergel, 2016; Kergel, 2018 for more details). This form of dialogic communication and process organization is also becoming established in management theory and practice in the digital age with agile management.

Agile management – a conceptual approach

Like all key terms used in social discourses on self-understanding, the concept of agility has a wide range of meanings. Accordingly, it is not surprising that agility is becoming a buzzword in which seemingly everyone sees a solution but means different things (cf. Krapf, 2018, p. 33). It can be stated that agile management is based on a dialogic understanding of social practices in the sense of Web 2.0.

Agile management can be defined as dialogical and thus flexible, forward-looking, and proactive organizational action used to implement change processes. Agile management is a response to the demand for flexibility in the digital world of work – Digitaization is driving the pace of many business processes. More and more tasks must be completed in the shortest possible time and in parallel. Results and developments in the business environment become unpredictable and unplannable (cf. Preußig & Sichart, 2018, p. 7). The dynamic working world of the digital age can be met using process management strategies developed in the field of software development. The answer to digital transformation and its immanent wealth of complexity is increasingly being located in the buzzword agility (cf. Krapf, 2018, p. 32). Proactive flexibility corresponds to the dynamics of disruptive, digital transformation. This proactive flexibility is semantically conveyed by the word agile:

> In its original physio-logical sense the word refers to the capacity of a body to move itself in quick, light, and well coordinated ways. In zoological contexts, it is used in a positive sense to describe the movement and manner of any animal which displays nimbleness, speed, fluidity, and suppleness.
>
> (Gilles, 2010, p. 1)

Due to its dynamic structure of interaction and the extensive abandonment of strict taxonomic orders, agile management represents a deconstruction of established management processes: Established organizational structures and management practices are either process-oriented (e.g., government agencies) or project-oriented (e.g., aid organizations). Hybrid forms can also be identified at times. Actors who argue for an agile understanding of management problematize that established management forms do not meet the new demands of the digital market, which increasingly challenges companies. "The self selects the identity which suits the market: "the agile self anticipates the market and reshapes itself" (Gillies, 2010, p. 6f.).

Gilles defines agility as an ephemeral form of process organization that makes it possible to react flexibly to the unpredictability of a free market:

> Agility is defined as a competence to operate within a competitive environment, which is coined by permanent but unpredictable customer requirements. Thus, agility signifies an organization-theoretic approach which is coined by an ephemeral structure: In summing up 'agile' as an epithet, therefore, the defining features would include such concepts as movement, speed, fluidity, and lightness. It should be noted, however, that there is no verbal form of the word: it is instead descriptive of action in the form of movement or potential movement, of the physical capacity or capability for certain types of action.
>
> (Gilles, 2010, p. 2)

The ephemeral structure of agile manifests itself in the characteristics of customer-oriented corporate structure, the establishment of iterative process structures:

- Customer-oriented corporate structure: Instead of a rigidly hierarchical process organization structured like a taxonomy, the agile process organization must be aligned with the customers' needs. A dialogic, team-oriented organizational structure replaces taxonomies and hierarchies.
- Implementation of iterative process structures: According to the negotiation process that defines dialogic communication, an iterative work process is required to implement agile management. The product to be created must be flexibly adapted to customer requirements during the development process. It is necessary to develop iterative work processes at short notice to achieve this. This ensures efficient, customer-oriented product development: The customer receives parts of the products/services quickly. This strategy allows the customer to point out optimization potential. In a subsequent, new, short-term work process, the product/service can be adapted to customer requirements and evaluated again by the customer. In terms of agile management, the production process is iterative and dialogical.

According to agile management theory, "the supervisor" should support the process but let "the employees" take responsibility for the iterative production process. Together with the customers, the teams – not the supervisor – define sub-goals. Instead of a taxonomic structure that restricts "the employees" movement space, an agile organizational structure is characterized by a dialogic, transparent communication culture.

Agile management is thus based on the assumption of a dialogical relationship between customer and service provider. Both parties are involved in a permanent dialogic communication process. This endless dialogue requires a performative negotiation process between the service provider and the customer. The product is produced within the framework of this dialogical negotiation process due to the dialogue.

This concept of agility is the result of the workflow developed in software development and led to the Agile Manifesto formulated by the Agile Alliance in 2001, or the "Manifesto for Agile Software Development," which has been translated into over 60 languages to date.

Manifesto for Agile Software Development

We are uncovering better ways of developing software by doing it and helping others do it. Through this work we have come to value:

Individuals and interactions over processes and tools
Working software over comprehensive documentation
Customer collaboration over contract negotiation
Responding to change over following a plan

That is, while there is value in the items on the right, we value the items on the left more.

Agile Manifesto: The agile manifesto is the reference text for the discourse around agile management.[1]

The Agile Alliance was founded by some software practitioners committed to the concept of agile development. As an ephemeral understanding of organizational processes, Agile is given the status of a philosophy: "Agile is a philosophy, not a set of business practices. The four bullets outline a way of thinking, a framework for prioritizing all the complicated parts of a project" (Mimbs, 2017: 34).

Conclusion: from agile management to agile-orientated media pedagogy

From an epistemological perspective, an agile understanding of social practice can be analyzed as a socio-constructivist, dialogic, performative-pragmatic, and hermeneutic understanding of the world:

- Reality is not given as an essence but produced in dialogical negotiation processes.
- These negotiation processes are infinite, but at the same time goal- and action-oriented.
- At the center of the negotiation processes is an action-pragmatic-dialogical discussion about the following (project) steps.
- To reach a level of reciprocity, a hermeneutic understanding of the other/interlocutors is required.
- Agile management is based on a socio-constructivist understanding of the subject from an epistemological perspective. The subject constructs its knowledge and organizes/manages projects in an action-oriented manner and through (digitally based) dialogic communication.

The socio-constructivist, action-pragmatic, and dialogical process-based management strategies of agile management need to be transferred into the context of media pedagogical practice.

Privileging a process orientation over a product orientation is the guiding principle for pedagogical practice. Here lies a difference to agile management: Agile management is defined by a market-like output orientation. The creation of a product as a commodity is the focus of the work. Education theory and practice, on the other hand, is concerned with learning processes that focus, among other things, on strengthening self-efficacy and explorative curiosity in a social context (cf. Heidkamp & Kergel, 2019). The implementation of market logics must not – despite all employability discussions in the context of the Bologna process – suspend a critical approach to the commodity-like structure of interaction processes or even lead to an equation between agile management and media-pedagogically supported teaching/learning processes. A difference can also be seen in the difference between the relationship constellation of agile management and the relationship constellation of media pedagogical work. The roles of customers and employees, who form two central dialogue partners in the agile management process, coincide in the education process: The learners are – entirely in the sense of socio-constructivist learning theory – the "customers" of their learning process. They co-produce in the social or dialogic-collaborative context. Therefore, the product orientation of agile management is replaced by a process orientation in the media pedagogical learning process. In the media-pedagogical learning process, media competence must be generated. For this process, elements from agile management can be adopted.

Note

1 Source: https://agilemanifesto.org/, zuletzt zugegriffen: 11 January 2019.

References

Baudrillard, J. (1986). *Requiem for the media*. Retrieved from http://shmacek.faculty.noctrl.edu/Courses/MediaCritSyllabusSPR2_files/19-baudrillard-03.pdf. Last accessed: 3 May 2017.

Gilles, D. (2010). *Agile bodies: a new imperative in neoliberal governance*. Paper presented at the British Educational Research Association Annual Conference, University of Warwick, 1–4 September 2010. Retrieved from http://www.leeds.ac.uk/educol/documents/197804. pdf Zuletzt zugegriffen: 16. Januar 2019.

Han, B.-C. (2005). *Hyperkulturalität. Kultur und Globalisierung*. Berlin: Merve.

Heidkamp, B., & Kergel, D. (2016). Der ʻDigital Turnʼ – Von der Gutenberg-Galaxis zur e-Science. Perspektiven für ein forschendes Lernen in Zeiten digital gestützter Wissensproduktion. In Kergel, D., & Heidkamp, B. (Hrsg.), *Forschendes Lernen 2.0. Partizipatives Lernen zwischen Globalisierung und medialem Wandel* (S. 19–45). Wiesbaden: VS Springer.

Heidkamp, B., & Kergel, D. (2019). *E-Inclusion – Diversitätssensibler Einsatz digitaler Medien. Überlegungen zu einer bildungstheoretisch fundierten Medienpädagogik*. Bielefeld: Bertelsmann.

Kergel, D. (2018). *Kulturen des Digitalen. Postmoderne Bildung, subversive Diversität und neoliberale Subjektivierung im Digitalen Zeitalter*. Wiesbaden: VS Springer.

Krapf, J. (2018). Agilität als Antwort auf die Digitale Transformation. *Synergie – Fachmagazin für Digitalisierung in der Lehre Nr.*, 3, 32–33.

Mimbs, C. (2017). *The winter getaway that turned the software world upside down: How a group of programming rebels started a global movement*. Retrieved from https://www.theatlantic.com/technology/archive/2017/12/agile-manifesto-a-history/547715/. Last accessed: 31. July 2022.

Preußig, J., & Sichart, S. (2018). *Agiles Führen. Aktuelle Methoden für moderne Führungskräfte*. Freiburg: Haufe.

Chapter 7

Moving forward in social constructivist theories through agile learning in the digital age

Ingrid Noguera

Introduction

Learning theories advance, or must advance, as far as the society progresses. Nevertheless, the conceptual foundations and researches are always a step backward from the continuous advancing societies. Furthermore, once theories are investigated and developed, it takes time to prove it and test it into practice. Therefore, it is fair common to observe a lead time between the characteristics and needs of new generations and the theorization of its impact on teaching and learning.

In the last two centuries, several learning theories have proliferated. The social constructivism approach to learning implied a step forward on the interpretation of how learning occurs and the critical role of the group in such a process. However, several approaches have been previously developed until this view became relevant. At the beginning of the 20th century, the "behaviorist" theory (i.e., Bandura, Pavlov, Skinner, Thorndike, and Watson) described learning as a behavior's change derived from the reaction of students to the stimuli of the environment. Under this perspective, the behavior is learned in relation to the consequences of the undertaken actions. During the fifties, "cognitivism" (i.e., Anderson, Gagné, Gardner, Novak, Rumelhart, and Norman) gained protagonism criticising that learning could not be understood limited to the observable behavior but had to be interpreted considering the mental processes associated to knowledge, language, and information processing, among other elements. One of the relevant changes was to consider the student as an active subject. In the late nineties, the "constructivist" theories (i.e., Bransford, Bruner, Grabinger, Hasselbring, Piaget,[1] Spiro and cols.) introduced the idea that knowledge is built individually, so that each person creates a unique interpretation of the reality. According to this approach, learning is a process of adaptation of new information to prior knowledge. Knowledge is actively built in a process of generation of new ideas (schemas) and generalization. The individual, thus, learns when interacting with the environment. A step forward on this view was the "social constructivism" theory (i.e., Cole, Engeström, Lave and Wenger, Leontiev, Rogoff, and Vygotsky) which

DOI: 10.4324/9781003188728-9

reinterpreted previous constructivist approaches considering that knowledge is built through the interaction with others. Learning, then, is social-mediated and is considered to be more effective if it is constructed with and from others. In this regard, the culture transforms the individual, and the individual transforms the culture.

Nevertheless, after these disruptive views, it has taken long until a new approach to learning has emerged. We had to wait until the irruption of the digital technologies to reflect on the changes that the digital age implied for the learning paradigm. In this chapter, we will deepen into the social constructivist approach and the connectivism theory to establish the foundations of the so-called "collaborative agile project-based learning." The agile method is a well-known project management approach for regulating teamwork processes. Agile learning is nourished from this method and introduces a renewed view to collaborative knowledge building. The following sections will develop these ideas (in the form of foundations) to demonstrate how agile management, with the support of digital technologies, can be introduced in learning processes to make social constructivism advance into practice.

First foundation: learning is a social-mediated process

The individualistic approaches to learning have been superseded nowadays. Although learning is an individual and intrinsic process (none can learn for you), it is widely accepted that the sociocultural context and the interpersonal communication play a fundamental role in learning when we are immersed in society. The social constructivist theory gives the culture a central position. Under this view, learning occurs when the individual interacts in a determinate situation. This theory defense that learning, referred as knowledge building, is situated that means that is affected by the activity done, the context and the culture where you're involved. This theory criticizes previous approaches that consider the learning process as something that just occurs inside the mind, independent from the environment.

Vygotsky (1978), following Piaget's approach, describes the learning process as the interaction between the subject and the environment. To this view, they added two main elements to explain how this interaction is supported: cultural tools and the people who accompany the subject during learning. Cultural tools can be either physical (e.g., a book) or psychological (e.g., language). Vygotsky defended that the appropriateness of the ways of thinking and doing is modelled through social interaction. What they called zone of proximal development (ZPD) describes the difference between what a learner can do without help and what the learner can do with the support from a skilled partner. In consequence, learning with and from others may raise us to a higher competence level.

Over the years, several authors have extended and incorporated new ideas to this primary approach (for an extensive review of social constructivist theories consult Gros, 2008). For example, Leontiev (1978) developed the "activity theory" that described the human activity as the interaction between the subject (the person/group who is performing the activity) and the object (the thing being done). The subject incorporates motives to the activity while the object is related to the purpose. The tools used mediate, and are mediated by, the social context of the activity. Grounded on Leontiev's theory, Engeström (1987) developed the concept of "collective activity system." This approach maintains the idea that the activity is a relationship between the subject and the object that mediate, and is mediated by, tools and the social context, however, three elements are incorporated: rules, community, and division of labor. Once more, there is a distinction between the motive and the outcomes, which not always are as expected.

Taking up the notion of community, Lave and Wenger (1991) formulated the concept of "Community of Practice" to describe a group of people with a common interest who collaborate to learn about a subject. They defended learning as a co-participating process within a community (Legitimate peripheral participation – LPP) where learners are engaged "in the practices of social communities and constructing identities in relation to these communities" (Wenger, 1998, p. 4). In this sense, the learner does not create structures as previous theories interpreted, but it is the context of the community itself that has a structure. According to this approach, learning occurs within an activity, under an authentic context of practice. Knowledge should be learned in the context that will be applied. Learning, then, is situated in a context and culture where learners move from being legitimate participants to full participants in a community of practice. Focusing on learners, Rogoff (1990) described three planes (nonhierarchical) of development in sociocultural activity corresponding to personal (apprenticeship), interpersonal (guided participation), and community processes (participatory appropriation). Rogoff distinguishes diverse levels of roles and responsibilities in a community of learners. Apprenticeship refers to active individuals participating with others in an organized activity; guided participation refers to the mutual implication (communication and coordination) of people in a culturally valued activity; and participatory appropriation refers to the transformation process of individuals derived from their implication in an activity.

Table 7.1 summarizes the principal approaches to social constructivism described earlier.

Social constructivist theories have eventually been transferred into the educational world as actions for scaffolding (i.e., technique for supporting students to achieve a stronger understanding and progressively master the domain of a task), tutoring (it may include individual, peer, and group tutoring), situated learning (e.g., service-learning or case-based learning), inquiry-based learning or conflict-cognitive strategies (i.e., presenting motivational or discordant questions to investigate about a topic), contextualized learning (e.g., problem-based learning), and cooperative learning (e.g., project-based learning). Nevertheless,

Table 7.1 Social constructivism approaches to learning.

Author	Theory	Core elements on learning processes
Vygotsky	Social constructivism	• Interaction between the subject and the environment • Cultural tools • People • Zone of proximal development • Social interaction
Leontiev	Activity theory	• Interaction between the subject (the person/group who is performing the activity) and the object (the thing being done) • Subject (motives the activity), object (activity's purpose) • The tools mediate/are mediated by the social context of the activity
Engeström	Collective activity system	• Interaction between the subject and the environment • The activity mediate/is mediated by tools and the social context • Elements: rules, community, and division of labor • Distinction between the motive and the outcomes
Lave and Wenger	Community of practice	• Group of people with a common interest to learn • Legitimate peripheral participation • Learning is situated in context and culture • Community gives context • Learning occurs within an activity in an authentic context of practice
Rogoff	Human development as a cultural process	• Community of learners • Planes of development in a sociocultural activity: personal (apprenticeship), interpersonal (guided participation), and community processes (participatory appropriation) • Roles and responsibilities.

from a reductionist view, it is usually put into practice as any type of group work.

There are several concepts used interchangeably, and mistakenly, to describe group work, for instance, teamwork, cooperative learning, collaborative learning, and group dynamics. First, we must distinguish formal and informal grouping. If a group of people accidentally congregate in a determinate place (e.g., a bus stop), we cannot say they are working in "group." On the contrary, if we formally ask some individuals to carry a learning task together, we are creating a "team." Hence, the first distinction is between group (informal) and team (formal). "Teamwork" may be simply described as a set of people working together for a common goal. From our perspective, "cooperation" is necessary in teamwork as it implies the exchange of information, resources, or ideas from individuals to support each other's. However, under our view, "collaboration" goes a step further as it implies a shared vision, interdependence, equal participation, and a collective effort, not only the sum of individualities with a guiding leader.

Learning in collaboration may increment students' motivation, persistence, and efficiency due to the exchange of ideas (Laux et al., 2016; Liaw et al., 2008). Nevertheless, for effective collaboration (Johnson & Johnson, 2004), students may be trained on self-regulated collaboration (Miller & Hadwin, 2015; Tseng & Yeh, 2013). Consequently, to effectively learn in collaboration, we must offer students strategies to regulate teamwork and help them to structure the joint learning process.

The review of social constructivist theories presented earlier describes the basis to understand learning as a social-mediated process. Some challenges are also presented when attempting to apply such theories into practice in the form of collaborative learning. What all these theories bring, then, to the approach to effective collaborative learning that we aim to defend in this chapter? Firstly, to consider learning as an individual cognitive process mediated by social interaction. In consequence, any collaborative activity is a continuum between individual and social processes. Secondly, to understand learning as an active process that must be situated into an authentic context. Hence, collaborative learning activities require students to be actively involved in meaningfully designed tasks. Thirdly, to firmly believe that the immersion in a community of learners offers the opportunity to learn more and better from others and to learn from its structure, rules, and values. Hereafter, collaboration requires skilled partners and structure. Lastly, to understand that learning is not static and is affected by a sort of elements; thus, the outcomes of a collaborative activity may not always be as expected. We need to assume that the difference between the expectations and the results is not an error but inherent to the learning process.

All these considerations help to draw our approach to social learning. In the following section, we intend to define how social-mediated learning occurs within the context of the digital age. How is learning affected by the information society? Has the concept of knowledge building changed due to the easy access to information? What is the impact of digital technologies on learning? We believe that the connectivist theory establishes the principles to understand learning as a process of information management and interaction through the net.

Second foundation: learning is connecting information

Previous approaches to learning were occupied with solving questions as "how the learner learns?" (Constructivism) or "why the learner learns?" (Social constructivism). However, after the emergence of digital technologies into society and, consequently, into the education sphere, some researchers started to question "How the digital age affects learning?". This is the starting point of the connectivism theory.

However, before launching into this theory, it is necessary to reflect on the social contexts that have impacted on the approaches to learning. The development of theories in the educational area is intrinsically linked to the historical and cultural moment. They must be interpreted considering the characteristics of the society where they are immersed. Previously cited theories (i.e., behaviorism, cognitivism, constructivism, and social constructivism) were mainly developed in the 20th century. During the first half of 1900, societies lived the two World Wars which dramatically changed the way of life. Once societies started to recover from the havocs, changes in the industry, the economy, the society, the culture, and the education occurred. A society of illiterate and agricultural workers led to an urbanization process with new industries and the need for more skilled professionals. As a result, the education system got adapted and new schools, universities, and adult education centers proliferated. Thus, there was an extension of public education systems (and the shift to compulsory education) that augmented the number of people attending schools.

In the second half of 1900, a strong commitment to continuous education emerged and public educational systems proliferated around the world. As a result, some pedagogical practices started to be reconsidered. Although along the history diverse teaching methods have existed and been implemented, it was fair common until 1960–1970 to find a teacher-centered and religious-based education. From the 1950s to the latest nineties, several laws emerged to reform educational systems and scientific knowledge started to substitute religious instruction. In consequence, there has been a proliferation of teaching methods and claims for a more student-centered education that give the learner the opportunities, scaffolding, and tools to learn actively. As we have seen in previous sections, there is also an increasing role given to the community as a mediator of learning.

The 21st century is characterized as the information age where there has been a tremendous change in the industry. The industrialization has shifted to an economy based on information technology. It is derived from the advent of the World Wide Web (around 1990) which opened to the world a new paradigm for accessing and sharing information. The digital age refers, thus, to the period in which computers and related technologies have been used to share information easily. The intensive use of the Information and Communications Technology (ICT) has impacted the economy, society, politics, and culture. Current citizens require different competences from the citizens of the past century. For instance, 21st-century skills include, among others, critical thinking, communication, collaboration, and media literacy (Ananiadou & Claro, 2009).

Within this context, where professionals and citizens require to develop a set of complex skills, there has been a new shift into the learning conception. If "knowledge" has been the focus of attention in previously cited research, in the digital age, learning is characterized by "critical thinking skills, knowledge creation and learning through connections" (Starkey, 2011, p. 19). In such approach, the use of digital technologies facilitates collaborative knowledge building (Jonassen et al., 1999). Under this view, the connectivism theory has emerged. It has caused controversy; some researches consider it as an updated version of constructivism in the digital age and some even doubt if can be understood as a theory (Anderson & Dron, 2012; Clarà & Barberà, 2014; Mattar, 2018). We will not get into this discussion. We consider that connectivism opens an exciting understanding of learning in the digital age and, therefore, we analyze it with a view on how information management and digital technologies are impacting on social learning.

In 2005, George Siemens and Stephen Downes developed a theoretical framework to comprehend how learning occurs when is mediated by technologies and in a context where information flows. From their perspective, learning is a process of connecting nodes or information sources (e.g., people, tools, Internet, and libraries). Contrary to constructivism, in the connectivism theory knowledge is not conceived to be constructed by the individual, "knowledge is distributed across a network of connections, and therefore that learning consists of the ability to construct and traverse those networks" (Downes, 2007). Although the starting point of connectivism is the individual, as in the theories of learning presented in previous sections, under this view, there is a cyclical process of knowledge development that passes through three spheres: personal, network, organization. Learning occurs in different contexts and the individual is the one connecting them.

As well as previous theories of knowledge acquisition introduced the necessary role of the environment and the social interaction in learning processes, the connectivism include social networks as the neuralgic point. Social networks and ICT are used to generate knowledge, however, under this approach, the "ability to learn what we need for tomorrow is more important than what we know today" (Siemens, 2005, par. 33). Learning is continuous and continuously updated and nurtured from connections. This means that what one knows may vary and be affected by alterations in the information.

Table 7.2 summarizes the main differences between the theories of the 20th and 21st centuries.

To sum up, social constructivist theories introduced a shift into the understanding of knowledge development transforming it as an active social process immersed in a specific context. Meanwhile, connectivism deepen on the current information flow and defend learning is connecting such existing information and knowledge is the result of the information networks. The two ideas "learning as a social process" and "learning as connecting information" are impacting education nowadays. However, as previously noted at the beginning of this chapter, the theoretical perspectives are hard to transfer into practice.

To understand the application of connectivism into classrooms, it is necessary to reflect on the incorporation of computers into the teaching-learning process and the digital competence of both teachers and students. The introduction of computers into education is being a slow process with diverse levels

Table 7.2 Characteristics of the 20th and 21st learning theories.

	20th century	21st century
Main question	• How learners' behavior change as a result of the stimuli of the environment? (Behaviorism) • How do learners store and process information? (Cognitivism) • How does the learner learn? (Constructivism) • Why the learner learns? (Social constructivism)	• How the digital age affects learning? (Connectivism)
Society	• Marked by the two World Wars • Shift from illiterate and agricultural workers to the need for skilled professionals • Extension of public education systems and people attending schools	• Marked by the digital age and an economy based on information technology • 21st-century skills (e.g., critical thinking, communication, collaboration, and media literacy)
Education	• Teacher-centered and religious-based • Focused on knowledge	• Science-based, active, student-centered, and competency-based • Focused on connections

of adoption depending on the educational level and countries (for exhaustive research on ICT integration in education, consult Noguera, 2015). In general terms, computers entered in schools in large numbers around 1970–1980 (historically, the USA is always advanced on the technological adoption respect to Europe). Since 1990, the Internet took place into the educational sphere in the form of distance education or as a source for teaching and learning. Currently, the use of computers and the Internet is widespread in the first world; however, there are inequalities and there exists a digital divide. Although digital technologies are widely used in our daily life, their effective use for learning and instruction still is called into question.

The digital competence among teachers and students is still insufficiently developed (Instefjord & Munthe, 2015; Ramírez-Montoya et al., 2017; Reisoğlu & Çebi, 2020). Even if the needs of the society have changed and the way learners learn has dramatically been transformed, there still are traditional practices that are reproduced with and without the use of technologies in classroom. At the European level, there has been an effort to support teachers in innovative practices and efficiently adopting digital technologies. This is the case of the European Framework for the Digital Competence of Educators (DigCompEdu) (Redecker, 2017) that provided a reference for educators to support the development of digital competences. Nevertheless, despite the efforts, digital competences are still underdeveloped in teacher education programs (Amhag et al., 2019). From our perspective, apart from other reasons (e.g., reluctance, investment, policies, and training), one of the motives of the low level of innovation and digital technologies inclusion in education is the difficulty to transfer the theory into practice.

Along with the applications of social constructivism that can be reduced to noneffective teamwork practices, the transference of the connectivism theory into real learning scenarios can be misunderstood. Some applications that could be labelled as connectivism practices could be, for instance, learning through a MOOC, developing a Personal Learning Environment, writing a blog, or using groups for learning in social media tools. If these strategies are designed for active engagement of students in a process of accessing/sharing information and building knowledge within a network (or several networks), one can interpret close to the nature of connectivism (for specific learning activities applying the principles of connectivism, consult Utecht & Keller, 2019). On the contrary, if these practices respond to an isolated process of merely aggregating information where there is not an intensive use of technologies, it is a simplification of a complex approach to learning in the digital age. According to Kop (2011), the application of connectivism may imply some challenges as learner autonomy (must be able to learn independently and to be engaged in aggregating, relating, creating, and sharing activities), presence (there is a need for some presence in online activities), and critical literacies (learners must master 21st-century skills to get the most of the learning environment).

From our the perspective, and according to Starkey (2011), the effective use of digital technologies aligns with effective teaching practices, but teaching practices will not change "until teachers understand and can apply theories of learning that are relevant to a digital age" (Starkey, 2011, p. 36). In that vein, the transference of some theories into practice remains unsolved. What this chapter suggests is leaving the comfort zone and searching for effective technology-supported teamwork practices outside the theoretical and academic sphere.

Third foundation: we can learn from the professional world

One of the recurrent principles for engaging learning is the involvement in authentic contexts. It is fair common that students react negatively to working in groups due to their prior negative experiences, the lack of regulatory skills for group management, or inaccurate learning design and teaching support. However, in the professional world, it is rare to find a job where employees do not cooperate with others. When working in projects, there is a real need to cooperate with co-workers to achieve the goals (even if it is fair common to do it ineffectively). The author observed that phenomenon and searched for a method that was of help for professional teams to achieve their aims effectively. This is how we get to agile project management.

Traditionally, in the context of software development companies, teamwork has been carried out through sequential methods (such as the "Waterfall method"), in which consecutive phases are performed (i.e., requirements' analysis, design, implementation, verification, and maintenance). The requirements are gathered at the beginning, so changes on the needs are rarely incorporated during the project. Consequently, these methods often lead to unsuccessful projects and inefficient work processes. To deal with this situation, the agile method emerged. It can be described as a team process for project management characterized by iterative work sequences, constant collaboration, adaptation, and continuous improvement.

Fowler and Highsmith (2001) developed the "Manifesto for agile software development" where four main principles were drawn: a) individuals and interactions over processes and tools, b) working software over comprehensive documentation, c) customer collaboration over contract negotiation, and d) responding to change over following a plan. There are diverse methods that aim to make teamwork agile, for instance, the "Scrum method" which is based in an iterative and progressive process of decision-making, the "Kanban method" that aims to display the working flow characterized by frequent deliveries and tasks prioritization, and the "Extreme programming method" that is built upon the principle of continuous improvement to get a quality product based on clients' needs. To sum up, all these methods are characterized by teamwork, frequent communication, adaptation to change, and decision-making in ongoing projects.

Agile project management is based on agile methodologies. It combines diverse agile methods' characteristics to manage projects from any discipline to reach effective teamwork processes. As reported by Masood and Farooq (2017), some of the accepted benefits are reduction in the cost of rework, fast completion of projects, improved customer satisfaction, greater creativity and innovation, improved performance visibility, and individual and team development. The challenges include difficulties in scheduling tasks, controlling quality, managing knowledge, managing large projects, managing distributed teams, and managing people related. To help with some of the difficulties previously listed, agile project management is usually accompanied by the support of digital technologies and software that support the teamwork process. Currently, some well-known tools are JIRA (https://www.atlassian.com/software/jira/free), Trello (https://trello.com/), ActiveCollab (https://activecollab.com/), and Basecamp (https://basecamp.com/).

Despite the challenges, the recognized benefits of agile project management have attracted the attention of academics and educators (Dewi & Muniandy, 2014; Krehbiel et al., 2017). Several manifestos have been developed to transfer the principles of agile software development to the field of education. Table 7.3 summarizes the main ones.

All these manifestos, considering their particularities, claim for a change in teaching and learning practices. They call for a more active, meaningful,

Table 7.3 Agile manifestos in the educational field.

Author	Manifesto	Principles
Peha (2011)	Agile Schools Manifesto	a) individuals and interactions over processes and tools, b) meaningful learning over the measurement of things, c) stakeholder collaboration over complex negotiation, and d) responding to change over following a plan
Kamat (2012)	Agile Manifesto in Higher Education	a) teachers and students over administration and infrastructure, b) competence and collaboration over compliance and competition, c) employability and marketability over syllabus and marks, and d) attitude and learning skills over aptitude and degree
Royle and Nikolic (2016)	Agile Pedagogy Manifesto	a) practice preferred to theory, b) learner choice and agency preferred to learners being limited and controlled, c) learning and applying skills preferred to learning facts, d) collaboration preferred to competition, e) customized learning preferred to standardized one-size-fits-all, and f) co-constructed learning preferred to teacher-led learning
Krehbiel et al. (2017)	Agile Manifesto for Teaching and Learning	a) adaptability over prescriptive teaching methods, b) collaboration over individual accomplishment, c) achievement of learning outcomes over student testing and assessment, d) student-driven inquiry over classroom lecturing, e) demonstration and application over accumulation of information, and f) continuous improvement over the maintenance of current practices

collaborative, applied, personalized, and competence-based learning. Under this view, teaching is more adaptive and subject to the students' needs. Computer Science teachers were the first to experiment with these principles into their classrooms, although they have been progressively incorporated in other disciplines. For instance, Lembo and Vacca (2012) have explored the integration of the agile method (Extreme programming) for problem-based learning. Results show positive findings concerning the redefinition of the role of the teacher, the active role of students, and collective instructional design. Monett (2013) presents an experience of "agile project-based teaching and learning." Findings demonstrate that the use of agile strategies in project-based learning is effective (as it is based on performing a realistic project through a collaborative and self-organized team) although it requires an adaptation of teaching and more time for completion. Tesar and Sieber (2010) report successful findings of using the agile concepts for developing blended and e-learning scenarios.

In an extensive review of agile methodologies in education, Salza et al. (2019) conclude that "applying agile methodologies to learning and teaching transforms from knowledge transfer to knowledge generated from rich collaboration and experience" (18). In this regard, Stewart et al. (2009) evaluated the

118 Ingrid Noguera

agile principles in active and cooperative learning. As a result, four characteristics of the agile pedagogy were extracted: a) students over traditional processes and tools, b) working project over comprehensive documentation, c) student and instructor collaboration over rigid course syllabi, and d) responding to feedback rather than following a plan. Related publications have defended the connection between agile education and active, project-based, and collaborative learning (López-Alcarria et al., 2019; Kropp et al., 2014, Stewart et al., 2009). Following this trend, the next section describes an approach to "collaborative agile project-based learning."

Fourth foundation: learning in collaboration is effective if it is agile

Throughout this chapter, we have defended the need for an applied and effective solution to learn in collaboration in the digital age. The current educational paradigm urges to define specific strategies to move from the theoretical sphere of social constructivist and connectivist theories to the practical application of their main principles into classrooms. Figure 7.1 attempts to summarize the key ideas expressed in the sections above and that serve as a basis to understand the author's approach to "collaborative agile learning" (Noguera et al., 2018).

Under our view of an approach to learning based in the social constructivist and connectivist theories, learning is an interactive and social process where the learner generates knowledge in collaboration with peers (skilled peers or

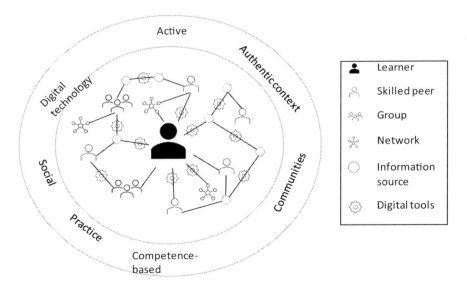

Figure 7.1 Learning process under a social constructivist and connectivist approach.

groups) through an authentic activity. Such activity requires developing knowledge and applying it in a real-based context. Digital tools are intensively used to connect with peers, groups, networks (already established relations between people and nonhuman artefacts), and information sources. Such interactive knowledge sharing process occurs within a community (or diverse communities) of learners where there is a specific purpose of collaborating to learn. The community gives structure, rules, and responsibilities. The learning product may not be as expected, but the individual always must achieve higher competence levels as a result of the active learning process.

The notion of "collaborative agile learning" (Noguera et al., 2018) was first described as the incorporation of agile principles into online project-based learning (PBL). In this chapter, we would like to reconsider such approach and make it extensible to face-to-face education. In this sense, we propose the concept of "Collaborative agile project-based learning" as a methodology that combines the benefits and characteristics of collaborative learning, project-based learning, and agile learning. We consider that PBL offers the perfect framework to develop collaborative practices through authentic, real-world, and situated activities. PBL has proved useful in planning, accountability, social learning, active learning, motivation (as it is based on students' interests and choices), scaffolding, meaningful incorporation of curriculum contents through a project, safe and effective use of technology, and the development of 21st-century skills (Bell, 2010). There is evidence that PBL also increases the ability to communicate, problem-solving abilities, and resource management skills, among others. However, there are also some weaknesses when implementing PBL as "difficulty in making students to concentrate on learning tasks, difficulty in helping students to connect new content with their prior knowledge, and difficulty in performing cooperative learning activities efficiently" (Sumarni, 2015, p. 482).

Some of the challenges expressed earlier for collaborative learning as well as for PBL can be improved with the use of agile strategies. In this sense, we suggest incorporating the following agile-based strategies in any collaborative learning project to overcome the barriers that often led to unsuccessful practices.

Phases

The development of a project is usually considered as a unique complex activity. Sometimes students get discouraged due to the considerable effort it requires to concentrate on a long-time task, and it is fair common they devote excessive time to define the project and to assume the bulk of the work when little time is left. We suggest dividing the project into phases with incremental complexity. These phases may allow us to adapt the project to needs and incorporate changes regularly. These phases are focused on improving the management process and could be organized as follows: Preparation, Development, and Closure. The

Preparation phase includes constituting the group, distributing roles and responsibilities, defining the topic, planning the tasks, and creating a document of agreement. The Development phase is divided into iterative Work Cycles (periods of one to two weeks with specific tasks associated, from now on WC). The Closure phase involves creating the final product, reviewing it, and disseminating it.

Roles

Social constructivist theories defend the need for roles' distribution. Informal roles (those that arise spontaneously) emerge from individuals; however, formal roles are designated by the group to a person. In a formal educational context, and for successful project management, it is necessary to assign predefined roles that help to organize and cover all tasks within a project. We suggest two mandatory roles (Project Manager and WC Manager) and varying PBL roles such as reporter, resource manager, timekeeper, or recorder. The Project Manager is a continued position in charge of the general management of the project (e.g., updates the project tasks list and monitors team collaboration). The WC Manager is a rotatory position responsible for the successful development of a WC (e.g., coordinates WC tasks or creates agendas for meetings).

Decision-making

Commitment is one of the challenges of collaborative learning. The interdependence among team members and the shared responsibility have to be managed and organized to be effective. One solution is to define initial agreements in respect to a general list of tasks, distribution of roles/responsibilities and agreements (e.g., communication, organization, motivation, and collaboration) that may serve as the basis for future decisions and for solving conflicts.

Time management

Time management is one of the main challenges when working in projects and groups. Time self-management is challenging and is even more difficult when it has to be collectively coordinated. In this respect, making decisions about time and having a time-structure could be of help to deal with excessive or inefficient time dedication to tasks. We propose organizing WC with a duration of one week, predefining and agreeing on the duration of each task per WC and limiting the meetings to 10–15 minutes.

Tasks

As previously commented, a project is a complex activity challenging to embrace. A useful agile strategy is to divide the work into small and more graspable tasks. We suggest creating a general list of tasks for the entire project at the beginning of the course and one task list per each WC. The lists of tasks must include the responsible person, time dedication, value (low, medium, and high), indicators, deadlines, and status (in process, done, and pending). Tasks must be reviewed at the end of each WC and decisions about their status must be made.

Monitoring

It is fair common to maintain meetings during a PBL. However, in our view, they usually last more than necessary and are inefficient. To deal with this, we propose establishing regular meetings per each WC (two meetings per WC, for example), creating an agenda per each meeting, generating minutes at the end of each meeting and limiting the time to 10–15 minutes. We bet for regular operational meetings oriented to solving problems and making decisions.

Review

PBL processes are quite linear and finish with an assessment or review that can be individual and/or in group. As in professional projects, leaving the review to the end implies limiting the opportunity to improve, to learn from errors, and to adapt to changes. We suggest a continuous review process that can take the form of one meeting at the end of each WC where the team reflects on the collaborative process and the learning products. These meetings must be prepared in advance through an agenda and agreements and decisions collected in minutes.

Digital tools

Throughout the application of all these strategies, it is highly recommended the use of project management tools (see examples in Section "Third foundation: we can learn from the professional world"). The combination of these tools together with the individual and collaborative use of tools for managing information sources (including features for aggregating, relating, creating, and sharing information) may involve more efficient practices.

Teacher's role

Furthermore, although the focus of the strategies has been placed on students and teams, it is crucial to mention the role of the teacher within this process. Considering the three main approaches to learning reviewed in this chapter, namely constructivism, social constructivism, and connectivism, the teacher's role has shifted from a guide to a mediator to a curator. Under the agile approach, the teacher takes the role of team facilitator or Project Owner. From our perspective, in "Collaborative agile project-based learning," the teacher acts as a facilitator who collaborates with teams and offers continuous feedback. The teacher scaffolds the individual and team process by solving doubts, offering strategies and tools for team self-management. The teacher presence is essential, particularly at the beginning of the process, to establish the foundations of collaborative, project-based learning and agile learning.

Conclusion

This chapter has reviewed the main learning theories that have been developed during the 20th and 21st centuries. Special attention has been placed to the social constructivist approach to learning, understanding that it establishes a solid framework to comprehend how knowledge is socially built. Several teaching methodologies derived from the core elements of social constructivism proliferate in our times because such an approach to learning fit with the principles of the 21st-century education (e.g., collaborative, active, situated learning). However, some considerations are needed for the effective application of collaborative learning in the digital age. Connectivism has proven to offer a renewed perspective to the collective knowledge-building process, incorporating suggestive ideas to understand how learning occurs in a society mediated by technologies and surrounded by information. Nonetheless, as in the case of social constructivism, the application of connectivism into practice does not always lead to effective learning. To deal with inefficient collaborative and connectivist teaching and learning practices, we suggest applying the principles of PBL and agile learning into educational contexts. They offer practical strategies that may be of help for team regulation and project management.

In conclusion, we wish to draw attention to the need for effective methods to transfer the theory into practice. In this regard, in the context of PBL, teams need specific orientations for successful work management. The agile principles demonstrate to be suitable to advance on collaborative knowledge building. "Collaborative agile project-based learning" is a teaching methodology fostered by project-based and agile strategies, which offers specific recommendations to advance on the application of effective collaborative learning processes. This is a working example of specific strategies grounded on theories that demonstrate the interdisciplinary dialogue might result beneficial to advance on successful learning practices.

Note

1 Piaget has been identified as a cognitivist and a constructivist theorist. In this chapter, we consider that Piaget defended a cognitive constructivism position, so we classify him under the umbrella of constructivism.

References

Amhag, L., Hellström, L., & Stigmar, M. (2019). Teacher educators' use of digital tools and needs for digital competence in higher education. *Journal of Digital Learning in Teacher Education*, 35(4): 203–220. https://doi.org/10.1080/21532974.2019.1646169.

Ananiadou, K., & Claro, M. (2009). *21st century skills and competences for new millennium learners in OECD countries*. Organisation for Economic Cooperation and Development. EDU Working Paper no. 41. Retrieved from http://www.olis.oecd.org/olis/2009doc.nsf/linkto/edu-wkp(2009)20.

Anderson, T., & Dron, J. (2012). Learning technology through three generations of technology enhanced distance education pedagogy. *European Journal of Open, Distance and e-learning*, 15(2). Retrieved from https://files.eric.ed.gov/fulltext/EJ992485.pdf.

Bell, S. (2010). Project-based learning for the 21st century: skills for the future. *The Clearing House: A Journal of Educational Strategies, Issues and Ideas*, 83: 39–43. Retrieved from https://www.academia.edu/34971404/Project_Based_Learning_for_the_21st_Century_Skills_for_the_Future.

Clarà, M., & Barberà, E. (2014). Three problems with the connectivist conception of learning. *Journal of Computer Assisted Learning*, 30(3): 197–206. https://doi.org/10.1111/jcal.12040.

Dewi, D.A., & Muniandy, M. (2014). *The agility of agile methodology for teaching and learning activities*. 2014 8th. Malaysian Software Engineering Conference (MySEC), Langkawi, pp. 255–259. https://doi.org/10.1109/MySec.2014.6986024

Downes, S. (February 5, 2007). *What connectivism is* [Blog post]. Retrieved from https://www.downes.ca/post/38653

Engeström, Y. (1987). *Learning by Expanding: An Activity-Theoretical Approach to Developmental Research*. Helsinki, Finland: Orienta-Konsultit.

Fowler, M., & Highsmith, J. (2001). *The Agile Manifesto*. Software development. Retrieved from andrey.hristov.com/fht-stuttgart/The_Agile_Manifesto_SDMagazine.pdf

Gros, B. (2008). *Aprendizaje, conexiones y artefactos. La producción colaborativa del conocimiento*. Barcelona: Gedisa.

Instefjord, E., & Munthe, E. (2015). Preparing pre-service teachers to integrate technology: an analysis of the emphasis on digital competence in teacher education curricula. *European Journal of Teacher Education*, 39(1): 77–93. https://doi.org/10.1080/02619768.2015.1100602.

Johnson, D.W., & Johnson, R.T. (2004). Cooperation and the use of technology. In Jonassen, D.H. (Ed.), *Handbook of Research on Educational Communications and Technology*. Mahwah, NJ: Lawrence Erlbaum, pp. 785–811.

Jonassen, D.H., Peck, K.L., & Wilson, B.G. (1999). *Learning with Technology: A Constructivist Perspective*. Upper Saddle River, NJ: Merrill/Prentice Hall.

Kamat, V. (2012). *Agile manifesto in higher education*. Proceedings 2012 IEEE Fourth International Conference on Technology for Education, 18–20 July 2012, Hyderabad, India (pp. 231–232). Retrieved from https://ieeexplore.ieee.org/document/6305978. https://doi.org/10.1109/T4E.2012.49

Kop, R. (2011). The challenges to connectivist learning on open online networks: learning experiences during a massive open online course. *The International Review of Research in Open and Distributed Learning*, 12(3): 19–38. https://doi.org/10.19173/irrodl.v12i3.882.

Krehbiel, T., Salzarulo, P., Cosmah, M., Forren, J., Gannod, G., Havelka, D., Hulshult, A., & Merhout, J. (2017). Agile manifesto for teaching and learning. *The Journal of effective Teaching*, 17(2): 90–111. Retrieved from https://files.eric.ed.gov/fulltext/EJ1157450.pdf

Kropp, M. Meier, A. Mateescu, M., & Zahn, C. (April2014). Teaching and learning agile collaboration, *2014 IEEE 27th Conference on Software Engineering Education and Training (CSEE&T)*, 23–25, Klagenfurt, Austria (139–148). https://doi.org/10.1109/CSEET.2014.6816791.

Laux, D., Luse, A., & Mennecke, B.E. (2016). Collaboration, connectedness, and community: an examination of the factors influencing student persistence in virtual communities. *Computers in Human Behavior*, 57: 452–464. https://doi.org/10.1016/j.chb.2015.12.046.

Lave, J., & Wenger, E. (1991). *Situated Learning: Legitimate Peripheral Participation*. Cambridge: Cambridge University Press.

Lembo, D., & Vacca, M. (2012). *Project based learning + agile instructional design = extreme programming based instructional design methodology for collaborative teaching*. Depardemento di Informatica, Sapienza, Universita di Roma, Technical Report no. 8. Retrieved from https://citeseerx.ist.psu.edu/viewdoc/download?doi=10.1.1.910.6944&rep=rep1&type=pdf

Leontiev, A.N. (1978). *Activity, Consciousness, and Personality*. Englewood Cliffs: Prentice-Hall.

Liaw, S., Chen, G., & Huang, H. (2008). Users' attitudes toward Web-based collaborative learning systems for knowledge management. *Computers & Education*, 50(3): 950–961. https://doi.org/10.1016/j.compedu.2006.09.007.

López-Alcarria, A., Olivares-Vicente, A., & Poza-Vilches, F.A. (2019). A systematic review of the use of agile methodologies in education to foster sustainability competencies. *Sustainability*, 11(10): 2915. Retrieved from https://www.mdpi.com/2071-1050/11/10/2915/htm

Masood, Z.A., & Farooq, S. (2017). The benefits and key challenges of agile project management under recent research opportunities. *International Research Journal of Management Sciences*, 5(1): 20–28. Available online at http://www.irjmsjournal.com

Mattar, J. (2018). Constructivism and connectivism in education technology: active, situated, authentic, experiential, and anchored learning. *Revista Iberoamericana de Educación a Distancia*, 21(2). Retrieved from https://redined.mecd.gob.es/xmlui/bitstream/handle/11162/166929/20055-45152-1-PB.pdf?sequence=1

Miller, M., & Hadwin, A. (2015). Scripting and awareness tools for regulating collaborative learning: changing the landscape of support in CSCL. *Computers in Human Behaviour*, 52: 573–588. https://doi.org/10.1016/j.chb.2015.01.050.

Monett, D. (2013). *Agile project-based teaching and learning*. Proceedings of the 11th International Conference on Software Engineering Research and Practice, Las Vegas, NV, pp. 377–383.

Noguera, I. (2015). How millennials are changing the way we learn: the state of the art of ICT integration in education. *RIED. Revista Iberoamericana de Educación a Distancia*, 18(1): 45–65. https://doi.org/10.5944/ried.18.1.13800.

Noguera, I., Guerrero-Roldán, A.-E., & Masó, R. (2018). Collaborative agile learning in online environments: Strategies for improving team regulation and project management. *Computers & Education*, 116: 110–129. https://doi.org/10.1016/j.compedu.2017.09.008.

Peha, S. (June 28, 2011). *Agile schools: How technology saves education (just not the way we thought it would)* [Blog post]. Retrieved from http://www.infoq.com/articles/agileschools-education

Ramírez-Montoya, M.S., Mena, J., & Rodríguez-Arroyo, J.A. (2017). In-service teachers' self-perceptions of digital competence and OER use as determined by a xMOOC training course. *Computers in Human Behavior*, 77: 356–364. https://doi.org/10.1016/j.chb.2017.09.010.

Redecker, C. (2017). *European framework for the digital competence of educators: DigCompEdu*. Joint Research Centre (JRC) Science for Policy report. https://doi.org/10.2760/159770

Reisoğlu, İ., & Çebi, A. (2020). How can the digital competences of pre-service teachers be developed? Examining a case study through the lens of DigComp and DigCompEdu. *Computers and Education*, 156: 103940. https://doi.org/10.1016/j.compedu.2020.103940.

Rogoff, B. (1990). *Apprenticeship in Thinking: Cognitive Development in Social Context.* Oxford University Press.

Royle, K., & Nikolic, J. (2016). *Agile work practices for learning and teaching: What we can learn from agile work practices about learning and teaching in schools.* Unpublished white paper. https://doi.org/10.13140/RG.2.1.3501.0161

Salza, P. Musmarra, P., & Ferrucci, F. (2019). Agile methodologies in education: a review: bringing methodologies from industry to the classroom. In Parsons, D. & MacCallum, K. (Eds.), *Agile and Lean Concepts for Teaching and Learning.* Singapore: Springer, pp. 25–45. https://doi.org/10.1007/978-981-13-2751-32.

Siemens, G. (2005). Connectivism: a learning theory for the digital age. *International Journal of Instructional Technology and Distance Learning,* 2(1). Retrieved from https://jotamac.typepad.com/jotamacs_weblog/files/Connectivism.pdf

Starkey, L. (2011). Evaluating learning in the 21st century: a digital age learning matrix. *Technology, Pedagogy and Education,* 20(1): 19–39. https://doi.org/10.1080/1475939X.2011.554021.

Stewart, J.C., DeCusatis, C.S., Kidder, K., Massi, J.R., & Anne, K.M. (2009). *Evaluating agile principles in active and cooperative learning.* Proceedings of Student-Faculty Research Day, CSIS, Pace University, NY, USA (p. B3). Retrieved from http://citeseerx.ist.psu.edu/viewdoc/download?doi=10.1.1.510.3904&rep=rep1&type=pdf

Sumarni, W. (2015). The strengths and weaknesses of the implementation of project based learning: a review. *International Journal of Science and Research,* 4(3): 478–484. Retrieved from https://www.ijsr.net/archive/v4i3/SUB152023.pdf

Tesar, M., & Sieber, S. (2010). *Managing blended learning scenarios by using agile e-learning development.* International Association for the Development of the Information Society, 2, 124–129. Retrieved from http://www.iadisportal.org/digital-library/managing-blended-learning-scenarios-by-using-agile-e-learning-development

Tseng, H., & Yeh, H. (2013). Team members' perceptions of online teamwork learning experiences and building teamwork trust: a qualitative study. *Computers & Education,* 63: 1–9. https://doi.org/10.1016/j.compedu.2012.11.013.

Utecht, J., & Keller, D. (2019). Becoming relevant again: applying connectivism learning theory to today's classrooms. *Critical Questions in Education,* 10(2) 107–119. Retrieved from https://files.eric.ed.gov/fulltext/EJ1219672.pdf

Vygotsky, L.S. (1978). *Mind in Society: The Development of Higher Psychological Processes.* Cambridge: Harvard University Press.

Wenger, E. (1998). *Communities of Practice. Learning, Meaning, and Identity.* New York: Cambridge University Press.

Chapter 8

The magic of digitalized educational projects

Nikolaj Kure

Introduction

During recent decades, the Nordic welfare state model has changed radically. When first developed in the 1950s and 1960s, the focus was on delivering universal rights to the state's citizens (Kuhnle, 2000). However, as free trade commerce and financial deregulation in the 1980s and 1990s created a situation of economic entanglement across nations, new ways of defining the role of the state emerged. In Denmark, this stimulated the development of the concept and the practice of "the competition state" whose primary role is to ensure Danish companies' ability to compete in the globalized market place (Pedersen, 2013).

One way of favoring Danish companies in the globalized competition is to develop a highly efficient and effective public sector that delivers low-cost public services, such as infrastructure, education, and healthcare (Babu, 2002). However, most public services are messy and expensive and so a streamlining of these services would be a significant step in the right direction. An important strategy to deal with this challenge is to digitalize public services. Decision-makers hold a strong belief that digitalization is a key component in developing an effective and efficient public sector; a belief which has resulted in a flurry of digitalization projects across the Danish public sector.

While some of these projects have been successful, it is fair to say that a significant number of high-profile projects have been digital failures. Most recently, it was discovered that an effort to digitalize the Danish tax authorities, which included massive layoffs, paved the way for enormous fraud schemes where foreign fraudsters tricked the Danish state out of app. EUR 2bn in relation to stock yields. And the list goes on: The police, the court system, the ministry of defense, the ministry of employment, and many others have been involved in digital projects that eventually turned out to be extremely costly and unfit for use (Lauesen, 2020). Thus, the language-game surrounding the discourse of digitalization seems to be akin to a mythical language, characterized by broad and ambiguous concepts, dogmatic authority, and a unified world view (Nørreklit et al., 2012).

DOI: 10.4324/9781003188728-10

However, such failures have not had politicians and decision-makers modify their claim that digitalization is the most effective means of streamlining public services. This raises the question of why decision-makers do not assume a more nuanced position toward digitalization in the face of evidence which clearly suggests that digitalization is not the panacea that it is assumed to be. In this chapter, I will discuss this question and put forward the proposition that digitalization has been imbued with distinct magical qualities, which may help understand decision-makers' voluntary blindfolding. I will do so by drawing on Marcel Mauss' definition of magic as put forward in his seminal work *A General Theory of Magic* (1902/1972) and by showing how distinct traits of magic can be found in the argumentation that supports the digitalization of the Danish educational sector. The analysis is followed by a discussion where I argue that the existing *a priori* belief that digitalization is good *per se* should be replaced by a much more nuanced and critical approach.

Magic in management

As one would expect, the academic realm of management is not ripe with papers on the subject of magic. Magic has primarily been studied by anthropologists who have mainly seen it as a way of controlling the external world, yet a control which is essentially pseudo-scientific and futile. This perspective, originally worded by one of the founders of modern anthropology James George Frazer (1854–1941) (1911–1915/2013), has since gained foothold in science in general, which goes a long way to explaining why magic is regarded with a certain degree of aloofness from conventional scientific communities. In line with a traditional scientific logic, magic is simply not seen as a proper scientific object as it cannot be observed directly and has no real efficacy. However, a number of quasi-academic papers and some authors of management literature still use the concept of magic to describe three organizational features:

First, magic is used as a concept to describe the unique personal traits that some managers display. These managers are sometimes described as "management wizards," a characteristic coined to encapsulate the fact that some managers possess an extra-rational X-factor that gives them the ability to inspire employees, hold people's attention and develop new creative solutions. This perspective is richly illustrated in Caravantes and Bjur (1996) who explore how magic can be used to develop executive potentials.

Second, magic is also used as a way of explaining the phenomenon that sometimes very small efforts may translate into very large organizational effects. For instance, this point of view is touted by a former Disney executive, Lee Cocherell (2008) who argues that small gestures such as remembering people's names and appreciate, recognize, and encourage employees have the almost magical effects of stimulating people to take responsibility for the business and "do the right thing." These mechanisms cannot be explained from a traditional scientific perspective with the underlying assumption that employees are motivated by maximization of individual wealth, and thus the conclusion is that some kind of magic is at play. By taking very small initiatives, managers may stimulate the organization to practically operate on its own in a positive and reinforcing feedback loop.

Third, magic in management is used as a way of representing the beauty that arises when people work together and create processes and results that go beyond what they could achieve as individuals. This perspective, for instance, illustrated in Mette Vinther Larsen's book *The Magic of Organizational Life* (2017), thus describes the aesthetics and subliminal aspects to work life that cannot be captured by the more mundane language of management science.

This brief review serves to show that the academic field of management studies is not too preoccupied with the concept of magic. In contrast, studies of digitalization of the public sector is high on the academic agenda (see, for instance, Greve, 2015; Plesner et al., 2018). This cluster of research is kept together by the underlying assumption that digitalization is a means of making established practices and processes more agile and effective. As the prominent management consultancy company Gartner puts it, digitalization does not change the process itself, it simply accelerates it:

> Digitization is the process of changing from analog to digital form, also known as digital enablement. Said another way, digitization takes an analog process and changes it into a digital form without any different-in-kind changes to the process itself.
>
> (Gartner, 2020)

The assumption is that when a process is translated from an analog form to a digital one, the process fundamentally stays the same, yet it may now take place in a much more quick and effective manner, which makes it very difficult to oppose digitalization. In this chapter, I will discuss this situation by showing that digitalization seems to be embedded in a magical context (which is not to be confused with the argument that digitalization *is* magic). Digitalization mimics the logic of magic, which creates a context where digitalization cannot be questioned. In order to carry out this discussion, I draw on two classics within the study of magic, Marcel Mauss and Bronislaw Malinowski.

Marcell Mauss' theory of magic

In Marcel Mauss' analysis, magic is not confined to indigenous tribes or archaic cultures, nor is magic isolated to particular individuals who claim to possess mystical powers. Instead magic is contemporary and woven into society's social fabric. Later, I shall briefly outline the most important characteristics of magic.

As a starting point, magic is believed to *do* something to the world. In particular, magic is used as a helping tool to make traditional professions such as fishing, hunting, or farming more effective. In effect, magic does not change the mechanics of how things are done, instead it changes the pace or the efficacy with which things are done. Moreover, magic works on the assumption that there is an automatic or mechanical relationship between the magical ritual and its efficacy. When magic is called upon, "the objects or beings involved are placed in a state so that certain movements, accidents or phenomena will inevitably occur" (Mauss, 1902/1972, p. 76). In practice, this inevitability is construed by means of what Mauss coins the "law of contiguity." This implies two operations. First, a part of the process which is the object of the magical rite is identified as a symbol of the process as a whole. For instance, a fish bone may be chosen to represent the entire fishing process. Next, the magical bone is brought into contact with the actual fishing process, for instance, by transforming the bone into a bracelet which is worn during fishing. The magical causality thus established is distinguished from scientific causality in so far as no *a posteriori* evidence or confirmatory experiments are required for its acceptance. In fact, magic relies on a social *a priori* belief in its efficacy. However, as opposed to many other *a priori* beliefs in society (for instance, the belief that it is generally good to follow the traffic rules), magic is imbued with such powers that even contradictory evidence cannot be used to reject it. In the face of events where magic does not deliver the desired effects, we know magic is in play if people still believe it works. As Mauss puts it,

> even the most unfavorable facts can be turned into magic's advantage since they can always be held to be the work of counter-magic or to result from an error in performance of the ritual. In general, they are seen to stem from the fact that the necessary conditions of the rite were not fulfilled.
> (1902/1972, p. 114)

As a final characteristic, magic is given its efficacy through the use of rituals. A ritual is an act or a set of acts which are "traditional, formal and clothed in effectiveness which is *sui generis*" (Mauss, 1902/1972, p. 71). Thus, when magic is called upon, it is always embedded in some sort of traditional setting where magicians draw on the rituals of previous generations of magicians. Moreover, the rituals are formalized in the sense that the acting magicians cannot simply develop their own rite but must meticulously follow the script of the tradition. All these efforts are put in place in order to fulfil the overarching aim of magic: The generation of a power that ensures that efficacy is actualized.

As we shall see later, the implementation of digitalization projects often follows the script of a transition ritual. Therefore, I shall spend a few words describing these particular rituals. In general, transition rituals follow three phases. First, the *isolation phase* is the part of the ritual where the object of the magical process is dissociated from its conventional context and celebrated as something unique and important. For instance, when adolescents are celebrated as adults in confirmation or *bar mitzwah* rituals, they are often taken away from their everyday surroundings, dressed in clothes designed for the event and placed in a position where they can be gazed upon and celebrated. The next phase is called the *transcendence phase* which is where the magical object is transferred to a new state. Often the object is reset or brought back to some kind of original starting point before they transcend this state and become something new. For instance, the process of initiating new students at universities is ripe with these kinds of rituals where new students are asked to carry out all sorts of degrading and demeaning actions – for instance, to dress and act like babies – before they can be welcomed to the group of "proper" students. Finally, the magical process is finalized in the *incorporation phase* where the object of the process returns to its everyday context, albeit in a transformed shape or with a new identity.

Methodological analysis

The chapter is based on the analysis of central documents that reflect the reasoning behind the introduction and integration of digitalization in the public education sector. These documents include policy papers on digitalization in education, research papers, and reports from think tanks and consultancy houses from the recent two decades. A full list of the documents can be found in the appendix. The reasons behind this choice are twofold. First, documents of the types used in the chapter are reservoirs of meaning that reflect the logic of digitalization. The aim of this chapter is to discuss if digitalization mirrors the logic of magic and so the empirical background for this discussion is best found in documents where decision-makers – broadly defined as politicians, civil servants, management consultants, advisory boards, and interest groups – formulate the benefits and potentials of digitalization. Second, the archive is restricted to include documents no more than 20 years old. Research on public digitalization has gained momentum during the last two decades, indicating that the phenomenon of digitalization has picked up speed since the early 2000s. This is supported by the numerous digital projects in the Danish public sector, which have been implemented in the same time frame. Therefore, the relevant empirical data must allow for a study of the reasoning behind digitalization in that time space.

Analysis

As argued by Mauss, the public sphere of modern society is ripe with magical rituals. For instance, think of the tossing of rice at weddings which everyone seems to do but no one knows why (as it turns out, rice symbolizes fertility and is used as a way of blessing the newly married couple). Essentially, the tossing of rice is an empty ritual; no one truly believes that it has any impact on the couple's future. This could indicate that while some behavioral structures in society have a magical shape – the ritual – they no longer carry any magical content. While this may be the case, I will try to show that the magical content seems to have migrated away from public ceremonies and into public organizations. I will do so by showing how the arguments behind digitalization of education draw heavily on the semantics and code of magic.

The first indication of digitalization as magic is the fact that digitalization is presented as a helping tool to make teaching and learning more efficient. This tallies with an overarching neo-liberal articulation of the public sector that extends free-market ideologies to all areas of society, including education. The view is highly prevalent in a 2017 report from the Danish Growth Advisory Board (an independent council that advices the government on economic growth measures) where it is argued that a comprehensive use of digitalization across the Danish public sector will stimulate enormous productivity gains (p. 9). The specific category of teaching is treated in more detail in an evaluation report from EVA (the Danish Evaluation Institute) in which the authors make a differentiation between what is considered a negative pedagogy, namely "teaching" that connotes an uninspiring teacher who tries to push information into the minds of passive recipients, and a more progressive strategy – the so-called "learning" – that focuses on how students may play a much more active part in their own learning. The point in the report is that digitalization will help both of these education strategies to become more efficient. First, digitalization will help speed up the way traditional teaching unfolds:

> Teachers also use digital technologies to make more traditional more efficient. The use of Internet-connected projectors and electronic blackboards means among other things that the teacher may more quickly present the information.
>
> (EVA, 2015, p. 12)

However, digitalization is also posited as a driving force in turning teaching into learning. While traditional face-to-face pedagogical practices may stimulate learning to a certain extent, digitalization has the potential to make these processes even more innovative. The list of positives include: Digitalization stimulates new innovative ways of handling information, it offers new ways of giving feedback, it frees the teacher's time to pedagogical activities, it enhances flexibility, it offers a possibility for more individualized teaching, it supports different learning styles, it enhances cooperation across geographical borders, it motivates students, and it makes it more interesting and fun to be a teacher (EVA, 2015, pp. 12–15). The problem, however, is that very little empirical evidence provides backing to the aforesaid positive effects of digitalization in teaching. Balslev (2020) devotes an entire PhD dissertation to showing that there is virtually no hard evidence to support that digitalization of teaching has a positive effect on learning.

In the face of these findings, one would expect that decision-makers would hesitate and at least consider the option that the linear causal link between digitalization and improved teaching effects is not as clear cut as expected. However, the analyzed documents clearly indicate that this is not the case. Instead of questioning the causal link itself, the authors point to various external factors that may explain the lack of effects. Again, the EVA publication is illustrative as it puts focus on a "number of barriers linked to the implementation of digitalization in the class room" (p. 24). For instance, the lack of success may be due to a failure on the behalf of local management to properly support the introduction of new technologies, teachers' negative attitudes toward digitalization, and teachers' lack of IT-competencies. It seems to be the underlying position that if these barriers were simply absent, digitalization would work as expected.

A striking feature of this argumentation is that the EVA report makes no reference to pedagogical literature at all. The causality between the introduction of digital tools and their positive learning effects is not well-argued or substantiated; it is simply posited as a matter of fact. And in the face of contradictory evidence, these findings are explained with reference to external conditions that presumably make it impossible to establish the link. This position is echoed by the Association of Primary School Managers where the implicit assumption seems to be that digitalization works *per se* and that there is therefore no point in waiting for empirical evidence:

> At this point in time, students and teachers alike are already enthused about the use of modern information technology and when this engagement is used in the pedagogical process it will promote the further integration of digitalization in the class room. However, digitalization is only one of many changes in the class room. Economical as well as technical issues need to be dealt with and potential skeptics may point to the fact that no evidence has yet made clear that an increased use of digitalization in teaching translates into better teaching results.
> (Association of Heads of Danish Primary Schools, p. 2)

Not even the conspicuous lack of empirical evidence in favor of digitalization makes the Association of Primary School Managers dither. The *a priori* belief is that digitalization works and people who do not accept this are branded as backward-looking "skeptics." This analysis goes to show that the causality implied by proponents of digitalization has the characteristics of a magical causality. There seems to exist an *a priori* social belief that digitalization inevitably makes learning more efficient; a point of view which cannot be rejected, even in the face of contradictory empirical or experiential evidence.[1] Thus, the classical scientific falsification logic as proposed by Karl Popper (1935/2010) is bracketed when it comes to digitalization. Popper proposes that science should first formulate hypotheses — for instance, that digitalization makes teaching more efficient — and then try to falsify the hypotheses empirically. If they still stand after vigorous falsification efforts, they are the best available. If falsified, the hypothesis should be ruthlessly rejected. In the case of digitalization, this logic is short circuited as even very compelling evidence that digitalization does not work is simply disregarded. A straightforward explanation is that a magical rationality is at play.

A second indication of digitalization as magic is the way digitalization is proposed to function as a learning tool. As we have seen, magic produces a sense of efficacy by means of the "law of contiguity." This law implies two operations. First, a part of the process is identified as a representation of the process as a whole. Next, the magical object is brought into contact with the process which is to be made more efficient.

In the case of teaching, digitalization does something similar. This, however, must be seen in the light of a more general development in the education system, namely the increased focus on formal learning targets. At all levels in the Danish education system, any course is driven by a set of learning targets. This is built on the idea that learning activities may be decomposed into a set of analytically distinct competences that students are supposed to train during the course. The implication is that specific parts of a very complex process may be identified and treated as particularly essential or privileged to the process as a whole. For instance, when I teach a university course, I have to choose four or five learning targets which implicitly define the essentials of the learning process. Although I know that learning is a much more multidimensional process than that, I need to reduce the complexity of the pedagogical process by defining a set of specific competences that indirectly claim to represent the essence of the entire process.

The point here is that proponents of digitalization seem to contend that digital learning tools possess the ability to bring these essences of teaching into the actual teaching process. For instance, look at this description of the so-called "flipped class room technology" where teachers provide videos and literature on the basis of which students are asked to develop questions and points of discussion, which are then treated in the actual class room:

> Instead of spending time on the traditional lectures, the shared time in the class room can be used for discussions, exercises and problem solving. Here the students are active while the teacher assumes a supervisory role and may concentrate on facilitating the students' learning process. The point is that the students are to deal with the lowest level of learning – remembering and understanding – through reading and video lectures while learning at the highest level – application, analysis and assessment – are trained in the class room.
>
> (EVA, 2015, p. 13)

The argument is clear: The use of digital technologies creates a situation where the essentials of learning – often the students' ability to use theory to analyze and discuss empirical phenomena – can be brought into the teaching process in a much more focused way than if conventional teaching techniques were used. The result is an improvement of the teaching process as a whole.

This entire approach mirrors Mauss' law of contiguity: A part of a complex process is generalized as a representation of the entire process – for instance, the fish bone or the learning targets – and digital technologies are then used to place the essential parts in close physical proximity with the actual teaching process. This produces a magical-like belief that digitalization will inevitably work, even in the face of contradictory evidence. As it is, the entire discourse of digitalization in education seems to be saturated by a strong belief that digitalization works, just like magic uses the law of contiguity to build its own efficacy.

A third and final indication that magic is at play can be found in what appears to be ritualistic initiations of new IT systems. When magic is called upon, it always draws on a formalized ritual, which imbues the magical process with efficacy. The archive does not contain descriptions of these processes with regard to the specifics of IT systems in learning. However, the general guidelines on the implementation of IT systems developed by two central governmental agencies, namely the Agency of Digitalization and the Agency of Economy, reveal that a specific script is followed, namely one that mirrors Mauss' transition ritual with the three phases of resetting, transformation, and incorporation.

The first phase when bringing IT systems into public processes is about defining and describing the process that is supposed to be made more efficient by means of a new IT system. The guidelines are ripe with procedures as to how participants in project groups may engage with local users to gain insights about how the process is run and which problems it entails, etc. Often the existing process is considered problematic or somewhat derailed and so the idea is to get an analytical overview of the building blocks of the process and define the essentials of the process.

When the process has thus been reset and isolated from its context and social life, the next phase involves a transformation of the process from its current perverted form to a smarter or simpler one which is better aligned with the original purpose of the process. For instance, in its digitalization strategy (2016–2020) the Danish government argues,

> Digitalization can strengthen citizens' experience of closeness and influence on their own life situation as citizens are now offered easy access to services and information of a high quality from their own homes, no matter where in the country they live. Digital services may increasingly be tailored to the individual, so that individual needs are the main focus point. And as digital welfare solutions are introduced, the citizens may become co-creators in the welfare. With more efficient digital solutions, it is possible to increase the quality of public services.
> (The Danish Government, KL, and the regions, p. 7)

The logic seems to be that digitalization allows processes to be brought back to a simpler or smarter form, making the public sector better equipped to living up to its purpose of meeting the citizens' needs. In the context of New Public Management (Hood & Dixon, 2015), this constitutes a crucial feature of the legitimacy of public organizations, and so the crucial challenge is to incorporate the new smarter practices in the everyday life of the public organizations. To this purpose, the Agency of Governmental Management has developed a so-called "implementation strategy," which describes how this should happen in practice. The central idea in this document (Agency of Governmental Management, 2020) is that if the new systems are to be properly and lastingly integrated in the actual everyday organizational processes, there is a need for a thorough change in the organizational logic. Thus, the publication draws heavily on the literature on organizational change, for instance, by insisting that the key to a successful implementation are concepts such as "ownership," "organizational commitment," "communication," and "partnerships" – all concepts that aim to incorporate the new technology into the workings of the organization. While this process may resemble a rational implementation strategy, it also mirrors the structure of a magical transition ritual: isolation, resetting, and incorporation. This is not trivial as the ritual is the institution that guarantees magic's efficacy. Only if magic is embedded in a traditional ritualistic context – just as the earlier transition ritual – may we believe in its effectiveness.

Conclusion and discussion

In this chapter, I have shown that digitalization of teaching mimics the logic of magic in three important ways: Digitalization is, like magic, presented as a helping tool that makes public sector processes more efficient; it builds its own efficacy by means of the "law of contiguity"; and it makes use of rituals. If this argument is correct, it is the equivalent of a management accounting horror show. In contrast to management accounting's insistence on empirical proof and control of operations, magic creates a situation where these factors are rendered irrelevant. In fact, magic escapes all control as it is constituted as an *a priori* belief that cannot be rejected in the face of empirical evidence. Therefore, if the argument of the current chapter is accepted, it should give rise to critical reflections and efforts to establish a more evidence-based approach to digitalization.

Next, we may begin to reflect on why magic has gained foothold in Danish public institutions in the shape of digitalization. Bronislaw Malinowski, one of the founding fathers of structural anthropology, perhaps offers an explanation in his essay "The Role of Religion and Magic" (1931/1979). Here they argue that magic, in fact, is to be expected in any society that has reached its limits but still has to continue its pursuit:

> Magic is to be expected end generally be found whenever man comes to an unbridgeable gap, a hiatus in his knowledge or in his powers of practical control, and yet has to continue in his pursuit. Forsaken by his knowledge, baffled by the results of his experience, unable to apply any effective

technical skill, he realizes his impotence. Yet his desire grips him only the more strongly. . . . Standardized, traditional magic is nothing else than an institution which fixes, organizes and imposes upon the members of a society the positive solution in those inevitable conflicts which arise out of human impotence in dealing with all hazardous issues by mere knowledge and technical ability. The spontaneous natural reaction of man to such situations supplies the raw material of magic.

(Malinowski, 1931/1979, p. 83)

When a society is no longer able to control what it aspires to control; when society can no longer "apply any effective technical skill," magic makes itself available to offer a positive solution to this impotence. At least in one instance does the Danish government display this kind of impotence, namely in its lack of ability to control public agencies such as universities, hospitals, etc. The historical context for this discussion is the installation of new public management (NPM) in the 1990s. With this came also the *desire* to control. Until the 1990s, the allocation of resources to public institutions was primarily based on the so-called framework allocation system. This system describes the practice that institutions such as hospitals and universities are allocated a yearly sum of money and made responsible for spending this money most efficiently. Effectively, this means that the government hands over the decision autonomy to the individual agencies. With NPM, this changes radically. In this new context, governments begin to control their agencies much more strictly in accordance with political targets. One of the preferred steering mechanisms is the contract (Merchant & Van der Steede, 2014), allowing governments to define KPIs and motivate agencies to meet them by tying the allocation of resources to the KPIs. By this, legitimate public agencies are the ones capable of living up to their contractual bindings (or at least communicate what they do) (Suchman, 1995).

On the face of it, it appears that governments are actually capable of controlling their agencies. There is an almost frenetic production of KPIs and other performance measures and an overwhelming production of reports to show that the institutions do live up to their contractual bindings. However, an increasing number of empirical studies have begun to question not only the effectiveness of central steering (see, for instance, Arnaboldi et al., 2015; Bevan & Hood, 2006; Hood & Dixon, 2015) but also the very idea that central governments are capable of controlling what plays out at the operational level. For instance, Kure, Nørreklit, and Røge (2021) argue that the contractual steering of Danish universities is actually more akin to pseudo-steering as the semantic content and structure of the contracts are bordering on meaningless.

On this basis, it appears that Western governments are now faced with a situation where they try to steer their agencies to become ever more efficient while also realizing that their ability to do so is significantly constrained. In such situations, magic traditionally presents itself as a means to recreate a sense of certainty. However, in modern societies based on values such as rationality and empirical evidence, it is simply not feasible to call on magic in its traditional forms. However, it is feasible to disguise magic and make it appear in an acceptable clothing. *The argument in this chapter is that this acceptable clothing is digitalization.* Digitalization is posited as the most rational solution ever devised for solving the problem of making the public more efficient. As such digitalization makes for the perfect camouflage for magic. As the earlier analysis has shown, digitalization displays all the characteristics of magic, yet it is also embedded in magic's exact opposite, namely the ideas of rationality and technical solutions that hark back to the period of the Enlightenment. In other words: Digitalization simultaneously displays signs of both rationality and magic, which may be why it is accepted so willingly. After all, in the face of mounting problems to control the public sector, decision-makers firmly *believe* in digitalization despite a conspicuous lack of evidence of its benefits.

One may argue that the use of magic is relatively innocent. Magic has always been used and the fact that contemporary societies has changed its format just shows that magic is useful for all kinds of societies. However, I would argue that it is not innocent. In fact, the installation of magic is highly problematic. While proponents of digitalization argue that digitalization simply speeds up processes, the fact of the matter is that digitalization radically changes them. The logic of digitalization builds on the idea that all features of an analog process may be computed in simple binary yes/no sequences. But to believe that this provides the basis for sound and effective public sector processes seems to be illusory. Take the example of taxing. In an analog world, taxmen use their professional experience to assess whether people are fraudsters or not by analyzing a *continuous* space of reality from which a variety of observations is compiled into a conclusion: Observations X, Y, and X indicate that this man is most likely a fraudster (which may then call for further investigations). Yet the digital tax system reduces this array of observations to a simple set of binary ones. An extremely complex analog world is reduced to simple yes/no observations. Thus, in contrast to the conventional take on digitalization, I will argue that it radically reshapes the processes. This has at least one implication: The risks of fraud and mistakes increase. When a system is based on binary observations, it is simply a matter of detecting systematic flaws in the system where a binary "yes" should have been a binary "no" (or vice versa). Incidentally, this was the case when foreign fraudsters tricked 2 bn EUR out of the Danish tax authorities in relation to refund of stock taxes. The fraudsters simply tested the system for digital mistakes and when they found one, they exploited it to the full. An analog process where the professional competences of experienced taxmen were employed would most likely have put an end to this scheme before it was up and running. Such failed projects do not do any good to the general trust in the public authorities and when it is all wrapped in a magical flavor the risk is compounded. The causality of magic cannot be falsified empirically, yet when this logic is transferred to the management of public processes, the risks of mistakes, fraud, and inherently the loss of trust to the authorities are imminent.

Note

1 A possible reason for this contra-empirical position is that digital tools are assumed to stimulate a learner-centered learning process, which is considered more robust and effective than more traditional teacher-centered approaches. Thus, the fact that digital tools have the potential for putting students at the center of the teaching process may obscure the lack of empirical evidence in favor of digitalization of teaching.

References

Arnaboldi, M., Lapsley, I., & Steccolini, I. (2015). Performance management in the public sector: the ultimate challenge. *Financial Accountability & Management.* 31: 1–22. https://doi.org/10.1111/famm.12049

Babu, Suresh. (2002). Competition and competitiveness among states. *Economic and Political Weekly*, 37(13): 1281–1284.

Balslev, Jesper. (2020). *Evidence of a Potential. The political arguments for digitizing education 1983–2015*. PhD dissertation, Roskilde University. https://forskning.ruc.dk/en/publications/evidence-of-a-potential-the-political-arguments-for-digitizing-ed

Bevan, G., & Hood, C. (2006). What's measured is what matters: targets and gaming in the English public health care system. *Public Administration*, 84: 517–538. https://doi.org/10.111/j.1467-9299.2006.00600.x

Caravantes, Geraldo, & Bjur, Weslay. (1996). *Magic and Management – Developing Executive Potential*. New York: iUniverse, Inc.

Cocherell, Lee. (2008). *Creating Magic – 10 Common Sense Leadership Strategies From a Life at Disney*. New York: Random House.

Gartner. (2020). Retrieved from https://www.gartner.com/en/information-technology/glossary/digitization

Greve, Vagn. (2015). Ideas in public management reform for the 2010s: digitalization, value creation and involvement. *Public Organization Review*, 15: 49–65.

Hood, C., & Dixon, R. (2015). What we have to show for 30 years of new public management: higher costs, more complaints. *Governance*, 28: 265–267. https://doi.org/10.1111/gove.12150

Kuhnle, Stein. (2000). The scandinavian welfare state in the 1990s: challenged but viable. *West European Politics*, 23(2): 209–228.

Kure, Nikolaj, Nørreklit, Hanne, & Røge, Kristian. (2021). Objective and results-based management of universities – constructing reality or illusions? *Financial Accountability and Management*, 37(2): 204–230.

Larsen, Mette Vinther. (2017). *The magic of organizational life*. Taos Institute Publications.

Lauesen, Lars. (2020). IT project failures, causes and cures. *IEEE Access*. Chagrin Falls, Ohio. 8: 72059–72067. https://doi.org/10.1109/ACCESS.2020.2986545

Malinowski, Bronislaw. (1931/1979). The role of magic and religion. In Lessa, William, & Vogt, Evon (Eds.), *Reader in Comparative Religion* (4th ed.). New York: Harper & Row.

Mauss, Marcell. (1902/1972). *A General Theory of Magic*. New York: Routledge.

Merchant, K., & Van der Stede, W.A. (2014). *Performance Measurement, Evaluation and Incentives*. New Jersey: Pearson Prentice Hall.

Nørreklit, Hanne, Nørreklit, Lennart, Mitchell, Falconer, & Bjørnenak, Trond. (2012). The rise of the balanced scorecard! – Relevance regained? *Proceeding of Pragmatic Constructivism*, 2(1): 16–29. https://doi.org/10.7146/propracon.v2i1.16673

Petersen, Ove Kaj. (2013), Political globalization and the competition state. In *Introduction to Political Sociology*. Copenhagen: Hans Reitzel.

Plesner, Ursula; Justesen, Lise, & Glerup, Cecilie. (2018). The transformation of work in digitized public sector orginazations. *Journal of Organizational Change Management*, 31(5): 1176–1190.

Popper, Karl. (1935/2010). *The Logic of Scientific Discovery*. New York: Routledge.

Suchman, M.C. (1995). Managing legitimacy: strategic and institutional approaches. *Academy of Management Review*, 2: 729–757. https://doi.org/10.5465/amr.1995.9508080331

Empirical material

The Agency of Governmental Management. (2020). *The implementation concept*. Retrieved from https://oes.dk/systemer/digitale-services-paa-vej/statens-hr/implementering/

The Danish Evaluation Institute (EVA). (2015). *A digital elevation. a management perspective on digitalization in teaching*. Retrieved from https://www.eva.dk/videregaaende-uddannelse/digitalt-loeft-ledelsesperspektiv-paa-digitalisering-undervisningen

Chapter 9

Lightschools® space and freedom for the co-creation of new possibilities, opportunities, and valuable solutions

Britt van Mensvoort – in creative collaboration with Mar Cano Mesa

Introduction

Imagine removing all the walls. We are breaking down the literal walls of the schoolhouse and instead have the world as our "classroom." Imagine removing the metaphorical walls between education and life, between education and the market, and between sectors, disciplines, and departments, and instead, creating a diverse education and innovation ecosystem. Welcome to *Lightschools®*!

Lightschools® is a reimagining of human development and organization. An opportunity to think outside the "big box," providing a new and innovative perspective on living, learning, and working. It creates an open structural form in which Students, Business Entrepreneurs, Households, Teachers, and Connectors[1] partner up. They co-construct a life-learning path allowing them to become the best version of themselves while facing today's worldly challenges and creating valuable solutions together.

We humans love stories. We interpret the things that happen around us and within us in a framework of mental constructs that we, not always consciously, build up in our lives. Our stories influence the way we interpret the world around us and within us. When events occur that are inconsistent with our story, we tend to question, deny, or rationalize them away. Anything rather than changing our story. For a long time, this has been the normalized way of operating around the globe. People, organizations, products, services, and insights have been evolving and have gradually improved within our story. However, the oil in the machine, that is our story, seems to be running out. The machinery is sluggish. The flaws are abundant, and the stories no longer always offer satisfactory answers.

The world has been changing rapidly. We are confronted with big social, environmental, and economic challenges. It requires committed and active participation to make change for the good of humanity, the Earth, and all that inhabits it. The predominant stories and the rigid, linear thinking, managing, and organizing fall short. Globalization and technological innovations

DOI: 10.4324/9781003188728-11

have made the world a lot more volatile, uncertain, complex, and ambiguous (VUCA) in recent years. Flaws are more visible than ever before, confronting us with an even stronger need for radical sustainable change.

Change is the constant, and the world is more messy and unclear than we could have ever imagined. We need a new story. A story that embraces and works with the complexity and ambiguity of the world, as well as that of ourselves. Our human nature is complex, ambiguous, and changeable, like the world we live in. In efforts to make things simpler and clearer, we have become further removed from that which is natural, to the point where we have to maintain our created systems in a forced way.

According to Yunus (2017), our stories and systems are based on the assumption that "every human being is driven by self-interest." Based on that assumption, theories, models, and legislation were created with the aim to control, regulate, and train the selfish beings we may be. There is great distance between the people and the controlling powers. There is little real knowledge of people and trust is lacking. We don't trust each other, and because leaders don't act out of trust in us, we have a hard time trusting ourselves. There is an increasing amount of research and examples in practice that show a natural commitment and intrinsic motivation of people when they feel part of something. Selfishness does not come naturally. It must be learned. When people are approached differently, there is more room for their selfless nature and the unique power they have within them. Of course, it is easier to play safe than to stand in your full power and the responsibility that comes with it. It is more open and vulnerable. It takes courage in a fertile breeding ground.

The systems nowadays don't start from our human nature and our authenticity. Many people don't live aligned with their nature and with the world as it is today, but rather, fight against it. The stories and systems impose something that pulls us away from that which is natural to us. Our own nature and today's world are complex.

The natural world is full of complex systems and is agile, diverse, resilient, and resistant. Its structures, rhythms, workings, and movements offer plenty and continuous inspiration as infinite sources of knowledge and possibilities. The more we attune ourselves and live, learn, and create in harmony with our own nature and the natural world, the more flow, creativity, and synergy arises. Living, learning, and creating with natural time is an important part of this process.

With *Lightschools®*, we co-create an education and innovation ecosystem, starting from our human nature, authenticity, the world of today, and the natural world. The essence of a person is at the core of a humane organization. Understanding both our own nature and the natural environment that surrounds us, guides us in the co-creation and continuous development of the conditions necessary to live, learn, and co-create in space and freedom. In this chapter, we will take you through the fundamental elements within *Lightschools®* that allow this.

Fractal organization

Nature is full of fractals. Fractals are characterized by repetitive patterns on different levels. Just look at the leaves of a fern. You see the same structure and patterns within the small leaves as you see them in the bigger ones. Similarly, a cauliflower floret is a fractal of a whole cauliflower, and capillaries are a fractal of our entire blood vessel system. Fractals are created based on relatively simple principles or elements shared among parts of a larger whole. The principles and elements at a higher level are consistent with those at a lower level in natural complex systems. Rather than directing top-down and enforcing rules, the smallest level determines the organization of all levels. Organizing all levels based on universal principles and elements creates consistency, transparency, and harmony. It makes it easier to create alignment between the levels. *Lightschools®* organization is inspired by fractals and behaviors of natural complex systems. It is based on the smallest and most essential level in *Lightschools®*, which is the individual human being. Principles and elements have been designed that recur and are embedded on every level.

The five levels of *Lightschools®* are as follows:

1. The individual: a single and unique member
2. The group or team: a small collective of three to six individual members
3. The Lightschool: local education and innovation ecosystem
4. Partnering *Lightschools®*: regionally and/or translocally partnering local education and innovation ecosystems (see number 3)
5. *Lightschools®*: global education and innovation ecosystem. All *Lightschools®* together.

All levels live, learn, and co-create with the following principles and elements, creating repetitive patterns:

- Why-what-How (WwH) emergent curriculum
- 13 Common Principles
- Potential Development Habits
- Distributed living, learning, and co-creating among people and spaces
- Natural Time and the PDRAC-spiral
- EduScrum
- Nature as Teacher

These principles and elements create structure, culture, and guide the process at every level. They are explained in more detail later. When we talk about *Lightschools®* in the rest of the article, we also talk directly about all levels within it as they are all aligned.

Emergent curriculum

Lightschools® sees the world and life as the space for learning opportunities. We learn by living and we live by learning. Living, learning, teaching, and co-creating happens everywhere, and from and with everyone. The interaction between Students, Small-to-Medium Business Entrepreneurs (SMBE), Households, Teachers, and Connectors is central; and that creates a complex system. As *Lightschools®* members develop as individuals, as a team, and as a community, the interactions change over time. That makes *Lightschools®* a **complex adaptive system**. As the interactions create complexity, dynamics, uncertainty, and change, they are reflecting the complexity, chaos, and ambiguity of the world around us and within ourselves. They thereby provide us with ongoing opportunities to learn how to deal with ourselves and the world constructively and authentically.

In natural complex adaptive systems, the behavior cannot be predicted by looking at the properties of the individual components. You can know everything about the system, and yet, its behavior and development can be unpredictable. Properties emerge from the interactions in the collective. That is why, within *Lightschools®*, we speak of an emergent curriculum. The curriculum is constantly developing and dynamic. Meaningful learning experiences are co-created responsive to the interests, needs, and desires of the community. Teachers gain greater understanding of each member's interests, needs, and desires, which enables personalized planning. The way of teaching and planning is therefore also of an emergent nature. Teachers in *Lightschools®* need to be flexible to be able to adapt and use different strategies, teaching methodologies, methods, etc. which at the same time cater for self-determined members (Stacey, 2009).[2]

We are confronted with challenges that affect us as a person daily. Those challenges test us, and the way we deal with them makes a world of difference. It determines whether we learn, what we learn about ourselves, others, and the world, and how we learn that. It also influences the way we shape the world. One of Mahatma Gandhi's famous sayings tells us to "Be the change you wish to see in the world." When we think about that for a moment, it actually tells us that *how* we go through life and *how* we learn and create are essential. It puts the process or the journey central instead of the result or the destination. That goes along with looking at ourselves and questioning the why. Why are we challenged? And why do we want to change ourselves or something in the outside world? The why takes you to the essence of things. The essence of yourself. Why are you here and what is it you truly care about? The *how and why* are therefore central to *Lightschools®*.

Let us use a natural metaphor to clarify the foregoing. Instead of focusing on gathering more knowledge and results, the branches and fruits of the tree, *Lightschools®* focuses on developing strong roots and a sturdy trunk (the Why and How), so that those branches and fruits continue to come naturally (the what). In *Lightschools®* we therefore speak of the **Why-what-How (WwH) emergent curriculum**. As you, others, the environment, and the world are developing and changing, the topics you want to learn about, or the things you want to create, change over time. The what is therefore variable. The Why underneath, however, is more consistent, and drives you to keep exploring new possibilities and opportunities. Besides, the focus on the How ensures that you learn how to deal with yourself, others, the environment, and the world in a personally and socially meaningful way, while continuously developing your potential in your own way.

13 Common Principles

Lightschools® acts using 13 Common Principles (see the overview of all Principles later). These Principles have been defined together with the initial global community and are continuously re-examined according to emergent events and needs. They are living definitions that can be adjusted after inclusive democratic discussion (Principle 9), because everyone has an authentic perspective and their role to play. Within *Lightschools*®, it is all about empowerment (Principle 1) – the empowerment of ourselves, the empowerment of each other, in teams and in the community, on local, regional, translocal, and global level. This goes hand in hand with a commitment to the entire ecosystem (Principle 13). We believe in the power of together, because together we know and can achieve much more than on our own. That is only possible in a culture of trust and respect (Principle 2), where we take the autonomy (Principle 3) and responsibility for a balanced and sustainable (Principle 8) development of ourselves, our teams and communities, the environment, and the world. We keep developing ourselves to stay true to ourselves and learn to express ourselves in new ways (Principle 6). We continue to learn from life (Principle 5), by taking part in the dynamics of the interactions in the community, by making mistakes and playing (Principle 10). We are open to what comes our way, find out who we truly are, what drives us, and continuously align ourselves with that (Principle 4). We take a holistic approach to living, learning, and co-creating at all times (Principle 7). We know that value can only be created when we connect compassionately with ourselves and each other and collaborate creatively (Principle 11), while remaining open to feedback and regularly pausing to reflect in order to learn and adapt (Principle 12).

13 Common Principles

1 – Empowerment	8 – Balance and Sustainabil ty
2 – Trust and Respect	9 – Democracy and Inclusiveness
3 – Autonomy	10 – Play and Flexibility
4 – Authenticity and Openness	11 – Compassionate Connection and Creative Collaboration
5 – Life-Learning	
6 – Self-development	12 – Reflection and Feedback
7 – Holistic approach	13 – Commitment to the entire ecosystem

The 13 Common Principles provide structure, guide the process, and are imbued in the culture in *Lightschools*®. Let's start by explaining how the Principles

shine light on the structure and process. The 13 Common Principles guide the WwH emergent curriculum, and emphasize and set the basis for the "How": the way we do things collaboratively. At the same time, they also guide the "what," as developed products or services should foster the Principles for the chosen target group. They provide a powerful framework, but are not a ready-made road map that can easily be consulted. The Principles provide directions along the way to help you find the right way. They leave room for every Lightschool to let them flow in their own way. The differences between *Lightschools®* are there because meaning is given to the Principles from their own perspectives and in dialogue with each other. The uniqueness of all those involved and the local culture and environment play a role in the translation of the Principles into practice. Traditions, customs, and religion, for example, can play a role. Each Lightschool is free to translate the Principles into practice in their own way, as long as it is in line with the definitions as agreed within the global community.

A Lightschool invents itself. It is a conversation that is conducted over and over again in order to co-create the space in which members feel at home and which, at the same time, becomes a valuable and inspiring context. Together, the Lightschool comes to a translation of the Principles that suits them and their context, and makes sure that they can justify their chosen working methods at all times.

Talking about culture, the Principles are sensible and tangible everywhere. They are "the smell of the place," as Prof. Sumantra Ghoshal called it so beautifully. Besides, they are a touchstone in practice. Are we acting in accordance with the Principles? How do we see that reflected in our everyday actions? And when we notice that a certain principle is not fully lived and integrated by an individual, a team, or the community, how do we hold each other to account? How do we deal with a situation that presents itself, when we look at it through the lenses of the Principles?

Potential development habits

Ecosystems are examples of complex adaptive systems. They organize themselves in a nonlinear way. There is an interdependency between the individual components and there are multiple possible outcomes of dynamics (Levin, 1998). Power is distributed all over the place. Within *Lightschools®*, all members discover, explore, and grow the power that they have in themselves. By bringing out and emphasizing personal talents and qualities, members automatically become more aware of their own abilities. From there, they feel strengthened to naturally and playfully find creative and effective ways to face challenges. In discovering who they are, what they love, what they are good at, what the world needs, and what they can get paid for in service to others, also known as Ikigai (Garcia & Miralles, 2016), a very powerful source of learning arises.

Information and resources are available all over the world. In projects, we explore how to use them in an intelligent, responsible, and meaningful way.

For that purpose, we bring people's powers – their talents, qualities, passions, and ideas – together with the collective backpack of knowledge, skills, and resources, in teams and community projects.

However, a team or community only really flourishes on the basis of individuals who are highly personally developed and authentic. That is the true basis of healthy relationships from which valuable creations can emerge. The focus within *Lightschools®* therefore lies with the development of the person, their intelligences, character, mindset, values, skills, and resilience. Such development does not take place in isolation, but in relation to people and the environment. Reflective mindful practice is important in the development of the above. Excellence results from a combination of practice and talent. Not through practising memorization of knowledge, but by practising habits. Because all members invest in their own development through reflective mindful practice of habits, they are aware of their interests, needs, and desires. As a result, the WwH emergent curriculum can be and remain aligned with their interests, needs, and desires.

With the aim of empowering every member to develop their own ways, Potential Development Habits – guiding questions and tools – have been co-created together with the global community. These Habits have been developed based on the criteria within the Potential Development Profile. This Profile includes nine Domains with five related themes each. The nine Domains are Being, Feeling, Daring, Loving, Expressing, Seeing, Knowing, Doing, and Co-Creating.

The Habits make the person's development in line with the Profile part of daily practice. The Habits leave room for authenticity and individuality and, thus, for the development of their own practices. The Habits do not stand alone. The way in which they are used depends on what emerges and the need in the moment. In their learning process during joint conversations, projects, and internships in the community, members are challenged as individuals, as a team or as a community. The Habits are there to support this process.

Measurement of development and impact

In addition to qualitative measurement methods such as the portfolio, we have also developed new quantitative measurement methods. We measure the development of *Lightschools®* members around the nine Domains, and the impact of using the Habits on their development, that of others and the environment. With our measurement methods, we aim to visibly capture our complex lives and the ways we develop and impact each other. By making the process visible, we are becoming aware of the development and transformation that is going on and are able to make the most out of that as we see the connections and recognize patterns. A visual representation allows us to learn, improve, transform, make aligned decisions, and celebrate the big and small steps along the way. We never live, learn, and co-create alone. It happens in interaction with other **people** and with the **space** in which we move. Finally,

time also influences our development. That makes our measurement methods multidimensional. In the next section, we will take a closer look at these dimensions: the diverse people, the various spaces, and the utilization of time that characterize *Lightschools*®.

Distributed living, learning, and co-creating among people

All *Lightschools*® members are part of a distributed collective education and innovation ecosystem, based on a self-determined learners' approach. Regardless of their roles, they are regarded as life-learners and entrepreneurs. They all find inspiration regarding the path they want to take in their life through living, learning, and co-creating in the community. In doing so, they demonstrate entrepreneurship both in character and in behavior. Based on an agile, life-learning, and entrepreneurial mindset, they take responsibility from their own ability and learn to flow with what comes naturally instead of forcing something to work. They explore possibilities assertively, and identify and utilize new opportunities for the development of themselves, others, and the environment (Iske, 2018).

Ecosystems with higher (bio)diversity tend to be more stable with greater resistance and resilience in the face of disruptive events. That is why *Lightschools*® aims for a community that is diverse in backgrounds and disciplines. *Lightschools*® brings sociocultural, technological, political, spiritual, ecological, and economical disciplines together and connects thinkers, doers, makers, and feeling people. We aim for diversity in backgrounds and disciplines among all five roles: Students, Teachers, Households, SMBE, and Connectors. Besides the common denominators and the diversity of the community, each role also has its specific characteristics and responsibilities.

STUDENTS

Students within *Lightschools*® are human beings of any age that fully commit their time and attention to their life-learning journey. An important criterion is that they are not employed by a company (as a major pastime) and are fully committed to their learning journey. A local Lightschool distinguishes itself primarily on the basis of the type of Student. The age of the Students, and a possible specialization, like arts, technology, health, fashion, or ecology, make for different types of local or partnering *Lightschools*®. While interacting with the other roles, Students bring a fresh perspective and are able to think outside the box more easily.

TEACHERS

Teachers cultivate the *Lightschools*® mindset, which means that living, learning, and co-creating in an agile, life-learning, and entrepreneurial way with the 13 Common Principles and the Potential Development Habits is part of their nature. They act in every situation based on the Principles and Habits, as well as guide and empower other members to do the same in their own way. Teachers continuously develop themselves along the nine Domains leading to authentic embodiment. With that they are examples to the community. How they go through life, in and outside their role as Teacher, breathes the genuine love and fascination for life and the personal and social development of people. They have a clear personal "why" that guides them every day. They recognize the inner strength of people and skillfully support them in developing it further in a sound and practical way. Teachers use their own qualities and passions in this regard, and are mature, socially just, and creative solution thinkers. Teachers have a healthy educational closeness to the Students and the community. They are servant leaders and agile facilitators, who take care of the communities by ensuring that the right conditions are co-created for everyone involved to develop their potential.

SMALL-TO-MEDIUM BUSINESS ENTREPRENEURS

Depending on the age and possible specialization of the local Lightschool or partnering Lightschools, the type of Business Entrepreneurs involved in the community may differ (as long as the community is diverse in backgrounds and disciplines). In a Lightschool with mainly younger students, where learning themes are varied and broad, there could be, for example, cooperations with a baker, greengrocer, shoemaker, carpenter, gardener, fitness instructor, restaurant and theater owner, artist, programmers, car mechanic, etc., of course depending on the inhabitants and conditions of the area. In a Lightschool with a certain specialization, partnerships could exist, for example, with some bigger (city) companies and centers specialized in fields such as housing, technology, health, infrastructure, ecologic design, energy and earth resources, food, permaculture and agriculture, the arts and culture, politics and alternative economy design.

CONNECTORS

Connectors explore the possibilities of including open-minded local Business Entrepreneurs with diverse backgrounds, and prepare them to be able to take part in the Lightschool community. Connectors create learning arrangements and facilitate and support the organization of community projects. Together with Teachers, Connectors develop a clear strategy to ensure active participation and ownership of the education and innovation process among the community. They build strong local, regional, and translocal networks, maintain relationships, and inform those involved about the course of events in a Lightschool. Sometimes, partnerships turn out not to go well and there might be even talk of an "invasive species." Connectors watch over the community and identify, transform, or remove potential threats on the basis of a powerful collective vision and mission and collective decision-making using the 13 Common Principles. In short, Connectors are true networkers, organizers, educators, and watchguards that build sustainable bridges within the Lightschool and between different *Lightschools®*.

HOUSEHOLDS

In this participative process, the degree of involvement of the Students' Households in the community depends on age, needs, and desires. Households are of key importance in *Lightschools®*, particularly with young Students. They are approached as partners in the education and upbringing of the Students. In this way, better use is made of the intelligence, knowledge, and skills present in the Households. Parents, carers, and tutors of children and adolescents actively participate in co-creating the Lightschool and can be involved as Business Entrepreneurs (from their work), Teachers, Connectors, experts, or partners.

Distributed living, learning, and co-creating among spaces

In an ecosystem, individual beings and different species interact with each other in relation with their environment. It is precisely this interaction with the environment that makes it an ecosystem and not just a community. The environment has an important influence on the development of a community. *Lightschools®* therefore also places great importance on the relation with the environment. The space in which we live, learn, and co-create influences our experience. Let's take the local Lightschool level as an example. Every Lightschool is rooted in its environment, its culture, traditions, and/or beliefs. Besides, the Lightschool community lives, learns, and co-creates distributedly. The different spaces, whether it be *at their households, at workplaces, in nature, in the city or town, in the Dojo, or on our online platform*, influence their experience.

HOME

Home, the environment where members live, greatly influences the potential development opportunities there. It is a starting point and basis for their outlook on life. Homes should be spaces which meet their physical and safety needs, nourish their need for love and belonging, and support emotional balance. The social economic status of the Household, the organization of the space, the ambiance, and the people with whom it is shared contribute to this. Households are co-responsible for aligning with the 13 Common Principles and the Potential Development Habits. They collaborate with Teachers and Connectors and are committed to purposefully turn their homes into stimulating and safe environments.

WORKPLACES

Lightschools® members take ownership of their life-learning journey and are free to follow their curiosity, interests, and passions. They go to the workplaces of the various affiliated Business Entrepreneurs to learn by doing. Immersing in real practice, they experience different things about themselves, the disciplines, crafts, and arts. These experiences are valuable to themselves and to the projects they work on. Depending on the plans, needs, and desires, workplace learning can take the form of orientation days, or weeks, or an internship. Business Entrepreneurs guide and mentor Students or other life-learners in these places from their expertise, whereby the process is coordinated together with Teachers and Connectors.

NATURE

There is a difference between learning "about" and learning "as," "with," "in," "from," and "for" nature (Green School, 2021). To really get to know and be able to learn and create for and with nature, hearing or reading about it is not enough. In *Lightschools*®, we learn as and from nature, using the local natural environment as a learning environment. We immerse ourselves in nature to truly understand life. We see the natural world as an endless source of inspiration. The structure, the rhythms, the workings, and the movements inspire innovations and increase our understanding of the world around us and within us. Besides, spending time in nature increases our mood, attention, memory, and cognitive abilities. It is also the best context to improve and nourish our social skills. Moments and trips into nature are part of *Lightschools*® as times of play, reflection, connection, and inspiration.

CITIES AND TOWNS

Cities and towns are human-made spaces that stimulate all the senses. There's a lot going on; hubbub, many people, many buildings, and a diversity of scenes and sights that can be perceived as we walk through the streets for an afternoon. It may be spaces for inspiration and perspective. Spaces to interact with people we know, or may not know yet. Spaces to learn and share experiences with the world about projects and solutions that *Lightschools*® members have created together. This way members spread the examples and are the positive change they wish to see in the world.

DOJO

One space plays a crucial, central, and coordinating role in the structure, process, and culture of *Lightschools*® and therefore for every level within it: the

Dojo. Dojo is Japanese for "place of the way." The Dojo is a protected, serene space. A space to be, to feel, to dream, to see and be seen, to listen and be heard. A space where we leave all our other responsibilities and daily tasks and worries outside, so that we can dedicate our attention and time fully to ourselves and each other. It's a space where members can learn and/or practice their Habits, gather as groups, teams, or as a whole community to discuss or align current developments, issues, or challenges, collaborate on projects and share stories, ideas, and experiences. The Dojo is designed in such a way that it immediately evokes a sense of safety and security. Teachers are mostly present in the Dojo, reinforcing a sense of stability and security through their presence, experience, and knowledge. More experienced community members also contribute to this, by providing beginners with the first instructions and explanation of how things work at the Dojo. Teachers guide and lead community members so that they learn to guide and lead themselves and are able to teach others. In this way, they become self-organized and independent in relationship and a learn-and-lead ecosystem is created.

GLOBALLY CONNECTED EMPOWERMENT

Both face-to-face and online meetings can be held, as a virtual platform has been created with the purpose of being a safe and protective virtual space for members to meet, share, learn, co-create, and discuss. All *Lightschools*® worldwide have their virtual home in our platform. Apart from that, it also facilitates learning, sharing, and co-creating between partnering Lightschools and *Lightschools*® as a whole, together with the international eduScrum community. Members learn from each other's failures and challenges, and exchange solutions that have been valuable in their contexts and can be transformed and translated in other contexts.

Within *Lightschools*®, we aim to empower all members at all levels. It is of vital importance for us to distribute available resources justly. Those resources can be (Avelino & Rotmans, 2009) human (experts, clients, supporters, (wo)manpower), mental (information, solutions, (best) practices and ideas), monetary (financial resources and funds), artifactual (tools, devices, products, infrastructure), and natural (physical spaces for living, learning, and co-creating, natural materials).

Members share their resources with the community. The Principles are used as lenses to look at situational needs and the context of each Lightschool. After democratic discussion and reflection resources are distributed among the different *Lightschools*® around the world. National and international authorities and organizations that believe in and wish to invest in *Lightschools*® and eduScrum can also empower the community with their resources. One globalized economy is being avoided. There is a focus on vibrant local or regional economies. Translocal partnering *Lightschools*® can carry out projects in close cooperation, which increases the possibilities and impact. Enterprises that may arise thereof can therefore bridge partnering *Lightschools®*.

In the end, the exchange on our online platform allows for ongoing opportunities to develop and improve. Every Lightschool has its own characteristics and integrity, due to the uniqueness of its members and their local context. Every Lightschool therefore shines its own light, creating a diverse and thereby more resistant and resilient global ecosystem.

Natural time and the PDRAC-spiral

In *Lightschools®*, we attune our development and creation processes to natural time. That means, for example, that we live and learn with the seasons and attune and tailor our festivities to moments of natural importance, such as the spring equinox, the summer and winter solstice, and the autumn equinox. We align our way of planning and organizing to the natural order in time, which means that we organize ourselves per day, week, moon, season, and year using the PDRAC-spiral.

The PDRAC-spiral is an adaptation to the Plan Do Check Act (PDCA) learning and improvement cycle (Moen & Norman, 2009). In *Lightschools®*, we Plan, Do, Reflect, Adapt, and Celebrate in a spiral instead of a cycle. Every single step is taken mindfully, allowing us to learn and improve gradually, one step at a time. Instead of staying on the same level, and learning and improving in response to the "Check" moment, we gradually rise to the next level through our reflective mindful practice during the entire process.

Firstly, all community members create a Potential Development Plan every year, in which they describe why, how, and what developments they wish to make in line with the Potential Development Profile. Based on these individually drawn up plans, the time is taken to talk to each other. During these community discussions, decisions are taken democratically concerning the year and seasonal themes within the Lightschool. Besides, mentor groups and project teams for the first season are composed. Mentor groups are created based on a common focus concerning a particular Domain(s) with guidance of a Teacher who is highly developed within that or those Domain(s). In the mentor groups, ways are sought to support each other during the process. Project teams are composed on the basis of common interest and complementary qualities, skills, and knowledge. Based on the community's decisions, the different living, learning, and co-creating spaces are coordinated and organized. The community jointly takes care of the execution of the plans in the different spaces. Helpful tools are designed and a rough year planning with room for change and what emerges are created. This planning process takes quite some time. It is a very important step to make flowing together in a smooth, effective, and efficient way possible.

Once plans are co-created, the community organizes moments to Do, Reflect, Adapt, and Celebrate together, again attuned to the natural time (weekly, moonly, and seasonal moments). At team and group level, we also see the PDRAC-spiral coming back, with a higher frequency of gathering moments (daily and weekly moments). Important community and natural milestones are celebrated. In thematic exhibitions, learnings and created products and services are presented and shared with the community and interested outsiders. These are important days for the community to be together, to pause, and celebrate. Days of pride!

The WwH emergent curriculum thus arises first from the individual, then communal, and later team and group Potential Development Plans. The Plans give rise to joint discussions on the different levels. Asking questions, facing conflicts, and making choices are inherent to the process. Challenging questions need to be asked in order to stay aligned to what truly matters to them and the world. A Lightschool constantly challenges the way in which is lived, learned, taught, and developed, to find a way that suits the present. That requires reflection, experimentation, and adaptation of ourselves and what we do to stay aligned to what is personally and socially meaningful. The 13 Common Principles guide the curriculum; every step of the PDRAC process.

Project-based learning

In *Lightschools®*, we learn by actively engaging in real-world, personally, and socially meaningful projects. In a safe and inspiring context, we learn to face the unprecedented social, environmental, and economic challenges today and co-create new solutions in projects, aligned with the 13 Common Principles. Solutions are translated into *regenerative* products, services, and educational programs.

In order to develop projects, time is taken for deep conversations. Challenging questions are broken down or divided into different parts by further conversation, deep thinking, and exploration. Only in this way, it is possible to truly get to the heart of the matter and influencing factors. That includes asking challenging questions, having an open mind, and a willingness to face uncomfortable situations. Only then meaningful projects with a new approach and aligned actions can be shaped.

eduScrum

Projects of any size within *Lightschools®* are managed using eduScrum. eduScrum is a refinement of Scrum (Schwaber & Sutherland, 2017), allowing not only the product but also the person and team to develop in a structural way. During the projects, team members bring their strengths, knowledge, and skills and actively put them in service of the team. There is plenty of cross-pollination between the teams and within the team, so that learning from and with each other, and co-creation can happen. By creating, experimenting, and reflecting on the developments in short cycles (or spirals in our case), which are called "sprints," the teams remain attuned to each other and the developments, and different paths and solutions can be explored. These solutions can form the basis for the emergence of diverse local enterprises with valuable impact. Developing local enterprises are the benefits that can be reaped from a thorough approach based on the focus on the Why and How. Every individual, every team, and therefore every Lightschool, is unique and so are the solutions they come up with around challenges of different scales.

eduScrum is a framework for an active, collaborative, and co-creative education and innovation process. Using the eduScrum framework, teamwork becomes more effective, efficient, and fun. With "trust, transparency, review, and adapt" as its pillars, eduScrum focuses on the journey, in other words, the process, instead of solely striving toward results and goals. It attaches great importance on enjoying the journey. Participants in an eduScrum team develop into valuable members with an agile mindset that aims for constant improvement. Moreover, teams gradually build and take ownership of their learning process. It is up to the teams to think about how they want to meet the predefined "celebration criteria" and how they want to work and learn. As a result, they are intrinsically motivated and take responsibility. The framework and process are clearly structured, empowering the flow of the team.

Teams consist of a diverse complementary group of Students and Business Entrepreneurs. They plan their own activities and tasks and keep track of their own progress. Business Entrepreneurs participate in the project, bring in their expertise where possible, and could act as mentors to the Students.

Teachers coach, support, and guide the team(s) or the individuals, tailored to the needs, during the process. During the projects, teams have to acquire content knowledge themselves to be able to continue their work. If the teams need outside expertise for their projects, they will look for the necessary experts themselves. They guide their own learning, add their own meaning and experiences, dig into material, and actively engage with the content. Of course, this process is supported by both Teachers and Connectors. As a spectator, you see engaged and productive teams. Along the way, they discover who they are and what their abilities are. At the same time, they develop their skills concerning creativity, collaboration, communication, and critical thinking (also known as the 4Cs of learning and innovation, consolidated from the 21st-century skills) and strengthen their executive functioning, like planning, self-control, and time management.

SPRINTS

Teams work together in short cycles, called "sprints," according to the Plan Do Reflect (or Review in eduScrum terms) Adapt Celebrate (PDRAC) learning and improvement spiral. The teams define the time frame of the sprints with the support/guidance of the Teacher. In that time frame a certain amount of work has to be done for a context-concept-based project, in which one or more learning objectives will be achieved.

Every sprint starts with the planning of the work (Plan) to be done (Do) for the project and ends with a review of the learning and working results and a retrospective on team performance and personal development (Review). Teams have the space within the framework and goals to find their own way to deal with their work and to adapt (Adapt) according to their insights. Milestones in the process that are important to the team are celebrated (Celebrate).

Sprints get structured by the jointly defined and created Definition of Doing, Definition of Fun, and Definition of Communication, and the rules and artefacts of the framework. This creates a highly structured process. Teams plan and execute their work, keep track of their working and learning progress toward the goals set, to then be able to look back at team performance and personal development in a clear manner.

The "flap," the eduScrum visual framework, is co-created physically or virtually. It comprises the following areas:

- Stories
- Celebration Criteria
- Definition of Doing
- Definition of Fun
- Definition of Communication
- Run Up Chart
- Impediments

STORIES AND TASKS

The teams divide the project into several stories or subitems. Stories are a way to describe the products that this sprint should deliver. A story describes "what" and "why" it has to be done. Within the stories, celebration criteria are created, and stories are broken down into actionable and manageable small tasks to meet these celebration criteria.

Team members manage and show their process by moving tasks defined during the planning meeting(s) according to their status: from "still to do" (To Do), "working" (Busy) to "finished" (Done).

To Do: The "To Do" column summarizes all tasks for a sprint. The small tasks make clear what needs to be done so that results can be achieved.

Busy: Each team member chooses a task from the "To Do" column. Choices are made based on own preferences, but always in consultation with the team. A team member moves the task to the "Busy" column and starts working. Tasks can also be done together with other team members. Some tasks require the involvement of every member.

Done: A task will only be completed if it meets three conditions.

- All team members must agree that the task is done.
- The results must meet the celebration criteria.
- As accountable team members, they all are aware of what every task implies, so that the process continues to flow as best as possible despite possible impediments along the way.

To meet these conditions, each team member has to keep the others informed about their developments. They have to truly communicate and collaborate, think critically and creatively to really understand what has been done to complete the task and how they could support further development.

THE RUN UP CHART AND IMPEDIMENTS

The development process of each team is made visual with the Run Up Chart. The Run Up Chart makes the status of the project transparent to the team. Each task has a number of points. These points have been assigned to these tasks during the planning process using Planning Poker (Grenning, 2002). Planning Poker is a game approach to assign a relative score to individual tasks. It is a measure to make a relative estimate of the tasks to be done, according to the Fibonacci sequence. It allows for a quick insight into the relationships between the pieces of work and their workload within the total work backlog. By comparing the number of points accumulated with the agreed average number of points per time unit (velocity), teams get insight into their progress and whether they might have to change their way of working.

Within the "impediments" area on the flap, the team records everything that is preventing them from working efficiently. When a team encounters obstacles during the process, they put sticky notes with their struggles below "impediments." The main impediments are listed at the top. It is up to the team to remove impediments using their creative and critical thinking skills, guided and supported by the Teacher when necessary.

At the beginning of joint sessions, a so-called "Stand-Up" takes place regularly. In no more than five minutes, the team looks at their "flap" and each team member addresses the following questions:

- What have I done since the last Stand-Up?
- What will I do for my team during this time block?
- Do I have any obstacles or impediments? Do I see any impediments for my team?
- How will I support other team members? How can other team members support me?

Particular attention should be paid to possible obstacles and problems. Suppose one team member knows the solution to a problem of another team member. In that case, one can briefly state that to solve the problem directly after the stand-up so that the other teammates can continue working immediately. Some advice for practical application of eduScrum

eduScrum is a simple framework, which cannot be done partially because each part is there for a reason. It works as a whole and delivers more than the sum of the parts. Therefore, you can gain all the benefits that can be achieved only when you apply all the elements, no matter the project.

In learning to work with eduScrum, fail early and fail often. Your first attempt to use this new way of working could be flawless, but then the real journey begins. Learn by doing, learn by making mistakes and reflecting on them. Trust yourself and the learning process. The agile mindset is crucial to achieve successful implementation of eduScrum within *Lightschools®*.

Each new project, each sprint, or even every day you will feel more comfortable using eduScrum. Make mistakes, forgive yourself, and learn. The same applies to your life-learners' journey. Tell them to trust themselves and that they are allowed to "fail forward." The sooner you make mistakes the better. As long as you all work together as a team in an atmosphere of trust, it will work out well.

To conclude

As a diverse education and innovation ecosystem, *Lightschools®* has been born to create the conditions in which each member can get to know and endlessly develop oneself and one's potential in harmonious relationships with oneself, others, the planet, and all it inhabits. *Lightschools®* aims at empowering its members to live, learn, and co-create their own authentic path and make their own living. Using the elements of *Lightschools®*, we co-create personally and socially meaningful solutions in service of the greater whole. We take our human nature, our authenticity, the world of today, and the natural world as starting points to shape possibilities, opportunities, and solutions for sustainable living, learning, and co-creating. At all times during group process, in creating structure and designs, we start from what is natural. Nature is our Teacher.

Notes

1 Within *Lightschools®*, we (re)define what it entails to be a Student, a Teacher, etc. That is why these terms are written with capital letters.
2 The ideas of Dewey, Piaget, Vygotsky, and Tagore support the philosophy of the emergent curriculum.

References

Avelino, F., & Rotmans, J. (2009). Power in transition. An interdisciplinary framework to study power in relation to structural change. *European Journal of Social Theory*, 12(40): 543–569. https://doi.org/10.1177/1368431009349830

eduScrum team. (2020). *The eduScrum guide: the rules of the game*. Retrieved from https://www.eduscrum.nl/img/The_eduScrum_guide_English_2.pdf

García, H., & Miralles, F. (2016). *Ikigai*. Amsterdam: Boekerij.

Grenning, J. (2002). Planning poker or how to avoid analysis paralysis while release planning. *Hawthorn Woods: Renaissance Software Consulting*, 3: 22–23.

Iske, P.L. (2018). *Instituut voor briljante mislukkingen*. Amsterdam/Antwerpen: Business Contact.

Learning as, with, in, about and for nature. (March 29, 2021). *Green school*. Retrieved from https://www.greenschool.org/bali/principal/learning-as-with-in-about-and-for-nature/

Levin, S. (1998). Ecosystems and the biosphere as complex adaptive systems. *Ecosystems*, 1: 431–436. https://doi.org/10.1007/s100219900037

Moen, R., & Norman, C. (2009, September). *Evolution of the PDCA cycle*. Paper presented at the Asian Network for Quality Conference, Tokyo. Retrieved from https://www.westga.edu/~dturner/PDCA.pdf

Schwaber, K., & Sutherland, J. (2017). The scrum guide: the definitive guide to scrum. Retrieved from https://www.scrumguides.org/docs/scrumguide/v2017/2017-Scrum-Guide-US.pdf.

Stacey, S. (2009). *Emergent Curriculum in Early Childhood Settings*. St. Paul, Minnesota: Redleaf Press, pp. 17–18.

Yunus, M. (2017). *The 3 keys to eradicating poverty*. Retrieved on March 19, 2020, from YouTube. Retrieved from https://www.youtube.com/watch?v=UNu-OfYaLmM&ab_channel=OneYoungWorld.

Chapter 10

Agile learning and management in times of crisis in the digital age

Actor-reality construction in the COVID-19 pandemic

Tuomas Korhonen, Fabio Magnacca, Ossi Heino, Teemu Laine, Jakob Liboriussen, and Hanne Nørreklit

Introduction

While the impacts of the COVID-19 pandemic are felt virtually everywhere and by everyone, there is no common body that would define and coordinate all the necessary responses. The problem is global, but the responses are both global and local. This means we need both *generic* and *particular* sense-making, learning, and responses regarding the pandemic. The generic ones – provided by worldwide organizations such as the World Health Organization and researchers of medicine and virology – give generic guidelines (Van Bavel et al., 2020; Leoni et al., 2021). The particular ones result from the localization of these guidelines into national and regional contexts by local authorities (Ahmad et al., 2021; Ahn & Wickramasinghe, 2021; Ahrens & Ferry, 2021; Ferry et al., 2021; Huber et al., 2021; Leoni et al., 2021; Mitchell et al., 2021; Nikidehaghani & Cortese, 2021; Passetti et al., 2021; Sargiacomo et al., 2021). The response of each national, regional, organizational, and individual actor creates a reality construction that can display a more or less successful outcome (Nørreklit, H., 2017). On the basis of their experiences, each actor makes sense of the situation, acts, observes signals of the impacts, and essentially *learns* (Christianson & Barton, 2020; Müller-Seitz et al., 2014; Weick et al., 2005).

The knowledge formed regarding the pandemic can be seen as *actor based*, that is, relative to each individual actor's representation of the problem in situ (Nørreklit, H., 2017). Thus, learning about the global threats takes place in a situated manner: everyone reacts to a situation, interprets information, and translates their experiences into learning based on their personal epistemic systems. As the environment changes, so do the individual actors' interpretations and responses to it. Digitalization enables the actors to collect information from an ever-wider range of sources. However, the

DOI: 10.4324/9781003188728-12

context of creating information is often different from the local context in which this information is to be used (Quattrone, 2016). A generic model of knowledge creation, planning, and action, despite its possible efficiency, could entail an increasing risk of omitting central particularities of increasingly dynamic and complex environments. Accordingly, the essential thing is what the actors' attention focuses on and what it is limited to in decision-making, action, impact assessment, and transfer of learning from the particularities in context, and possibly from the generic level of knowledge as well (Roux-Dufort, 2007). To effectively manage in times of crisis and enable agile learning, actor-reality construction in such situations needs to be better understood.

This chapter is concerned about how actors can produce and use digital systems-based knowledge for agile learning to create effective responses to the COVID-19 pandemic. To create such understandings, we explore how processes of digitalization can more or less effectively affect an actor's reality construction in this context. We address this problem theoretically through the paradigm of *pragmatic constructivism* (PC) (Nørreklit, H., 2017), which provides a framework for understanding actor–world relational construction. We find that, to create a functioning reality construction, people produce local *language-games* about and learn from COVID-19. These language-games are influenced by digitalization. The actors' abilities to use digital information to learn in an agile way is influenced by their capabilities to integrate the *four dimensions of reality*, which, in accordance with pragmatic constructivism, are depicted as *facts, possibilities, values,* and *communication* (Nørreklit, H. et al., 2010, 2016; Nørreklit, H., 2017; Nørreklit, L., 2017). When these dimensions are integrated, practices can become successful and, vice versa, if they are not integrated, only illusions of success might appear with lesser chances of functioning practice (Nørreklit, H., 2017). With the help of empirical illustrations, we analyze agile learning through language-games used for the performance management of the COVID-19 pandemic in two European countries. We find that both integrative and non-integrative learning seem to exist due to several uncertainties and mis- and disinformation presented during the initial and later phases of the COVID-19 pandemic. Overall, the findings of this chapter contribute to the emerging knowledge of how different actors deal with crises from the viewpoint of digitalization in management, and how integrative, agile learning could be enabled by actor-reality construction.

The structure of the chapter is as follows. First, we provide some theoretical background on pragmatic constructivism, agility, and digitalization. The theoretical background is synthesized with the framework in use in the chapter. Then, building on the framework, we illustrate and examine integrative and non-integrative ways of learning in the COVID-19 pandemic. The chapter ends with concluding remarks.

Theoretical background

Pragmatic constructivism and the meaning of language for action

Pragmatic constructivism builds on the core assumption that human activities are organized around the use of language-games in which – according to the late Wittgenstein (1953) – thoughts, actions, and language are interwoven into a totality. Human beings are creative and reflective actors who use language to construct practices and coordinate activities in an effort to build functioning practices (Nørreklit, H., 2017; Nørreklit, H. et al., 2010, 2016; Nørreklit, L., 2017). Actors resort to the language toolbox to construe and develop their realities and the particular types of practices by which they aim to control their reality constructions. Pragmatic constructivism emphasizes that in order for actors to build a set of functioning actions, indeed the four dimensions of reality need to be integrated (Nørreklit, H. et al., 2010, 2016; Nørreklit, H., 2017; Nørreklit, L., 2017).

In order for intentional results to be realized, there must be action possibilities in place together with a factual basis for undertaking the actions. For instance, a vaccine has been an action possibility to protect the population against COVID-19 but, in order to obtain results, a vaccine with the protective features has had to be in place. Furthermore, it is crucial that the array of factual possibilities somehow reflects the actors' values. If an action cannot be interpreted as meaningful or valuable, actors will be disinclined to carry out the action in question. For instance, governments have had to be motivated to protect the population and citizens have had to be motivated to get vaccinated. Finally, if actors are to create a well-functioning reality, they must communicate to construct and coordinate functioning practices, for example, governments must communicate relevant information about the vaccine to citizens. The integration of the four dimensions is a sufficient condition for successful actions in practice (Nørreklit, H., 2017), but in contrast, if not integrated, any project can become an illusion (Nørreklit, L., 1987, 2017).

In local practices, actors use conceptual narratives and measurement models to control the integration of the four dimensions of reality. For the performance management of the pandemic, the managers involved need to develop a particular conceptual language, for example, using concepts such as "infected," "death," and "hospitalized." Effective performance management requires a linguistic structure within which each concept has a fairly well-defined meaning (Nørreklit, H. et al., 2016). First, a concept must be given an abstract meaning. Actors must define the concept's cognitive content and thereby outline its abstract idea. For instance, they must outline the cognitive content of "coronavirus," "COVID-19-infected," "death," and so on. Second, actors must agree on a specific set of exemplary references in order to establish a shared horizon of understanding of what the abstract idea implies in its practical use. For instance, in the specific case of COVID-19, virologists have had to be able to identify what a COVID-19 coronavirus is and what it is not. When relating a concept to an abstract idea, the results might be overly broad definitions that are inadequate for planning and control purposes. Therefore, criteria must be applied in order to overcome subjectivity issues by transforming the qualitative basis of the conceptual content into observations and numerical measures.

The establishment of the abovementioned qualities is crucial for the performance management of the pandemic. If concepts are properly constructed, they may assist actors in building functioning practices. However, from a PC perspective, it is imperative not only that concepts function as a result of their conceptual quality; concepts also need to be integrated into a narrative integrating the four dimensions of reality described: facts, possibilities, values, and communication. Therefore, these dimensions must be accounted for in a narrative that outlines the concept, in order to avoid producing illusions and confusion. For instance, the performance of a particular vaccine may look good, but whether it can correctly be described as performing well depends on whether people have actually received it (facts) and whether it can create the intended effects and avoid serious non-intended effects (possibility) and people intend to receive the vaccine (value). Furthermore, to create a social practice, the meaning of the concept must be communicated.

Drawing on such language, actors can develop, collect, calculate, and evaluate information about the nature of the coronavirus, human behavior, and action possibilities, and hence create and evaluate action plans. The meaning of language is learned and developed in local practices. Hence, the meaning of any concept is explained by the role it plays in actors' construction of functioning practices. However, for language-games to function in a certain practice, actors need to develop and adjust the meaning of concepts. Yet this is not, however, a simple matter; actors must engage in a reflective and dialogical process to adapt the concepts and make clear what a particular concept means in a particular reality construction. This requires actors having sufficient cognitive competences and abilities to observe, analyze, and act.

Digital language in times of crisis

Human beings have been immersed in uncertain and very transformative contexts where intense intertwining of live language and digital language in the construction of COVID-19 reality and in the control and coordination of human activities took place (Leoni et al., 2021; Mitchell et al., 2021). The performance management and measurement of COVID-19 reality has in fact been greatly boosted by information technology (IT) systems, which have facilitated the accumulation, retrieval, transmission, and elaboration of a large volume of data across social space at a speed and to an extent never seen before (Ahn & Wickramasinghe, 2021). Simultaneously, new analytical models were used to steer central operational decisions since the spread of

COVID-19 in the first months of 2020 (Siegenfeld et al., 2020; Leoni et al., 2021; Mitchell et al., 2021).

Continuous learning and adaptation are necessary to take place successfully in such an uncertain and transformative environment. This requires advanced habitus-based competences and insights to understand and analyze problems and to develop solutions to handle those problems successfully. The habitus can be defined as "principles of the generation and structuring of practices and representations" (Bourdieu, 1977, p. 72). At the core of such a learning process is the production and use of information for the performance management of the pandemic; digital language has constituted a major source of that information. However, the COVID-19 pandemic has shown the shortcomings of using digital language as a means to transfer knowledge quickly and reliably, and the unequivocality of using digital means for knowledge transfer (Piekkari et al., 2020; Quattrone, 2016). The digital language of IT systems operates with two-valued logic (Nørreklit, L. et al., 2019). Such digital logical structures imply that the statements of the phenomenon are shaped quantitatively, which facilitates advanced analyses, calculations, and operations. There are many benefits of such a symbolic language, but it differs from live language-games and hence is reductive. To intertwine productively with certain local actors' knowledge creation processes, the meaning of the digitalized information system should be controlled by the actors' advanced cognitive habitus. The cognitive habitus is required for the continuous creation of knowledge and learning about how to handle the pandemic most effectively. However, if the IT language takes control of the meaning overriding the advanced conceptual habitus, the many benefits of IT systems might transform themselves into drawbacks shaping dysfunctional reality constructions (Nørreklit, L. et al., 2019). Meaning produced in a reductive monologue communication undermines learning as it excludes the reflective, dialogical, and pragmatic functions of live language-games.

Reality construction and effective practice development (e.g., how to control the spread of COVID-19) presuppose dialogues among actors, and effective dialogues presuppose human beings' engagement in those dialogues by means of effective language-games made of effective concepts. This is central to learning and adaptation first and to action second. However, the COVID-19 pandemic has twisted this basic assumption to some extent, especially when it comes to the relationship between those who have the decision-making power and the rest of the population. That is because those in charge of managing the crisis very often have adopted a form of top-down communication based mainly on digital language without leaving space for live forms of language based on actors engagement in language plays and social interactions. An increasingly unbalanced intertwining of live language and digital language in favor of the latter has been dominating the pandemic. But how, then, can we acquire an integration of the dimensions of reality, to have a more balanced intertwining of these elements? We will go into this next.

Agile learning for faster integration of the dimensions of reality

The pandemic has turned out to be an enormous source of *uncertainty* that has required local responses – not because there is a lack of knowledge but a lack of knowing what knowledge is relevant. Indeed, decision-makers have had to face a lack of critical information in an unprecedented way and take this into account in their decisions; moreover, they have had to submit themselves to working under conditions in which they do not know what they need to know (Parviainen, 2020; Tovstiga & Tovstiga, 2020). Because of this, COVID-19 is not only a crisis of health but also a crisis of learning for administrators. From the viewpoint of learning, and the problem-solving capacity that develops through learning, it is particularly important for actors to constantly review their own presumptions and reconceptualize the phenomenon as new information and unexpected facts come to light (Greve, 2020; Henriksen et al., 2004; Lee et al., 2020). The acquisition of new information modifying established knowledge structures and the ability to examine oneself as part of learning systems are at the core of learning in such a field of not-knowing (Eschenbacher & Fleming, 2020; Feldman, 2004; Kallio, 2020; Wenger, 2000).

Due to the limited nature of information and knowledge relevant for resolving a crisis (any crisis) that is ongoing (i.e., it is not proven how the crisis is overcome), lessons should particularly be learned from crises at the conceptual level, as this allows us to understand the dynamic structures of events and respond to unexpected kinds of events as well (Borell & Eriksson, 2013). Thus, administrators could avoid the tempting opportunity to learn what is immediate, clearly visible, easily verbalized, and translated into action in and about a crisis. Following this tempting opportunity would mean that we might fail to understand the dynamics of the underlying mechanisms of crises (Sharpe, 2016), possibly leading to insufficient concepts in use and excessively rigid mechanisms that communicate information.

In a crisis situation, it is essential to translate the perceived, experienced, and obtained knowledge into lessons and to integrate the lessons into the operation of the system – already during the crisis, not only afterward (Müller-Seitz et al., 2014). But where can we learn from and how if the crisis is not over (i.e., it is ongoing or prolonged)? When the perceived knowledge of past events is the only thing available, one may ask which or how lessons should be learned from it so that what is learned serves the ability to face an ever-changing crisis. As noted, perceptions of the situation are constantly changing, but what is also characteristic of modern crises is that the mechanisms that produce that change are also inherently changing and uncertain. Information that may be useful in a context and over a period of time may not be as such transferrable to another context or period.

In this case, reconceptualization would be needed (Henriksen et al., 2004). Thus, actors need to revisit their understanding of how concepts work, that is, they need to reconceptualize different phenomena in the reality. For this, pragmatic constructivism offers a useful methodology. Through an alternation of successes and failures, humans experience life and accumulate knowledge that determines successful actions. PC could help to continuously develop effective conceptual models for handling problems, and ultimately to create successful outcomes. In times of crisis in the digital age, such help would be particularly necessary.

Tentative framework based on the theoretical background

All in all, our theoretical framework can be schematically represented as sketched in Figure 10.1. The x-axis represents time. The y-axis indicates the achieved degree of integration of the four dimensions of reality. The resulting graph illustrates the likely learning process actors go through in situations of crisis and high uncertainty in the digital age as extreme as the COVID-19 pandemic.

Faced with a new pandemic, the world in which all actors are immersed manifests itself into an uncertain and very transformative context that demands continuous learning and adaptation to act and succeed. The effectiveness of such a learning and adaptation process varies among actors and depends on their ability to successfully integrate the four dimensions of reality. Accordingly, the lower dotted line shows an archetype of non-agile learning where actors are not able to accomplish integration of the four dimensions of reality over time; the upper dotted line shows an archetype of agile learning with an ideal, fast, and linear integration of the four dimensions. Actual learning is an intricate transformative experience that follows a process of maturation over time, the agility and effectiveness of which depend on the quality of the actor–world relational complex construction (solid drawn line in the middle). In the perspective of pragmatic constructivism, such a construction implies the engagement of professional actors in the integration of facts, possibilities, values, and communication, and thus the creation of construct causality. In their professional habitus-based language-games (reported on the graph inside the cloud), actors make use of concepts, create meanings, develop narratives, and act based on the narratives they co-created. Since this process of reality construction happens in a world imbued with IT systems and digital language, the way actors construct their realities and the way they act accordingly is influenced by digitalization. Therefore, the way digitalization enters the process of reality construction impacts the outcome of actors' practices and actions. In this regard, we can imagine digital language as a "cloud" (dotted oval in Figure 10.1), rich in data and information always available "out there," which stands between the actor and their operating environment every time they attempt to establish a relational complex to it. In this task, digital language can function both as a catalyst and an inhibitor depending on the way it intertwines with live language and professional habitus-based language-games in creating narratives of action. When the two-valued logic of digital language is controlled by the

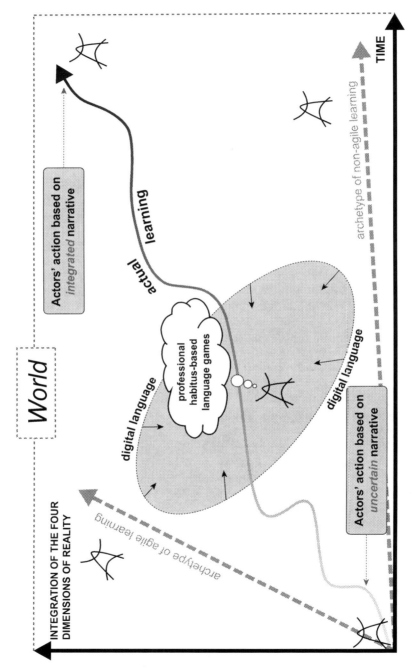

Figure 10.1 Actor–world relational construction.

cognitive habitus of the actors concerned, it acts as a catalyst that very likely leads to an integrated narrative and successful actions. On the contrary, when IT systems take the lead and harm social interactions, digital language might act as an inhibitor in the process of reality construction resulting in uncertain narratives that are likely to determine actors' failures or inaction. In the former scenario, learning tends to be an agile and effective process; in the latter scenario, it tends to move toward non-agility and less effectiveness.

Next, we will reflect upon the framework using empirical illustrations of the COVID-19 pandemic. The viewpoints were formulated in the spring of 2021.

Actor-reality construction in the COVID-19 pandemic: empirical evidence

From the early stages of the pandemic, countries struggled to create narratives that integrated factual possibilities within their value range and communicate them to citizens (Mitchell et al., 2021). Although many aspects of COVID-19 mean that there has not been proper knowledge to guide action, not everything about COVID-19 has been uncertain. Experts on infectious diseases have been quite unanimous across the board that the number of COVID-19 cases diagnosed, and deaths and hospitalizations depend on country-specific measures and on the extent to which people manage to change their behavior with respect to pre-COVID-19 times. Performance management of the COVID-19 crisis requires at least an acquired understanding of the illness and how it mutates and spreads accordingly in different environments, as well as the effects of measures and how these can be implemented to successfully affect the behavior of people from different groups.

The process of learning on these matters has been occurring in different ways in different countries with varying outcomes (Mitchell et al., 2021). Next, we first provide insights into attempting integration in two cases and, subsequently, a case of mis- and disinformation facilitating nonintegrated learning. We use pseudonyms for the countries because we do not wish to focus on specific countries but rather more generally on agile learning.

Case of attempting integration in the first phase in Country A

In Country A, measures for managing the prolonged pandemic were relatively successful over time (in terms of, for example, relatively low death toll). The country was fortunate that the first wave of the epidemic landed in the country relatively late, which is why control measures could be planned and implemented at a very early stage. The timing of control measures could be targeted as efficiently as possible regarding various factors, based on factual possibilities that had been established by agile learning. The country gradually moved to the hybrid strategy taking into account the values of health, economy, and human freedom. Thus, it sought to curb the spread of the disease and protect those at risk, but also to cause as little economic loss and interference with fundamental human rights as possible. (Tynkkynen et al., 2020; Tiirinki et al., 2020). Reflections on many details and specific measures enabled the emergence of an integrated narrative based on the "test–trace–isolate–treat" approach as a factual action possibility to achieve an outcome that is a compromise between the three sets of values. However, the factual basis for such narrative requires constant attention and development.

More specifically, during the first wave in particular, the effectiveness of contact tracing proved to be a significant factor in curbing the spread of the disease and proved its value in protecting the population's health. At this stage, there were only limited facts available on the actual mechanisms of the spread of the disease, despite the increasing availability of digital information from the first wave, both locally and globally. The development of a digital mobile app for contact tracking was started at an early stage as a means (a possibility) to help to build a *fact-based narrative* about the pandemic. The idea of the app was to report if a person (or actually their cell phone) had been in close proximity to a person (their cell phone) who had tested positive for COVID-19 and had indicated this in the app with a clear conscience. In terms of controlling the pandemic, the effectiveness of an app depended on the extent of the effective communication of its arrangement, its factual possibility of accurately detecting the people exposed, and people's opinion on its advantages and disadvantages in terms of their personal values (Currie, 2020; Trang et al., 2020; Coggin, 2020). In the beginning, the app was well received by people and authorities, as they were informed that it could provide the desired facts, making it possible to control the spread of the pandemic and thereby meet the values of protecting people's health. Later, critical discourse emerged, as the accuracy of the app was not always good enough for finding the contacts, as people needed to have the app switched on wherever they went. Thus, doubts were raised about the usefulness of the app in curbing the pandemic, that is, the actual possibility to detect the facts. All in all, the app provided a digital platform for learning about the pandemic, with citizens being able to learn whether they had been exposed to the virus themselves, and thus adhere to the wider *values of public safety*.

Another example of agile learning was the evolving information on the effectiveness of face masks, that is, their actual effectiveness in shielding people from the virus. At first there were not even enough masks available for healthcare professionals, let alone the public. Then, when masks became available, the possible benefits of the masks were interpreted differently because facts were uncertain. This led to strong political upheaval driven by conflicting values. Motivated by the prospect of protecting public health, strong recommendations for using the masks in public transport and later on more broadly in public places were communicated by the health authorities and by many individuals in social media, for instance. Concerned by the intervention made in humans' personal space, critical discourses emerged regarding the use of masks due to lack of evidence of their immediate effect on the pandemic situation. In particular, social media, that is, digital platforms, became an arena for antimask narratives, with people saying that they would not use masks or support their compulsory use.

However, the situation in Country A followed a more general trend in which, at early stages of the crisis, people generally set out to support the political leadership (Jennings et al., 2020; Moynihan, 2012). Trust in policymakers and authorities was exceptionally strong in the early stages of the pandemic. Later, this support declined even though the strategy could be classified as relatively successful in terms of the death rate. The later actions of isolation were not as successful as in the early stages of the pandemic because large-scale social isolation measures were thought to be detrimental to health. Although these measures were considered to be particularly important, there were shortcomings in the timeliness of the measures and their proper targeting (Miles et al., 2020). Confusion about the truth gave reason to doubt the relationship between policy-making and factual scientific evidence (Tynkkynen et al., 2020). On the one hand, there was criticism of politicians for not disclosing the information used in decision-making. It was not clear whether scientific facts or political interests were guiding decision-making. On the other hand, there was also a debate about whether the mathematical models of the spread of the virus should be judged based on their ability to predict future facts accurately (Siegenfield et al., 2020), or on their ability to serve decision-making on actions leading to intentional outcomes and hence pragmatic success.

All in all, the country followed a process of integrative learning although there were challenges of integrating factual possibilities along the way, that is, the agility of learning was not easily acquired all the time. Indeed, agility was sought for in the process as conflicting factual possibilities and values emerged (see the curves in Figure 10.1).

Case of attempting integration in the second phase in Country B

In Country B, as in many other countries, one of the most important processes in the management of the whole COVID-19 pandemic was the vaccination process. A vaccination plan was made and, at the same time, vaccines were procured. Those prioritized for vaccination (i.e., medical personnel) received an e-mail inviting them to register for a dose on a digital platform. Hence, the communication of such a pivotal process in the management of the whole COVID-19 crisis was based on digital language only, without any kind of interaction between those who set up the platform and those who were supposed to use it to obtain the vaccine. The objective of those who set up the platform was to find out the number of vaccines needed for the first phase of the vaccination program. The e-mail was received by medical personnel on the day before the date on which their chance to secure a dose of the vaccine was due to expire. Narratives around the use of the platform by the people to be vaccinated, on the rules governing that platform, and those governing the whole vaccination process were almost absent. Even though the e-mail reported some information about the vaccine and some informative material was attached to the e-mail, the material concerned another type of COVID-19 vaccine – the one that at that time was already available elsewhere and was different to the one that would have been available in Country B.

Lack of exhaustive information on the vaccine (facts), lack of actual integrated narratives around that type of vaccine, the short time frame to decide whether or not to attend the vaccination event (factual possibility), and the lack of social interaction (communication) with other people resulted in uncertainty that, in turn, resulted in many individuals not accessing the digital platform to secure a dose of vaccine, even if they were intrinsically motivated (values) to do so.

The process of learning about and adapting to the first phase of the vaccination process thus resulted in failure for many individuals. The communication that was based on digital language, the short time frame, and the lack of dialogue and social interaction meant that the actual possibility of getting the vaccine did not match (integrate) the reality construction of many individuals so, accordingly, they did not act. Digital language completely – but ineffectively – replaced live language, and the short time frame prevented parallel social interaction from taking place in the time available. Although country B cannot be classified as an example of pure non-agile learning (i.e., low integration of the dimensions of reality per time, see Figure 10.1), it could be said that the lack of social interaction among actors hindered agility to some extent.

Mis- and disinformation facilitating nonintegrated learning

Across the world, the COVID-19 pandemic has been characterized by the highly confusing effect of mis- and disinformation among the population. Mis- and disinformation spreads above all on social media platforms, making the formation and distribution of pandemic-related information less clear. This is a huge challenge for fact-based, agile learning in different societies. Fake news and conspiracy theories, for example, have created confusion about the nature of the pandemic, influencing people's ways to learn and behave – to integrate the dimensions of reality in a successful manner. People who tend to believe alternative facts and conspiracy theories are also less willing to follow the guidelines and instructions issued by authorities (Uscinski et al., 2020; Van Bavel et al., 2020).

Overall, the distorted and unreliable information spread by the Internet has created a risky environment for public health, hampering the realization of possibilities (e.g., masks and vaccinations). In response, administrations and authorities have been encouraged to develop strategies to counteract mis- and disinformation (Ali, 2020; Cuan-Baltazar et al., 2020; Jayaseelan et al., 2020). However, fact checking and the correction of erroneous information inevitably occur with a time lag, since the misleading information is diffused considerably faster, more deeply and more broadly than true information (Milewski, 2020; Vosoughi et al., 2018; Huynh, 2020; Brashier et al., 2021). This problem has hindered acting based on an integrated narrative.

The situation is aggravated by the fact that COVID-19-related information has rarely been clear-cut and easily definable as either true or false. Even scientific knowledge does not often form a consensus in this regard. In other words, as the information itself is constantly changing, this complicates actors' reconceptualization processes and agile learning. In such information environment that is tormented by ambiguity, learning has hardly been purely agile (cf. Figure 10.1). Integration of the dimensions of reality has been greatly influenced by local and global language-games of COVID-19.

Conclusion

This chapter focuses on the role of digitalization in the way actors produce and use knowledge for agile learning to create effective responses in times of (a pandemic) crisis. Drawing on pragmatic constructivism, the chapter proposes a framework for agile learning within the dynamics of a pandemic situation such as COVID-19. Yet, we claim that the chapter could be helpful in understanding different kinds of crises (e.g., financial, ecologic, and social) and agile learning therein.

Altogether, the chapter states that, to create a functioning reality construction in situ, professionals must engage through habitus-based language-games in learning about and developing solutions to handle different events such as crises. These language-games are influenced by digitalization. While digitalization enables quicker information dissemination and thus support for agile learning in crisis management, such information does not necessarily lead to an integrated, agile learning process. Also, drawing on pragmatic constructivism, the chapter empirically analyzes how authorities in different countries have responded to the COVID-19 pandemic based on different narratives. Thereby, the chapter provides the perspective of actor–world relational construction to the timely debate in academic research on the localization of general guidelines of responding to crises (Ahmad et al., 2021; Ahn & Wickramasinghe, 2021; Ahrens & Ferry, 2021; Ferry et al., 2021; Huber et al., 2021; Leoni et al., 2021; Mitchell et al., 2021; Nikidehaghani & Cortese, 2021; Passetti et al., 2021; Sargiacomo et al., 2021).

In particular, the chapter shows that the translation of live ideas into digital language raises serious concerns if not supported by live language-games and meaningful integrated narratives. Instead of reducing the high uncertainty already permeating the context of practice, the high digital reaction time demanded by IT systems can lead to uncertainty that is even higher than the initial situation. People need narratives and social interactions to learn effectively, generate meaning, adapt and act successfully. The better narratives are formulated by integrating factual possibilities into a value range, and the more actors are engaged in the formulation of those narratives, the more those narratives become meaningful, uncertainty is reduced and learning and adaptation become agile, virtuous, and effective processes that lead to action.

As a result, we conclude that, in a dynamic and uncertain context where IT systems and digital language play a predominant role, the role of narratives is pivotal. Individuals need compelling change-related stories (Aiken & Keller, 2009; De la Boutetière et al., 2018), which not only outline relevant factual possibilities but also put all actors in the position of partaking (Nørreklit, L. et al., 2019) to these stories, while understanding them in depth. Furthermore, such narratives should be orchestrated in advance by those in management positions, that is, in a time frame that fits not only the speed of digital technologies but also the different times when people are online. Not everybody is "glued to the screen" waiting for digital language to enter their reality construction. The digital vernacular notion, "in real life, IRL" is important from this perspective.

Prior research has provided comparisons between different countries through certain measures and indicators and has determined which measures or decisions have served to achieve the objectives of responding to the COVID-19 pandemic (Mitchell et al., 2021). The chapter contributes to emerging knowledge on how different actors deal with crises in terms of digitalization in management, and how integrative, agile learning could be enabled by actor-reality construction. In particular, the chapter contributes to literature by identifying the need to profoundly examine the motivations behind different response strategies: what guides an actor's response depends on the theory or model used by the actor to link the comparative information to the perception of reality and the logic that connects the pieces of information to each other (Nørreklit, H., 2017). Different crises such as pandemics then force actors to question the assumptions behind current theories, and thus revise those theories (Henriksen et al., 2004; Greve, 2020; Lee et al., 2020). A rapid response is then required and learning needs to be agile – that is, agile learning needs to take place. This chapter shows how that agile learning could be possible by integrating the dimensions of reality. It also adds to current academic understanding by showing that digitalization has changed how actors are able to consume and produce information and construct knowledge related to their responses to crises. To respond to the pandemic effectively, actors' actions need to be fact-based and knowledgeable. However, new types of uncertainties are posing continuous challenges to such knowledgeable actions. This viewpoint highlights the need for learning on multiple levels, partly enabled, but also complicated by digitalization.

Finally, while this chapter has unveiled some important aspects of responding to crises by agile learning, ample scope for future research exists. Researchers could examine how and through which cognitive processes agility is created. Or they could examine the types of actors and their roles in supporting agile learning. Furthermore, digitalization is a megatrend but only one among many, so researchers might find it useful to examine agile learning in relation to other megatrends or challenges that require both large-scale and grassroot responses (such as aging, global warming, or urbanization), and in relation to new ideologies that aspire to overcome some of those challenges (such as degrowth). Whereas the COVID-19 pandemic provides a very palpable example of an event for which agile, quick learning is needed (e.g., the new virus variants or returning to the "new normal"), some of these other grand challenges are more lingering and thus challenge the concept of agile learning. If a crisis manifests itself in less tangible but equally (if not more) grave and complex consequences, how could agile learning become a part of toolboxes used in responding to these challenges? We hope this chapter inspires such possibly relevant thoughts on overcoming future challenges.

Acknowledgments

We would like to express our gratitude to the Academy of Finland [Decision no. 315074] and Business Finland [NewBI5 project] for funding part of the research that yielded this chapter.

References

Ahmad, S., Connolly, C., & Demirag, I. (2021). Testing times: governing a pandemic with numbers. *Accounting, Auditing & Accountability Journal*, 34(6): 1362–1375.

Ahn, P.D., & Wickramasinghe, D. (2021). Pushing the limits of accountability: big data analytics containing and controlling COVID-19 in South Korea. *Accounting, Auditing & Accountability Journal*, 34(6): 1320–1331.

Ahrens, T., & Ferry, L. (2021). Accounting and accountability practices in times of crisis: a Foucauldian perspective on the UK government's response to COVID-19 for England. *Accounting, Auditing & Accountability Journal*, 34(6): 1332–1344.

Aiken, C., & Keller, S. (2009). The irrational side of change management. *McKinsey Quarterly*, 2(10): 100–109.

Ali, S. (2020). Combatting against covid-19 & misinformation: a systematic review. *Human Arenas*, 5: 337–352.

Bourdieu, P. (1977). *Outline of a Theory of Practice* (Vol. 16). Cambridge: Cambridge University Press.

Borell, J., & Eriksson, K. (2013). Learning effectiveness of discussion-based crisis management exercises. *International Journal of Disaster Risk Reduction*, 5: 28–37.

Brashier, N.M., Pennycook, G., Berinsky, A.J., & Rand, D.G. (2021). Timing matters when correcting fake news. *Proceedings of the National Academy of Sciences*, 118(5).

Christianson, M.K., & Barton, M.A. (2020). Sensemaking in the time of COVID-19. *Journal of Management Studies*, 58(2): 572–576.

Coggin, G. (2020). COVID-19 apps in Singapore and Australia: reimagining healthy nations with digital technology. *Media International Australia*, 177(1): 61–75.

Cuan-Baltazar, J.Y., Muñoz-Perez M.J., Robledo-Vega, C., Pérez-Zepeda, M.F., & Soto-Vega, E. (2020). Misinformation of COVID-19 on the internet: infodemiology study. *JMIR Public Health and Surveillance*, 6(2).

Currie, D., Peng, C., Lyle, D., Jameson, B., & Frommer, M. (2020). Stemming the flow: how much can the Australian smartphone app help to control COVID-19. *Public Health Research & Practice*, 30(2).

De la Boutetière, H., Montagner, A., & Reich, A. (2018). Unlocking success in digital transformations. *McKinsey & Company*, 1–14.

Eschenbacher, S., & Fleming, T. (2020). Transformative dimensions of lifelong learning: Mezirow, Rorty and COVID-19. *International Review of Education*, 66: 657–672.

Feldman, S.P. (2004). The culture of objectivity: Quantification, uncertainty, and the evaluation of risk at NASA. *Human Relations*, 57(6): 691–718.

Ferry, L., Hardy, C., & Midgley, H. (2021). Data, trust, democracy and Covid-19: the first parliamentary assessment of the UK government's approach to data during the pandemic. *Public Money & Management*, 1–3.

Greve, H.R. (2020). Learning theory: the pandemic research challenge. *Journal of Management Studies*, 57(8): 1759–1762.

Henriksen, L.B., Nørreklit, L., Jørgensen, K.M., & O'Donnell, D. (2004). *Dimensions of change: conceptualising reality in organisational research*. Copenhagen: Copenhagen Business School Press DK.

Huber, C., Gerhardt, N., & Reilley, J.T. (2021). Organizing care during the COVID-19 pandemic: the role of accounting in German hospitals. *Accounting, Auditing & Accountability Journal*, 34(6): 1445–1456.

Huynh, T.L.D. (2020). The COVID-19 risk perception: a survey on socioeconomics and media attention. *Economics Bulletin*, 40(1): 758–764.

Jayaseelan, R., Brindha, D., Kades, W. (2020). *Social media reigned by information or misinformation about COVID-19: a phenomenological study*. Retrieved from SSRN: https://ssrn.com/abstract=3596058.

Jennings, W., Valgardsson, V., Stoker, G., Devine, D., Gaskell, J., & Evans, M. (2020). *Political trust and the Covid-19 crisis: pushing populism to the backburner? A study of public opinion in Australia, Italy, the UK and the USA*. Democracy 2025. Retrieved from https://www.ipsos.com/sites/default/files/ct/news/documents/2020-08/covid_and_trust.pdf.

Kallio, E.K. (2020). From multiperspective to contextual integrative thinking in adulthood: considerations on theorisation of adult thinking and its place as a component of wisdom. In Kallio, E.K. (Ed.), *Development of Adult Thinking: Interdisciplinary Perspectives on Cognitive Development and Adult Learning*. London: Routledge, pp. 9–32.

Lee, S., Hwang, C., & Moon, M.J. (2020). Policy learning and crisis policy-making: quadruple-loop learning and COVID-19 responses in South Korea. *Policy and Society*, 39(3): 363–381.

Leoni, G., Lai, A., Stacchezzini, R., Steccolini, I., Brammer, S., Linnenluecke, M., & Demirag, I. (2021). Accounting, management and accountability in times of crisis: lessons from the COVID-19 pandemic. *Accounting, Auditing & Accountability Journal*, 34(6): 1305–1319.

Miles, D., Stedman, M., & Heald, A. (2020). Living with COVID-19: balancing costs against benefits in the face of the virus. *National Institute Economic Review*, 253: R60–R75.

Milewski, D. (2020). The analysis of narratives and disinformation in the global information environment amid Covid-19 pandemic. *European Research Studies Journal*, 23(special 3): 3–17.

Mitchell, F., Nørreklit, H., Nørreklit, L., Cinquini, L., Koeppe, F., Magnacca, F., Mauro, S.G., Jakobsen, M., Korhonen, T., Laine, T., & Liboriussen, J. (2021). Evaluating performance management of Covid-19 reality in three European countries: a pragmatic constructivist study. *Accounting, Auditing & Accountability Journal*, 34(6): 1345–1361.

Moynihan, D.P. (2012). A theory of culture-switching: leadership and red-tape during Hurricane Katrina. *Public Administration*, 90(4): 851–868.

Müller-Seitz, G., & Macpherson, A. (2014). Learning during crisis as a 'war for meaning': the case of the German Escherichia coli outbreak in 2011. *Management Learning*, 45(5): 593–608.

Nikidehaghani, M., & Cortese, C. (2021). (Job) Keeping up appearances. *Accounting, Auditing & Accountability Journal*, 34(6): 1502–1512.

Nørreklit, H. (Ed.). (2017). *A Philosophy of Management Accounting: A Pragmatic Constructivist Approach*. New York: Routledge.

Nørreklit, L. (1987). *Formale Strukturer i den sociale logic* [Formal structures in social logic]. Aalborg: Aalborg University Press.

Nørreklit, L., Jack, L., & Nørreklit, H. (2019). Moving towards digital governance of university scholars: instigating a post-truth university culture. *Journal of Management and Governance*, 23(4): 869–899.

Nørreklit, H., Nørreklit, L., & Mitchell, F. (2010). Towards a paradigmatic foundation for accounting practice. *Accounting, Auditing & Accountability Journal*, 23(6): 733–758.

Nørreklit, H., Nørreklit, L., & Mitchell, F. (2016). Understanding practice generalisation – Opening the research/practice gap. *Qualitative Research in Accounting and Management*, 13(3): 278–302.

Nørreklit, L. (2017). Actor-reality construction. In Nørreklit, H. (Ed.), *A Philosophy of Management Accounting: A Pragmatic Constructivist Approach* (1st ed.). New York: Routledge, pp. 23–71.

Parviainen, J. (2020). 'We're flying the plane while we're building it': epistemic humility and non-knowledge in political decision-making on COVID-19. *Social Epistemology Review and Reply Collective*, 9(7): 6–10.

Passetti, E.E., Battaglia, M., Bianchi, L., & Annesi, N. (2021). Coping with the COVID-19 pandemic: the technical, moral and facilitating role of management control. *Accounting, Auditing & Accountability Journal*, 34(6): 1430–1444.

Piekkari, R., Tietze, S., Angouri, J., Meyer, R., & Vaara, E. (2020). Can you speak Covid-19? Languages and social inequality in management studies. *Journal of Management Studies*, 58(2): 587–591.

Quattrone, P. (2016). Management accounting goes digital: will the move make it wiser? *Management Accounting Research*, 31: 118–122.

Roux-Dufort, C. (2007). Is crisis management (only) a management of exceptions? *Journal of Contingencies and Crisis Management*, 15(2): 105–114.

Sargiacomo, M., Corazza, L., D'Andreamatteo, A., Dumay, J., & Guthrie, J. (2021). COVID-19 and the governmentality of emergency food in the City of Turin. *Accounting, Auditing & Accountability Journal*, 34(6): 1457–1470.

Sharpe, J. (2016). Understanding and unlocking transformative learning as a method for enabling behaviour change for adaptation and resilience to disaster threats. *International Journal of Disaster Risk Reduction*, 17: 213–219.

Siegenfeld, A.F., Taleb, N.N., & Yaneer, B-Y. (2020). What models can and cannot tell us about COVID-19. *Proceedings of the National Academy of Sciences*, 117(28): 16092–16095.

Tiirinki, H., Tynkkynen, L-K., Sovala, M., Atkins, S., Koivusalo, M., Rautiainen, P., Jormanainen, V., & Keskimäki, I. (2020). COVID-19 pandemic in Finland – Preliminary analysis on health system response and economic consequences. *Health Policy and Technology*, 9(4): 649–662.

Tovstiga, N., & Tovstiga, G. (2020). COVID-19: a knowledge and learning perspective. *Knowledge Management Research & Practice*, 19(4): 427–432.

Trang, S., Trenz, M., Weiger, W.H., Tarafdar, M., & Cheung, K.M.K. (2020). One app to trace them all? Examining app specifications for mass acceptance of contact-tracing apps. *European Journal of Information Systems*, 29(4): 415–428.

Tynkkynen, L-K., Atkins, S., Keskimäki, I., Koivusalo, M., Rautiainen, P., & Sinervo, T. (2020). *Finland's response to the coronavirus pandemic – Now updated*. Cambridge Core blog, updated 15 May 2020. Retrieved 29 October 2020. Retrieved from https://www.cambridge.org/core/blog/2020/04/06/finlands-response-to-the-coronavirus-pandemic/.

Uscinski, J.E., Enders, A.M., Klofstad, C.A., Seelig, M.I., Funchion, J.R., Everett, C., Wuchty, S., Premaratne, K., & Murthi, M.N. (2020). Why do people believe COVID-19 conspiracy theories? *Harvard Kennedy School (HKS) Misinformation Review*, 1: 1–12.

Van Bavel, J.J., Baicker, K., Boggio, P.S., & Capraro, V., et al. (2020). Using social and behavioural science to support COVID-19 pandemic response. *Nature: Human Behaviour*, 4: 460–471.

Weick, K.E., Sutcliffe, K.M., & Obstfeld, D. (2005). Organizing and the process of sensemaking. *Organization Science*, 16(4): 409–421. https://doi.org/10.1287/orsc.1050.0133

Wenger, E. (2000). Communities of practice and social learning systems. *Organization*, 7(2): 225–246.

Wittgenstein, L. (1953). *Philosophical Investigations* (2nd ed.). Oxford: Blackwell.

Vosoughi, S., Roy, D., & Aral, S. (2018). The spread of true and false news online. *Science*, 359(6380): 1146–1151.

Part 3

The digital management of the lifeworld

Chapter 11

From the fordist self to the entrepreneurial self

Self-management in times of digitization

David Kergel

Introduction

The term management (Latin manus, "hand" and Latin agere, "to lead," "to lead by the hand") signifies a goal-oriented human course of action, organization, and planning in all spheres of life, based on economic principles. The main content of management is the organization, preparation, and execution of decisions in a complex environment. Management is not limited to companies or other associations of persons (such as public authorities) but also concerns sub-areas of lifestyle in private households (for example, time management). Anyone who is entrusted with management tasks in work and action systems can be called a manager. Above all, the manager needs management/leadership competencies. The social typus of the manager emerges in the course of Fordism.

Fordist consumer capitalism

Fordism signifies a form of industrial goods production which were developed in the USA after the First World War and established after the Great Depression.

As a capitalistic strategy, Fordism discovered the working masses as consumers, who had more money available for consumption due to Fordism. Consumer capitalism – the creation of capital by fueling consumer demand – roots in Fordism. In establishing Fordism and its consumer capitalism, the role of media was twofold:

On the one hand, media such as newspapers, journals, and commercial films were to be consumed.

On the other hand, advertising was used to create incentives to buy so that goods would be purchased.

To become a consumer, workers had to be able to afford the products. This was achieved by technical innovations and, above all, made possible by the assembly line work: In 1913, Henry Ford had the car "Model T" assembled for the first time. This new production method almost halved the price of the car from nearly 600 dollars to 360 dollars (cf. Schmitz & Daniels, 2006, p. 73), making it a standardized commodity that was also affordable for workers. Fordist

DOI: 10.4324/9781003188728-14

"assembly line production" is based on a radical division of labor: commodity production is divided into small work steps. Each worker carries out one work step. The assembly line dictates the pace of work, to which the workers must adapt. These processes were organized and supervised by the "managers."

A major publication in which proposals for standardized production were formulated came from the mechanical engineer Taylor. In the book "Principles of Scientific Management" from 1911, Taylor analyzes how the interface between machines and people can be optimized so that the workers' labor power can be exploited to the maximum.

Through the Fordist division of labor, production capacity increased. Goods such as telephones and an electrified household were affordable for the middle class, which gradually began to emerge as such. Workers could also buy consumer goods like the Model T. Still, they were told what to buy: The story about the Model T is that Ford said you could have the car in any color – provided the color you wanted was black. This also had a pragmatic background: black was said to dry the fastest (cf. Resch & Steiner, 2016, p. 233).

Fordist consumer capitalism was promoted by increasing purchasing power through an increase in wages. Thus, Ford introduced the "$5 workday." This $5 workday was tied to moral standards: Only "worthy" workers were included in the five-dollar category, morally stable and family-bound (cf. Resch & Steiner, 2016, p. 232).

Living standards increased, as did life expectancies. For example, the average life expectancy of a person born in 1930 is circa 61 years. Working hours in the industry are around 47 hours per week (cf. Schmitz & Daniels, 2006, p. 65). Capitalism reduces the pressure of exploitation somewhat, and the theory of pauperization seems to have been abandoned.

Fordism (and Keynesian economic policy) are closely related to mass consumption. To maintain this mass consumption, the need for consumption must be constantly restored. To fuel this consumer demand, mass media are increasingly used. For example, through mass media, needs are created via advertising – products are advertised, and thus a need is created via the goods.

In Fordism, the entertainment and advertising industries created desires that can be satisfied by acquiring goods. Thus, James Dean's portrayal in "For They Know Not What They Do" led to the establishment of the leather jacket as an expression for rebellion. The Che Guevara pictures stand for leftist counterculture and can be purchased as bed linen. These examples show that even anti-capitalist counterculture can also be "commodified" for the consumer capitalism.

According to Marcuse, the media – especially the advertising industry – deliberately produce false needs to turn citizens into uncritical consumers. In this way, values and norms are also (re)produced. Advertising becomes a "representation of domination" (cf. Steinert, 2018, p. 118). According to Steiner, the recipients of culture-industrial products get to know the façade that one have to hold up if one is not to be excluded (Steinert, 2018, p. 135). For example, when role models induced via media are taken up by recipients and reproduced in action.

Fordist self

The externally determined work and consumption in leisure time characterize the Fordist Self. The Fordist Self is externally determined. Through managers, the Fordist Self is put in their position in the production process. In the leisure time, a demand for goods is produced by advertising, which the Fordist Self has produced oneself with. The Fordist Self is a cogwheel in the Fordist production and consumption machine. This Fordist production and consumption machine is organized by managers. Subsequently, Fordism was accompanied by a leftist critique of alienation. According to the leftist critique of alienation, individuals are alienated from their actual needs and their actual potentials by the Fordist consumer culture. Boltanski and Chiapello refer to this phenomenon with the term artistic critique (Boltanski & Chiapello, corrected, p. 217). The thematic horizon and critical strategies of artistic criticism were developed in small circles of the political-artistic avant-gardes (*cf.* Boltanski & Chiapello, 1999 p. 217). The formulation of artist criticism took place before it experienced an unprecedented resonance in the 1968 student revolt (*cf.* Boltanski & Chiapello, 1999, p. 217). In the 1968 movement, an interplay between artist critique and social critique took place. A combination of types of critique resulted, which unfolded in the French, revolutionary movements of the second half of the 19th century and the first half of the 20th century (Boltanski & Chiapello, 1999, p. 216): While artist criticism up to the 1968 movement played a marginal role (artists were not very numerous and had practically no weight in the sphere of production), it moved to the center of protest during the student movement (Boltanski & Chiapello, 1999, p. 216).

Neoliberal mentality of the entrepreneurial self

With the crisis of Fordism, neoliberal ideas increasingly prevailed. The ideological approaches of neoliberal thinking took up forms of artist critique: Neoliberalism brought about a change in mentality throughout society. Basic assumption of neoliberal logic is the concept of a "free"/liberal market. According to this logic, economic processes are rational based and order themselves invisible for the individuals. Consequently any regulation should be avoided to not "disturb" the rational dynamics of the market. One feature of a neoliberal worldview is that welfare state services are to be judged according to efficiency criteria. The shift in mentality toward a neoliberal understanding of the self/world is accordingly also reflected in the fact that social relationships are increasingly permeated and shaped by economic calculations. Neoliberalism leads to a changing social climate.

> For neoliberals, there is one form of rationality more powerful than any other: economic rationality. Efficiency and an 'ethic' of cost-benefit analyses are the dominant norms. All people are to act in ways that maximize

> their own personal benefits. Indeed, behind this position is an empirical claim that this how all rational actors act. Yet, rather than being a neutral description of the world of social motivation, this is actually a construction of the world around the valuative characteristics of an efficiently acquisitive class type.
>
> (Apple, 2006, p. 60f.)

In the course of the neoliberal reorganization of society, a different understanding of social togetherness is constituted. The individual is less addressed as a fellow citizen in a society who behaves in solidarity with other citizens. Instead, individuals in a neoliberal society are addressed as entrepreneurs who are in competition with other entrepreneurs. According to neoliberal logic, the freedom of the individual unfolds on a free market. In this market, individuals face each other competitively. The neoliberal concept of freedom is based on competition, which structures the free market. Competition can only unfold its stimulating effect if it is not overridden by interventions that prevent or distort competition (cf. Bröckling, 2013, p. 106f.). If the unfolding of the free market is given, the individuals can unfold their potentials through neoliberal competition. In this context, neoliberal apologies of competition are Darwinian (cf. Bröckling, 2013, p. 97). Competition dissolves social solidary. The neoliberal individual is an individual who acts and decides (Bröckling, 2013, p. 106). This freedom of the individual is embedded in the constellations of neoliberal self-optimization and insecurity. Using one's freedom, the individual is supposed to position oneself as an entrepreneur by making one's own decisions in neoliberal society and taking care of oneself. Bröckling gives this neoliberal understanding of man the heading of the "Entrepreneurial self": Bröckling uses the metaphor of the entrepreneurial self. The entrepreneurial self can be understood as "the fundamental neoliberal interpellation." Neoliberal interpellations are directed at the individual and are required to act as a neoliberal entrepreneur. Via this metaphor, Bröckling condenses discourses, which actualize the narrative topoi of neoliberal thinking across different social fields. The entrepreneurial self-performatively reproduces the neoliberal concept of freedom – "ideal model for the future is the individual as self-provider and the entrepreneur of their own labour. The insight must be awakened; self-initiative and self-responsibility, i.e. the entrepreneurial in society, must be developed more strongly" (Bröckling, 2015, p. xi). One interpellation is that "[e]veryone should become an entrepreneur . . . Success at this can only be measured against the competition and therefore only temporarily" (Bröckling, 2015, p. 77). The entrepreneurial Self is thereby inextricably linked with the new spirit of capitalism.

The new spirit of capitalism

The neoliberal narrative is characterized by the so-called "new spirit of capitalism": With reference to the management literature of the 1990s, Boltanksi and Chiapello provide a discourse analytical study on the change of the self-understanding discourses of capitalism. One main result of their study was the observation that capitalism developed a "new spirit." This new spirit of capitalism absorbed the critique which was formulated in the course of the emancipation movements within the 1960s and 1970s and is characterized by an integration of demands from the 1968 protest movement. In the course of the student protests of 1968, anti-capitalist ways of life were demanded: Instead of living a life characterized by Fordist consumer culture and alienated labor, the ideal of a self-determined life and not alienated labor was demanded. Instead of standing at the assembly line, besides social justice and cultural freedom, work culture has been demanded in which people develop according to their "proper needs." These demands are absorbed by capitalism, leading to a "new spirit of capitalism".

> Thus, for example, the qualities that are guarantees of success in this new spirit – autonomy, spontaneity, rhizomorphus capacity, multitasking (in contrast to the narrow specialization of the old division of labor), conviviality, openness to others and novelty, availability, creativity, visionary intuition, sensitivity to differences, listening to lived experienced and receptiveness to a whole range of experiences, being attracted to informality and the search for interpersonal contacts – these are taken directly from the repertoire of May 1968.
> (Boltanski & Chiapello, 1999, p. 97)

The leftist, emancipative notion of freedom which combines artist critique, alternative culture, and anti-capitalistic critique was absorbed by a capitalistic self-understanding discourse. As a result, the alternative anti-authoritarian counterculture/life style and the anti-capitalist critique were detached from each other. In the course of this transformation process, a new spirit of capitalism emerged. This new spirit bases on the concept of an artistic-anarchistic individual: "It is not difficult to find an echo here of the denunciations of hierarchy and aspirations to autonomy that were insistently expressed at the end of the 1960s and in the 1970s" (Boltansky & Chiapello, 1999 p. 97). This new spirit of capitalism is still vivid in the digital embedding of the concept of entrepreneurial Self in times of digitization.

The narrative of neoliberal digitization

Digitization is the transfer of analog signals (e.g., sounds, colors, and measured values) into binary codes of values 1 and 0 that computers can process. Digital counterparts are increasingly replacing music CDs, letters, books, even keys and paper money. The term digitization thus refers primarily to the digital transformation of information. From a sociological perspective, digitization refers to a fundamental change driven by digital technology that encompasses all areas of life. Digitization has been discursively framed at the cultural level by neoliberal topoi.

In other words, Digitization was integrated into a neoliberal narrative. According to Kaerlein (2018), the California Bay Area of the late 1960s and early 1970s was an amalgam that consisted of individual performance enhancement with roots in the Second World War military research laboratories, aspirations for drug-induced consciousness expansion, countercultural ideals of individuality, Far Eastern spirituality, and hobbyist cultures. (cf Kaerlein, 2018, 103f.). It is to this "amalgam" or peculiar fusion of countercultural practices, artist critique, and computer-technical implementations that the image transformation of the computer is indirectly owed (cf. Kaerlein, 2018, p. 104). Apple's design language in particular expresses this new culture and aesthetic. Barbrook and Cameron point out the neoliberal implications of this amalgam and summarize it analytically in the term "Californian ideology." Californian ideology is defined by a neoliberal worldview in the context of emerging digitalization.

> Californian Ideology, therefore, simultaneously reflects the disciplines of market economics and the freedoms of hippie artisanship. This bizarre hybrid is only made possible through a nearly universal belief in technological determinism. Ever since the 1960s, liberals – in the social sense of the word – have hoped that the new information technologies would realise their ideals. Responding to the challenge of the New Left, the New Right has resurrected an older form of liberalism: economic liberalism [15]. In place of the collective freedom sought by the hippie radicals, they have championed the liberty of individuals within the marketplace.
> (Barbook & Cameron, 1997, para. 14)

Digital media provide the technological infrastructure for the neoliberal new spirit of capitalism, which manifests itself ideally in the entrepreneurial self.

> In this version of the Californian Ideology, each member of the virtual class is promised the opportunity to become a successful hi-tech entrepreneur. Information technologies, so the argument goes, empower the individual, enhance personal freedom, and radically reduce the power of the nation state. Existing social, political and legal power structures will wither away to be replaced by unfettered interactions between autonomous individuals and their software.
> (Barbook & Cameron, 1997, para. 185)

The neoliberal model of an "electronic marketplace" influenced the Californian ideology, which assumes a strong notion of the individual. The individual unfolds its especially economically priced – freedom with the help of information technology (cf. Kaerlein, 2018, p. 112). The model of the entrepreneurial

Self is given a "digital spin": For the often freelancing programmers, designers, and advertising professionals of Silicon Valley, the boundaries between work and leisure, colleagues, friends, and family are rapidly blurring (cf. Kaerlein, 2018, p. 112). The neoliberal worldview and the Californian ideology influenced coined digital age. This influence is paradigmatically evident in the social web.

The entrepreneurial self and the social web

Via Social Web communication platforms such as Facebook, Google+, Instagram, Twitter, Snapchat, and LinkedIn, users constitute their digital identity (Stalder, 2016, p. 139). In this constitution process, the most important resource is the attention of others, their feedback, and the resulting mutual recognition (Stalder, 2016, p. 139). The monadic starting point of this social dynamic is the creative individual, who produces data by being integrated into social networks and thus exhibits the characteristic of participatory content generation. At the same time, the users consume the data of other users, comment on it, and generate content themselves in the form of their "participatory consumption" of content by commenting on it. In this oscillating positioning between "producer" and "consumer" of content, the actor in the SNS universe becomes a "prosumer." Vis Social Media users are increasingly embedded in a normative space of possibility. Within the space of possibility the prosumer discursively enact themselves as actualizations of the entrepreneurial self, and evaluate each other via feedback.

These features constitute the normative possibility space of the unfolding of the entrepreneurial Self in the digital sphere Social Media. Social media lead to a flexible self-location and panoptic (self-)control: The individual must be permanently social to assert itself as a monad in a Social Network like Instagram. If this dynamic does not arise, the individual dies the symbolic death in the SNS universe in Lacan's sense. The evaluative interaction seems to be necessary to keep the prosumer actively in motion. The motion of the entrepreneurial Self is a movement of self-optimization in the competition of the neoliberal market. The social existence within Social Media is connected with normative pressure of neoliberal narratives. Evaluation is always present. Paradigmatic for this evaluation logic of the SNS universe is the so-called Facebook thumb. From a semiotic perspective, the Facebook thumb can be read as a performance evaluation for a successful self-narrative: Self-narrative can be measured by likes. The Facebook thumb or Facebook thump-up (and variations on other SNSs) represent "digitized gesture signaling approval, approbation, agreement, praise or even on occasion a reminder to the receiver of the sender's existence" (Faucher, 2013, S. 1). "Every social media user can be equally observer and observed, controller and controlled" (Mitrou et al., 2014, S. 12). Andrejevic (2005) signifies this phenomenon with the term "peer-to-peer monitoring":

> [P]eer to peer monitoring understood the use of surveillance tools by individuals, rather than by agents of institutions public or private, to keep

track of one another, covers (but is not limited to) three main categories: romantic interests, family, and friends or acquaintances.

(Andrejevic, 2005, S. 488)

Social Media performatively reproduce panoptic power structures and an economic logic in which more likes can be interpreted in terms of positive self-presentation. This neoliberal economic logic also makes it possible for companies to present themselves via Facebook pages. In this way, they move closer to the familiar and allow themselves to be included in the circle of friends. The spheres between the private and the public/commercial dissolve. The blurring of the boundary between these spheres can be understood from the results of a study conducted in 2012 by Harris Interactive on behalf of Careerbuilder, an online job portal. As part of the study, 2,303 HR managers were surveyed about the importance of social media in the hiring process. The HR managers indicated that to check an applicant's suitability, they also take a look at the applicant's social media activities. The primary source is Facebook with 65 percent, followed by LinkedIn with 63 percent. The review by HR managers focuses on the fit between the applicant's self-portrayal and the company's self-image:

When asked why they use social networks to conduct background research, hiring managers stated the following:

- To see if the candidates present themselves professionally – 65 percent
- To see if the candidate is a good fit for the company culture – 51 percent
- To learn more about the candidate's qualifications – 45 percent
- To see if the candidate is well-rounded – 35 percent
- To look for reasons not to hire the candidate – 12 percent (Careerbuilder, 2012, para. 7, H.i.O).

The view of HR managers has a normative disciplinary effect here. For example, 34 percent of recruiters who have already used SNS to review a candidate stated that they had found information in the SNS narratives of the candidates that led them not to hire them. The reasons are given range from uploading inappropriate content to the fact that candidates lied about their qualifications:

- Candidate posted provocative/inappropriate photos/info – 49 percent
- There was info about candidate drinking or using drugs – 45 percent
- Candidate had poor communication skills – 35 percent
- Candidate bad mouthed previous employer – 33 percent
- Candidate made discriminatory comments related to race, gender, religion, etc. – 28 percent
- Candidate lied about qualifications – 22 percent (Careerbuilder, 2012, para. 10, e.i.o.).

Twenty-nine percent of recruiters stated that they found information on SNSs that positively influenced them when hiring an applicant. The reasons given for the positive impression conveyed by SNSs range from intuitive assessments to positive feedback or that other users have posted positive things about the applicant:

- Good feel for candidate's personality – 58 percent
- Conveyed a professional image – 55 percent
- Background information supported professional qualifications – 54 percent
- Well-rounded, showed a wide range of interests – 51 percent
- Great communication skills – 49 percent
- Candidate was creative – 44 percent
- Other people posted great references about the candidate – 34 percent (Careerbuilder, 2012, para. 12, H.i.O.).

The normative gaze of HR managers is directed toward the private life, which is assessed under the parameters of an applicant's employability. Willey et al. (2012) state that the "utilization of social network sites for applicant screening will continue" (Willey et al., 2012, p. 307). Such a view of SNSs by HR managers is also affirmatively accepted by applicants: The results of a study by Martensen et al. (2011), which examined "the impact of social networking sites on the employer-employee relationship" is, that "members of SNS do believe that (potential) employers carry out research on the Internet and that users behave accordingly" (Martensen et al., 2011, p. 252). Among other things, SNS users were asked whether they would use the Internet as a platform for self-narration directed at potential employers: "[T]he 228 respondents (60.7%) agreed with the following statement: The Internet enables me to present myself the way I want to (n = 376, µ = 3.59, σ = 0.78)" (Martensen et al., 2011, p. 250, emphasis added).

Conclusion

Digital infrastructure is shaped by commercial Social Media such as Facebook, Instagram, and TikTok. This digital infrastructure requires a neoliberal self-presentation. Such a neoliberal self-presentation requires acting like an Entrepreneurial Self. Individuals must become Entrepreneurial Selves to participate in the social media infrastructure. In this process, manager logic is implemented into the private sphere. In the world of Fordist consumption, people worked according to predefined patterns. From this standardized and monotonous work, the workers could relax passively consuming in their leisure time. The Fordist Self was externally determined both in work and in leisure. At work, they were foreign-determined by the leading management. The management assigned the Fordist workers their tasks. And in the leisure time, the Fordist worker could use the offered world of goods for relaxation. An approach of artist critique countered this alienation through foreign determination. Instead of working passively, one should emancipate oneself. Self-actively they should realize themselves according to their needs. This artist critique, formulated mainly in the study protests of the sixties and seventies of the last century, was adapted by neoliberalism. In the sense of neoliberal thinking, man unfolds as an entrepreneurial self on the free market of neoliberalism. This free market of neoliberalism finds its expression in people's private lives in the social media world: In Fordism, leisure was the commercial freedom space beyond work. In the age of neoliberal digitalization, leisure is the neoliberal self-realization of the individual. As an Entrepreneurial Self, the individual unfolds in both work and leisure. The two spheres are inseparably interwoven. Work and leisure merge in the project of neoliberal self-optimization. This calls for a neoliberal self-management that demands flexible competitiveness and self-optimization as well as self-management.

References

Andrejevic, M. (2005). The work of watching one another: lateral surveillance, risk, and governance. *Surveillance & Society*, 2(4): 479–497.

Apple, M., W. (2006). *Educating the 'Right Way'. Markets, Standards, God, and Inequality*. New York: Routledge.

Barbrook, R., &, Cameron, A. (1997). Retrieved from http://www.imaginaryfutures.net/2007/04/17/the-californian-ideology-2/. Last accessed: 31. September 2021.

Boltanski, L., & Chiapello, È. (1999). *The New Spirit of Capitalism*. London: Verso.

Bröckling, U. (2013). *Das unternehmerische Selbst. Soziologie einer Subjektivierungsform*. Frankfurt am Main: Suhrkamp.

Bröckling, U. (2015). *The Entrepreneurial Self. Fabricating a New Type of Subject*. Thousand Oaks: Sage.

Careerbuilder.com (2012). *Thirty-seven percent of companies use social networks to research potential job candidates*. Retrieved from http://www.careerbuilder.com/share/aboutus/pressreleasesdetail.aspx?id=pr691&sd=4/18/2012&ed=4/18/2099&siteid=cbpr&sc_cmp1=cb_pr691_. Last acessed: 05 December 2016.

Faucher, K.X. (2013). Thumbstruck: the semiotics of liking via the "phaticon". *Semiotic Review*, 3. http://www.semioticreview.com/pdf/open2013/faucher_semioticsofliking.pdf. Last accessed: 05 December 2016.

Gökariksel, B., & Mitchell, K. (2005). Veiling, secularism, and the neoliberal subject: national narratives and supranational desires in Turkey and France. *Global Networks*, 5(2): 147–165.

Kaerlein, T. (2018). *Smartphones als digitale Nahkörpertechnologien. Zur Kybernetisierung des Alltags*. Bielefeld: transcript.

Martensen, M., Börgmann, K., & Bick, M. (2011). The *impact of social networking sites on the employer-employee relationship*. In Proceedings of BLED Conference 2011 Retrieved from http://aisel.aisnet.org/bled2011/54/. Last accessed: 23 December 2016.

Mimbs, N. (2017). *The winter getaway that turned the software world upside down. How a group of programming rebels started a global movement*. https://www.theatlantic.com/technology/archive/2017/12/agile-manifesto-a-history/547715/. Last accessed: 23.08.2021

Mitrou, L., Kandias, M., Stavrou, V., & Gritzalis, D. (2014). *Social media profiling: a panopticon or omnipoticon tool?* Retrieved from https://www.infosec.aueb.gr/Publications/2014-SSN-Privacy%20Social%20Media.pdf. Last accessed: 23 December 2016.

Nadkarni, A., & Hofmann, S.G. (2012). Why do people use Facebook? *Personality and Individual Differences*, 52(3): 243–249.

Resch, C., & Steiner, H. (2016). *Kapitalismus*. Münster: Westfälisches Dampfboot.

Schmitz, S., & Daniels, A. (2006). *Die Geschichte des Kapitalismus. Vom Wohlstand zum World Wide Web*. München: Heyne.

Stalder, F. (2016). *Kultur der Digitalität*. Frankfurt am Main: Suhrkamp.

Steinert, H. (2018). *Kulturindustrie*. Münster: Westfälisches Dampfboot.

Willey, L., White, B.J., Domagalski, T., & Ford, J.C. (2012). Candidate-screening, information technology and the law: Social media considerations. *Information Systems*, 13(1): 300–309.

Chapter 12

Between romance and market
The construction of partnership on dating platforms

Annick Ancelin-Bourguignon and Hanne Nørreklit

Introduction

Digitalization and datafication have been studied under various social perspectives, and on both macro and micro levels of analysis. For instance, Myers West (2017) has focused on how data commodification has changed capitalism, posing old questions of surveillance, transparency, and power in new terms (Zuboff, 2015, 2019). Other scholars have studied platforms – one of the most visible forms of digitalization and datafication – showing that, in collecting and aggregating data, they change everyday life, shape tastes (Alaimo & Kallinikos, 2017), and impact consumers' choices (Bialecki et al., 2017). Quantitative measures and rankings might also increase accountability (Scott and Orlikovski, 2012) and perception of trust (Jeacle and Carter, 2011). Combining digitalization and datafication under various forms (such as numbers and rankings), platforms shape individual representations and practices, and, beyond, are likely to contribute to changing social relationships and society.

Dating is a domain of social and private life which, over recent decades, has undergone significant changes, not least of which thanks to the rise of an online dating industry (Rosenfeld and Thomas, 2012; Bergström, 2011a). Dating websites are the continuation of matrimonial classified ads which have been issued in newspapers since the second half of the 19th century (Bergström, 2019). They developed from the mid-1990s in the United States and rapidly spread globally.[1] Dating websites have significantly changed dating conditions (Finkel et al., 2012). It is, as such, unsurprising that they have drawn the attention of scholarship from various fields (mainly sociology, psychology, and communication science). There is a general agreement that dating websites are shaped around market-like conditions regulating the encounter, which paves the way for various self-presentational strategies (Hancock and Toma, 2009; Toma and Hancock, 2016; Bergström, 2015, 2016b) that may be considered as "love marketing" (Lardellier, 2012, p. 160). However a debated point is the extent to which online dating leads to the commodification of intimacy. Exponents of this thesis view online dating as the irruption of economic and capitalist logics into the private sphere (Illouz, 2007), which would go hand-in-hand

DOI: 10.4324/9781003188728-15

with the hyper-sexualization of intimate relationships (Kaufmann, 2010) or the disenchantment of love (Illouz, 2012). Alternatively, based on significant empirical investigation, Bergström (2019) suggests that, except for the privatization of the encounter, dating websites have not deeply changed love representations and practices, which are still infused with the myth of romantic love and subjected to traditional social norms such as homogamy and gendered role expectations.

As with any social practice, traditional dating intertwines language with actions in a given environment. Since online dating changes the language of interaction, then, it changes the nature of the practice of dating. We argue that, to further study the debate regarding the commodification of romance, it is necessary to investigate the language used in dating websites, and how it differs from the language used in traditional dating practices. Accordingly, the objective of this article is to contribute to this debate by analyzing the language of online dating.

In particular, we are concerned about the use of language in relation to the first step of dating: *the users' decision to express their interest in establishing a relationship* with another user – paving the way first to a virtual, and then to a "real-life" encounter, if there is reciprocity. While the very first step is digitized in online dating, subsequent ones adhere closely to more traditional forms of dating (written exchanges, face-to-face encounters, etc.). To scrutinize the thesis of the commodification of love, we think it relevant to focus on the specific market-like first stage of dating, in order to show how the language used in the website constructs a particular understanding of relationships. Only then can the consequences of this on the dating process as a whole be gauged. Our analysis will also enable us to unveil new aspects of digitization and datafication in contemporary societies, and further, to contribute to the first research stream mentioned earlier.

More specifically, we study the dating website matchaffinity.com (also known by other names in different countries) (see Figure 12.1).[2] The site can be categorized as a "hetero-oriented" and a "serious" one, mainly targeting heterosexual individuals[3] looking for a long-term relationship, with love being supposedly its basis (Bergström, 2011a, pp. 235, 245). It promises efficiency, success, and the possibility to manage ones' search for a partner, and thus can be considered as part of the trend toward the "enterprising self" (Rose, 1992) that is an important feature of the commodification of romance. Thus as organizations do, the matchaffinity.com enables the professional management of partnership search on a "market" through digital information models and algorithms. Simultaneously, it appeals to the familiar cultural tropes of romance in the valorization of a "strong and lasting relationship." This twofold orientation in the idea of romance that matchaffinity.com puts forward makes it a very relevant case study for investigating the conflict between the "romance" and "market" constructions of personal relationships. On this basis, we raise the following research question: by which type of language does matchaffinity.com construct partnership relationships, and what are the respective parts of the figures[4] of market and romance in such constructions? Theoretically, drawing on the later Wittgenstein (1953), we argue that traditional dating is a complex habitus-based social practice organized around a set of language-games, where various types of language are intertwined with actions in a given situation. We contrast "language-games" with the "digital language" used in dating platforms, that can be understood in terms of the early Wittgenstein's (1922) conceptualization of language. Drawing on these categories, we show that most of the language used on the website is digital, making the digital lover a pseudo-objectified one – which is not only likely to have an impact on the virtual encounter but also constructs the lover as a market "product." We also suggest that the resulting overabundance of data, combined with the ambiguity of language, is more likely to confuse than help the user in their decision regarding whether or not to contact a potential partner. However, we also find enduring traces of appeals to romantic love, so that, all together, the various types of language used in the website are likely to conjure up different forms of partnership – which, again, may result in confusion and a sense of being lost. Finally, we suggest that this resulting confusion, as well as the discomfiting feeling of being treated as a "product," might explain why the myth of romance appears to be stronger than the market metaphor even in the context of such dating sites. The remainder of this text is structured as follows. First, after a brief historical overview of love and partnership arrangements, we provide a synthesis of existing academic work on online dating that has discussed the contemporary commodification of love. Then, we present our theory and method on the basis of Wittgenstein's (1922, 1953) theories of language. In the third section, we proceed to a detailed case study of matchaffinity.com, with a particular focus on its general pages (presenting its philosophy under the form of texts and photographs), the "affinity test" (which is taken during users' registration and is the source of almost all data), and the subsequent "affinity scores" and "affinity reports." Finally, the last section discusses our findings vis-a-vis prior research regarding the commodification of intimacy and suggests further views on the reification of online daters. The conclusion examines the limitations of our study and identifies paths for further research.

Market and romance – historical perspectives and online dating research

In this section, we present an overview of online dating research that has touched upon the contemporary commodification of love. Before doing so, we contextualize this debate by providing a brief historical overview of the various arrangements of love and partnership in the West through the ages, showing that, under other labels, market considerations are not a new feature in this domain, and, that subsequently, practices of partnership and love have always embodied a wide range of practices.

A brief history of partnership and love

Until the 20th century, marriage and love were hardly aligned in Western countries. Marriage was a matter of building economic or political alliances between families – as such, the future spouse was chosen by the parents. In this context, love was a construct that emerged in opposition to marriage. Along the ages, various figures have illustrated this conflict between passion and social order. De Rougemont (1983) views love as a Western invention, originating in the Middle Ages, where knights could be engaged in nonphysical but highly emotional relationships with the (most often married or engaged) lady they served. "Courtly love" (or *amour courtois*) was highly ritualized: the lovers subjected themselves to a series of trials involving physical but highly controlled closeness, to prove their commitment and love. In this form of love, emotional arousal and sex were clearly disconnected.

In the 19th century, romanticism highlighted the mythical figure of romantic love, which is traditionally considered as a mix of emotional and sexual desire for another person. Compared to courtly love, romantic love is above all a matter of feeling, with sex being seen as cementing the bond. Concurrently, social constraints and the role of parents in forming marriages have declined, so that love has increasingly come to be considered as the basis of marriage (Shorter, 1975). Until the 1950s, sexuality, cohabitation, and marriage remained broadly aligned. Since then, they have gained an increasing level of autonomy (Bergström, 2019). Today, "partnership" may label a variety of situations, ranging from ephemeral to enduring sexual relationships, from living independently to cohabiting, and from informal to various forms of contractual commitment, including not only marriage but also alternative arrangements such as civil unions. Emotional involvement is likely to be very unequal depending on the situation. To sum up, although romance and market considerations (which were implicit in arranged marriages) have long evolved as separate perspectives on relationships, it is likely that contemporary forms of partnership combine emotion- and pragmatism-based rationales, in other words the romance and market figures, in a variety of ways.

Tensions between market and romance in online dating research

The terms of the continuing debate regarding the contemporary constructions of intimacy are as follows. On the one hand, some scholars (notably Illouz, 2007; Kaufmann, 2010) highlight the marketization, or the commodification, of intimate relationships. Most such works are analytical, in that they examine the characteristics of dating websites, collect data from Internet forums or blogs, and, more rarely, draw on interviews to build their demonstrations. On the other hand, other empirical works contend that love as a romantic ideal still resists the marketed regulation of encounters. Well beyond the practice of online dating, this debate, as Dröge and Voirol (2011) argue, addresses the two "normative principles," namely economic rationality and romantic love, the radical opposition of which has been recurrently considered as being constitutive of modern societies (ibid., see p. 339 et s. for details).

Why the market has commodified (and is destroying) love

Heino et al.'s (2010, p. 442) empirical research shows that the "market metaphor" appears to influence "both [the users'] overall orientation towards the online dating process and the strategies they claim to use within it," encouraging a "more calculated and consumerist perspective towards mate selection." More critically, drawing on a performativity perspective, Roscoe and Chillas (2014, p. 797) show how the online dating industry builds "a market for love," leading to the "commodification and sale of relationships," alongside the "enactment of instrumentally rational, self-interested social relations."

For Illouz (2007, p. 85), the "spirit presiding over the Internet is that of an economy of abundance, where the self must choose and maximize its options and is forced to use techniques of cost-benefit and efficiency." Similarly, Kaufmann (2010, p. 222) mentions "a huge supermarket for love and/or sex, where everyone is both a consumer and a seller, displaying his/her desires and seeking their satisfaction in the most efficient way." As a consequence, rationalization would be substituted for feelings and traditional practices (Illouz, 2012), then making sex a banal "leisure" (Kaufmann, 2010, p. 127), and equating online dating to "liberalism conquering love" (Lardellier (2012, p. 114). To sum up, the contemporary conditions of dating generate "a radical departure from the culture of love and romanticism which characterized much of the nineteenth and twentieth centuries" (Illouz, 2007, p. 89).

Why love is stronger than market

On the other hand, drawing on in-depth empirical investigation, Bergström argues that market-like dating websites have not changed representations of love, and, accordingly, the practices of love survive largely unchanged. Indeed, Bergström's interviewees tend to "disqualify [online dating sites] as spaces for romantic encounters" (2013, p. vi)[5] because "romantic relationships are still largely considered the work of destiny rather than that of the actors involved" (ibid.). Bergström's interviewees also noted that there is nothing new in criteria-based mate selection. For Bergström, the main change brought by online dating is the privatization of the encounter – "privatization" here referring both to the industry running these activities, and to the anonymous and witnessless nature of the encounter (2019). Having studied the various stages of the encounter, Bergström highlights that once people are in contact, traditional norms (namely gendered role expectations and seduction conventions) and processes (homogamy) fully operate (Bergström, 2016b, 2019). Bergström's research demonstrates the strength of [users'] perception . . . of love as "unfathomable, unjustifiable, and therefore 'asocial' (in other words outside of human action)" (Bergström, 2013, p. vi, emphasis in original). Finally, Bergström highlights the fact that practices produce values and norms, and "are not the mere receptacle of cultural forces that prevail elsewhere" (2019, p. 216) – a thesis which is the exact opposite to the idea of the commodification of love. Finally, Dröge and Voirol (2011) address the specific question of the "tensions between economic rationalization and romantic love" in online dating. They view dating websites as "neoromantic media" (ibid., p. 344), blending romantic love and rationalistic market considerations. Thus, the overabundance of profiles and the facility of contact encourage projections and fantasies that nurture the ideal of romance, whereas the available "tools" (i.e., filters associated with a variety of data) allow for strategies of efficiency aimed at defensively preventing the disillusions of romantic expectations (ibid., p. 352). They conclude that "the tension between love and the market is apparently unsolvable and produces a double-bind situation," and like Bergström, conclude that "the romantic ideal of love is still in vigor today" (ibid.: pp. 353–354).

Theory and methodological analysis

Addressing our research question involves, first, defining our two categories of habitus-based "language-games" and "digital language" and providing examples of the former in traditional dating. Second, we explain the methodology we have used to analyze the language of partnership embedded in the dating site matchaffinity.com, and our selection of texts for this analysis.

Habitus-based language-games versus digital language

Our chapter is theoretically rooted in Wittgenstein's philosophy of language. His later works contend that practices are organized around the use of language-games in which language use, thoughts, and actions are woven together (Wittgenstein, 1953). A simple example of a language-game is the following "apple shopping scene," where a person needs another person to buy five red apples from the grocery for oneself:

> I send someone shopping. I give him a slip marked "five red apples". He takes the slip to the shopkeeper, who opens the drawer marked "apples"; then he looks up the word "red" in a table and finds a colour sample opposite it; then he says the series of cardinal numbers – I assume that he knows them by heart – up to the word "five" and for each number he takes an apple of the same colour as the sample out of the drawer. – It is in these and other ways that one operates with words.
>
> (inspired by Wittgenstein, 1953, §1)

In order for the buyer to obtain the apples, the participating actors need to develop a language (five, red, apples, go to, buy, shop) to organize a set of actions that constitutes a practice. Although there are language conventions for the use of words, their specific meaning is linked to the language-game within which they are learned and used. Hence, language-games are associated with forms of life (Wittgenstein, 1953, §23). A specific language-game is constituted using specific types of language and arguments, which makes it possible to discover and unfold a particular way of understanding and constructing a practice. Such complexities of human cognition producing and developing practices can be related to the notion of habitus (Nørreklit et al., 2019). For centuries, the practice of partnership has been governed by more or less complex habita, establishing more or less sophisticated language-games, including not only written and oral words but also other types of language (such as body language), and differing according to practices. For instance, when marriages were arranged by parents, language-games included the formal wedding proposal to the bride's father. More recently, during the first half of the 20th century and until the 1960s, when dancing was a prominent social activity (see Bergström, 2019, about France and Modell, 1991, about the United States), dating consisted of getting to dance – a combination of verbal and body language that followed particular rules, such as feminine reserve.

More generally today, dating mobilizes complex language-games. An example of a highly codified language-game is the question "Would you like a (or another) drink?", which, quite unambiguously in some cultural contexts, indicates that the path to sex is open after a social event (Kaufmann, 2010, p. 58). The places in which dating practices play out are influential to language-games. For example, when you date under your friends' or family's eyes, as was the case traditionally and as is still most frequently the case today (Bergström, 2019), language-games may be more implicit. Habitus-based language-games also vary with social class. Thus, direct compliments about one's smile, look, or attractiveness (the usual seduction pattern of lower-class men) are considered illegitimate by upper class women who prefer to be appreciated for what they like and do (Bergström, 2019).

The philosophy of habitus-based language-games contrasts with the language use that is structured according to the logic of information technology, which appears to adhere to an understanding of language rooted in the logical positivist ideas of the younger Wittgenstein (1922) (Nørreklit et al., 2019). Then Wittgenstein's project was that of formulating all kinds of knowledge in one unitary language. Complex meanings could be analyzed as an atomic set of basic observational statements (called elementary sentences) which could then be reassembled logically to constitute the whole meaning. For an elementary sentence to be true, the proposition must have the same logical structure as the fact it expresses. "True" and "false" are the basic values that determine the relation between proposition (sentence) and world (fact); either the logical structure of the proposition is mirrored in the world, or it is not. The sentence has a two-value logic; hence, the language is digital in nature. Accordingly, young Wittgenstein's digital[6] language is quantitative – its units can be counted. Whereas this approach to "digital" language was eventually defeated by the older Wittgenstein's philosophy of "living" language, it can be argued that it constitutes the philosophical basis for information technology (IT hereinafter).

The machine language used in IT is a digital language consisting of binary codes (ones and zeros), resulting from the symbolic (in the mathematical sense of the word) logical language of the software. Previously, these symbolic logical sentences have captured live ideas – for instance, the "living" student evaluation of a course is captured by Likert scales, resulting in a series of ones and zeros, thus making it possible to compute an average rating score. At the surface level, answers are formulated as elementary sentences regarding the students' experience. However, these students' expressions are not the objective observational statements they might purport to be, but rather pseudo-elementary sentences abstracted from an aggregation of quantifiable data echoing emotions and subjective values. Here, without dialogical interaction between the involved actors, this digital language is far from a habitus-based language-game – in fact, it might even eliminate the possibility of such language-games (Nørreklit et al., 2019).

Analyzing scripts

In order to address our research question, we analyze the language-games of partnership and love embedded in the language used by the dating site matchaffinity.com. The dating site includes the homepage, the test that is administered to users, pages of data, computed scores, and reports. In all these sections, the site draws on certain types of language, that is, vocabulary, metaphors, diagrams, images, numbers, argumentation, etc. By analyzing the specific uses of language on matchaffinity.com, we can identify its vision of a partnership relationship. More specifically, we analyze the textual parts of matchaffinity.com's homepage, test, scores, and reports. We look at the argumentative structure and the core linguistic features of the text. Also, we analyze the practice(s) presented by the images (photos, illustrations, tables, numbers, etc.) used on the website, which requires a semiotic interpretation and understanding of the signs included in the images. In the website, images and text are often complementary: they anchor each other and influence the user's interpretation (Barthes, 1964). We also try to establish linkages between language and the market and romance categories that are said to be in opposition in online dating research. Because the website contains overabundant material for study, the samples we have selected here for analysis are, in our view, the most relevant ones for our purpose. Because the website is constantly changing, it might be that the material presented here does not match the state of the website at the time of reading, but we have been careful about the overall coherence of our data. Quotes and screenshots presented in this article have been retrieved from the November 2017 version of the website.

Analysis of matchaffinity.com

The dating website matchaffinity.com was launched in 2008 in the UK. It is run by Match Group Inc., an American company owning and operating online dating websites around the world and, historically, the first actor in this industry. It is free to register and take the affinity test. Users also have free access to their "personality report" and ranked suggestions for matches, and are allowed to send a first message. However, to receive messages or view photos, subscription is required.

Our analysis of the structure of the website identifies four categories of pages: (1) *general pages* that any user can see, (2) the *affinity test* pages, (3) *personal pages* for the exclusive and personal use of each user, that is, mainly, a "profile page" and three personal reports including items of, respectively, "personal values, views, and personality," and (4) *partner's website-public pages*, including a summary and a full profile page of the potential partner (thereafter the "partner page"), mentioning "affinity scores" and giving access to comparative reports, regarding, again, personal values, views, and personality elements. The latter three categories are considered as pillars for compatibility, which is measured through affinity scores – that is, a percentage value computed for each potential couple. The higher the score, the more compatible the partners are assumed to be. We present now our analysis of these four categories of pages.

General pages

The homepage introduces the website's vision of a successful partnership relationship and its method to create it. Furthermore, it includes links to dating advices, love stories, registration and login, and user testimonials. First, when entering the site, three photos are displayed – of which we only present the first (and therefore most prominent) one. These photos evoke a loving and romantic relationship, and sometimes "love stories"[7] are explicitly mentioned in the text anchoring the images. Figure 12.1, which has no caption, shows a photo of a man and a woman walking closely together while smiling. They are dressed in a smart casual style and, while still relatively young, look old enough to conjure up the prospect of a mature relationship. Overall, they appear happy and connected. The woman is looking at the man, who holds his arm around her shoulders while he looks at the path ahead. The outdoor background points to sunny summer times with a clear blue sky that suggests the perspective of a cloudless relationship. Overall, the photo conveys the figure of a couple having found a partnership relationship of fondness and happiness. We witness elements of the language-games of romantic love, emphasizing unity and complementarity within the couple. The photo also shows the traditional roles of men and women (the former protecting the latter). The picture fully fits the archetype of imagery in "serious" sites (Bergström, 2011b, 2019, p. 59 et s.): light colors – especially blue – brown-haired women, and stereotypical gendered attitudes.

Figure 12.1 Matchaffinity.com homepage photo.

Second, the homepage texts provide the website's vision of "a strong and lasting relationship." Excerpts displayed in Figure 12.2 explain that the key to such a relationship is the matching of people with "common interests, values and the compatibility of personalities" (quotes 1 and 2). Those elements, referred to as "affinity" (quote 3), are key to happiness (quote 4). Overall, the following schema of causality is assumed: shared interests and values and compatibility of personalities > affinity > happiness > strong and lasting relationship. The idea of "being made for each other" (quote 3), as well as the strong statement about "natural" compatibility in "every" romantic relationship (quote 5), appeal to the ideal of romantic love. All these conjure up romantic love. However, the emphasis on shared values and compatibility might also suggest an image of a relationship that, while free of friction and conflict, might not necessarily suggest a great degree of intimacy either. Furthermore, the schema of causality suggests a simple direct way to successfully establish the desired relationship. We witness a mix of language features conjuring up language-games of both romantic love and impersonal forms of matchmaking, together with the idea that the user has control over the realization of the relationship.

The main tool for assessing affinity is the "affinity questionnaire (or test)," which is both a matter of getting to know oneself better (quote 6), and finding compatible profiles. Quote 7 unambiguously refers to efficiency ("from thousands of registered profiles, the singles who are the most compatible with you"). Furthermore, the test claims legitimacy and reliability by drawing on psychological and behavioral research and expertise. Overall, the text expresses a scientific approach to describing and analyzing values and feelings, which makes it easy and efficient to find a strong and lasting relationship.

1. Matching people […], based on a cross match of common interests, values and the compatibility of personalities, significantly increases your chances of meeting someone with whom you can develop a *strong and lasting relationship* (emphasis added).
2. Whether we're talking shared values, hobbies, plans or simply going through life at the same pace, these are all vital qualities that help light that initial spark, then help consolidate the relationship over time. Simple? Absolutely.
3. The idea behind it is that real affinity between two people often begins with *having something in common*. Or even better, several things ... the discovery that they are, in fact, *made for each other*! (emphases added)
4. A compatible couple is a happy couple!
5. Matchaffinity uses compatibility – something that emerges naturally in every romantic relationship.
6. Matchaffinity com is a compatibility-based dating and relationship site. We believe that to have the best chance of developing a successful relationship, it is important to start by taking a little time to consider your own character traits and personality, as well as thinking about the type of person you'd like to meet. **Our unique Affinity Questionnaire is designed to help you do just that** (original emphasis).
7. We will use your answers to select, from the thousands of registered profiles, the singles who are the most compatible with you.

Figure 12.2 Excerpts of matchaffinity.com front pages.

This analysis of the front pages suggests that matchaffinity.com blends language-games pertaining to three main fields: romantic love, managerial efficiency, and science – thus shaping the image of a love and partnership relationship that blurs the distinctions between romance and market.

The affinity test

The core measure of partners' compatibility is the overall affinity score which is computed from answers to the affinity test. This test includes 136 questions structured along sections, collecting data regarding "personality," "lifestyle" (holidays, films, music, hobbies, etc.), "values" (family relationships, children, education, money, fidelity, etc.), and "profile" (biographical and personal data such as income, level of education, and ethnic origin). There are three answer formats: direct answers (used for bibliographical data, such as date of birth or physical attributes), forced choice among pictures or among propositions. Figures 12.3 and 12.4 display a selection of the two latter categories.

---

1. If I had to describe myself in three words, I'd use:
○ emotive, spontaneous, open.

○ calm, thoughtful, controlled.

2. I would rather my partner:
be instinctive ○ ○ ○ ○ ○ think things through.

3. When I want to relax:
○ I go out: it's the best way to meet people.

○ I organise an evening with friends.

○ I phone my best friend.

○ I switch off my phone and spend time in the peace and quiet of my own home.

4. I would like to find a partner who prefers:
spending quality time alone together ○ ○ ○ ○ ○ going out.

5. Being organised is:
Necessary ○ ○ ○ ○ ○ boring

6. When I run into problems, I would prefer my partner to be good at:
Giving advice ○ ○ ○ ○ ○ listening to me

Figure 12.3 Affinity test – Examples of questions.

First, the test is organized around the supply-and-demand model, with persons both offering a "product" (their own personality and values) (see items 1 and 3) and demanding one (see questions 2 and 4). Questions may be paired so as to compare offer and demand. For instance, although their wording differs slightly, questions 1 and 2 point to the same aspects of personality, as well as questions 3 and 4.

At the surface level, the questions are formulated as analytical separated elementary sentences (propositions) projecting objective facts "out there." However, as there can be many different things and activities relating to being, for instance, "spontaneous," "thoughtful," or "going out": the references of the questions are very open for interpretation, and subjective in nature. Accordingly, the answers are not, in fact, observational propositions projecting facts, but pseudo-elementary sentences echoing emotions and subjective values. Furthermore, the questions are formulated on a forced-choice scale – under the form of either a binary choice between diametrically opposed alternatives or a Likert scale covering positions on a continuum between two such alternatives. Thus, in the previous examples, although the formulation of categories is open to interpretation, there is an apparent coherence, in that, in both cases, the alternative refers to the same phenomenon (e.g., going out or not). However, many other questions provide choices having no internal consistency. With questions 5 and 6, for instance, the poles of the continuum are not mutually exclusive: one can perceive being organized as both important and boring, and giving advice does not prevent one from listening (and vice versa). Consequently, the possible answers to such questions are not separated analytical statements.

Nevertheless, the use of binary choice and Likert scale formats implies that psychological characteristics and subjective values can be rendered in IT language. Thus, similarly to the binary digital language of computers, answers are a matter of true or false statements. Thereby, the test paves the way for describing users' personal characteristics, values, and wishes through the digital language of the computer, making it possible to quantify everything without taking into consideration either openness to interpretation or the potential overlap of concepts.

The answers to some forced-choice propositions are sometimes expressed through images. For instance, Figure 12.4 displays images showing various dishes as possible answers to what one would put on the menu if one were "throwing a dinner party." Some of the dishes are rather obvious, while others are more difficult to identify. However, the reader's interpretation of the images is anchored in caption texts such as "homemade burgers," "something experimental," or "a tasty salad." On the whole, the food categories are broad and imprecise: what is something "fancy," "tasty," or "experimental"? Again, those adjectives are not mutually exclusive. The choice, resultingly, forbids any complexity. Furthermore, when the answer to the question on a menu for a "dinner party" is retrieved on the partner page, it is converted into a piece of

Figure 12.4 Affinity test – Example of lifestyle questions using photographs.

information about "[his/her] favourite cuisine." Of course, what one cooks for a party is not necessarily what one prefers for themselves: situational constraints might be more of a factor than one's personal tastes.

Other questions about tastes ask the user to choose three items out of a long list (for instance, up to 45 possible answers for "favorite hobbies") – with, again, many overlaps and the well-known biases associated with this kind of answer format. Consequently, despite the fact that such forced-choice questions about lifestyle offer a variety of possible answers, and are not restricted to a bipolar digital scale, they produce a reductive or even faulty portrayal of users' lifestyle.

To conclude, the affinity test is organized around the *supply-and-demand* model, with users both offering a product (their own personality and values) and demanding one. This model is shaped around a set of more-or-less muddled pseudo-elementary and pseudo-separated analytical sentences. To enable the calculation of affinity scores, these sentences are computed as digits, that is, numbers on scales and categories. In addition, the lifestyle-related answers are very likely to provide a distorted view of the person. In other words, who you are and who you search for are quantified and objectified. It should, however, be noted here that, upon registration, the user is recommended to add photos and a "personal ad" to complement their profile. Those are the only "data" which are not standardized, and where the user's uniqueness can find a "free"[8] expression. Tellingly, unlike completion of the test, they are not mandatory.

The affinity score

The outcome of the affinity test is the affinity scores between prospective partners. The global affinity score is aggregated from three affinity sub-scores, concerning, respectively, values, views on life, and personality. All scores are computed for each potential couple. The global affinity score is displayed on different pages (selection of matches, partner page) and is assumed to be the primary consideration when making a decision on whom to contact. All three sub-scores are also available on click-through from the partner page (see Figure 12.5).

Figure 12.5 Affinity score display on the partner page.

The calculation of the affinity scores is based on the separated analytical empirical statements provided by the affinity test – translated, as we have seen, into quantifiable digital language. Not all test data is used for the calculation. On the one hand, some data (namely biographical and lifestyle data, both regarding oneself and the desired partner) can be changed at any moment without changing the scores. This suggests that they are not included in the calculation of the affinity scores. On the other hand, answers regarding values, views, and personality cannot be changed – which suggests that they factor in the affinity scores. We have unsuccessfully tried to find the underlying algorithms of both the affinity sub-scores and the global affinity score. We can only say that the global score is not a weighted average of the three sub-scores. However, we made a simulation of a man and a woman declaring the same values, which ended up with a value affinity score of 100 percent. This score attests that compatibility means similarity – a claim which, as we have already pointed out, is made repeatedly on the website.

Overall, we find that the affinity scores are meant to govern the relation to a potential partner. Embedded in the calculation of the affinity scores is the assumption that partners' compatibility can be assessed through the addition and comparison of pseudo-elementary sentences on personal features. The affinity scores are not based on observable fact but on the respondent's emotions and subjective values, making the statements produced pseudo-elementary sentences. Compatibility means similarity of values, views, and personality traits, expressed as percentages: the higher the percentage, the more compatible partners are. In other words, the affinity scores reflect the degree of utility of the "services" (values, views, and personality traits) offered by the potential partner. Accordingly, language features here are exclusively of the digital type and construct forms of love and relationships that conjure up market, not romance.

The affinity reports

Each affinity sub-score on values, views, and personality is supplemented by a report which comments on how compatible the user is with the potential partner on the relevant level. Although there is no explicit relationship between the affinity scores and the related affinity reports, these reports provide a broad explanation for the affinity scores. The value and personality reports, respectively, inventory ten values and twelve elements of personality, presented as being based on experts' views, namely Schwartz' model of universal values (Schwartz, 1992) and the Big Five model of personality. The view affinity report inventories eight life aspects, namely love and relationships, commitment and fidelity, day-to-day routine, sex, family, parenting, money, and religion. All reports compare the user's and the potential partner's answers, using diagrams that can take several forms, and remind that common points are a core factor for happiness in a relationship. We contrast "simple" (Figure 12.6) and

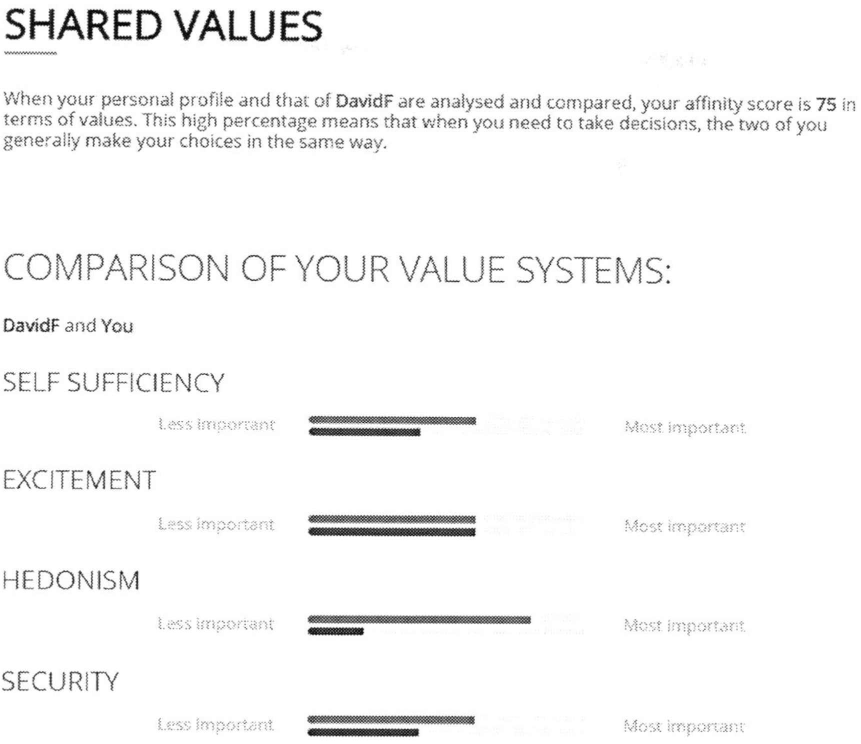

SHARED VALUES

When your personal profile and that of **DavidF** are analysed and compared, your affinity score is **75** in terms of values. This high percentage means that when you need to take decisions, the two of you generally make your choices in the same way.

COMPARISON OF YOUR VALUE SYSTEMS:

DavidF and **You**

SELF SUFFICIENCY
Less important ——————— Most important

EXCITEMENT
Less important ——————— Most important

HEDONISM
Less important ——————— Most important

SECURITY
Less important ——————— Most important

Figure 12.6 **Affinity report with simple comparison – Values compared.**

"computed comparison" since, in the latter case, the diagram relies on data treatments that are more extensive than in the former.

Simple comparison diagrams report the importance of each item to each partner, in a digital language that is simply derived from the questionnaire answers, with the use of a Likert scale-like image. Such diagrams are complemented by a comment on the suggested action for each point of agreement or disagreement between partners' values – which is also digital in that all suggestions are constructed from data, without sometimes much consistency with the diagram itself. Sometimes it also proves difficult to reconcile the diagram with the alleged model of the test (e.g., the Big Five model). Narratives always follow the following casual schema of "if-then" arguments: if partners are different, difference is viewed as a way of making one of them progress . . . provided that enough consideration is given to their needs. If partners are alike, there is a kind reminder that they should not forget to balance their behavior. The message is standardized depending on the degree of deviation between the two value scores, and digitalized in that it follows a binary scheme.

Similarly, affinity reports with computed comparison diagrams display four-square boxes, in which each square is shaped by two axes with scores retrieved from the test answers. In a diagram (that provides four different degrees of similarity and related comments) for instance, views on routine depends on flexibility (versus organization) and acceptance (versus avoidance); views on love and relationships are shaped by romanticism and daily division of labor. Here similarity means being plotted in the same square. As previously, comments tend to downplay differences, despite the fact that divergences of opinion may seriously impinge on the relationship. Thus appeals to negotiation and communication appear rhetorical, as well as the claim, that, in case of sharp discrepancy, it is the responsibility of the person to make the relationship work. To maintain the belief that the website is a key to finding a matching partner, the possibility of irreconcilable differences is denied.

To conclude, the presentation of the affinity reports is dominated by an extensive use of diagrams shaped around either dichotomous scales or categories involving bipolar formats. Personal values, views, and personality are presented in a digital language that ultimately, categorizes users. The standardized comments on recommended actions are also digital, in that they are automatically generated from the deviation between the users' scores. A causal line of "if-then" argumentation indicates that, in any case, there is always a path to the relationship. Here again, by comparing partners' position on diagrams (as any "product" could be), the language used points to forms of partnership that exclusively allude to market logics.

Summary of findings

Our analysis of the language use in the general pages reveals that matchaffinity.com shapes the image of a relationship that blurs the differences between romance and market. On the one hand, there are few occurrences of language features that can be linked with romance. Those are found in the texts explaining the purpose of the website and most notably, in the photographs on the home page, whose prominent position is likely to establish a strong foundational construction of love and partnership in terms of romance. On the other hand, the rest of the website (the test, the affinity scores, and reports) is infused with digital language. At the outset, the affinity test puts the users' perception of who they are and who they are searching for into the format of digital language that can be computed. The user's complex wishes for a partner are thus translated into digital scripted messages and, eventually, into a data set, which is then made visible to the other users, thus constructing the potential partner as a digital(ized) lover that might be far away from the "real" person.

Such a digital(ized) lover is tightly associated with, and embodies, the rationale equating similarity, compatibility, happiness, and the promised "strong and lasting relationship." The search is built on discourses and efficiency of utility: supposedly matching partners are those with the highest utility, the latter being defined in terms of similarity. Besides, the test explicitly refers to offer and demand in terms of personality traits and lifestyle – unambiguously evoking the idea of an efficient market place. All this is realized through the objectification of partners, whose subjective singularity is reified into a series of predetermined digital categories. The only unstandardized data are the personal photographs and ad, but these spaces of free expression are like a small island in the middle of the ocean.

To sum up, compared to the complex habitus-based language-games of traditional dating, online dating largely, but not exclusively, relies on digital language, the main traits of which are discrete, predetermined categories enabling the objectification and quantification of users. However, due to the presence of other language features (photographs and texts) strongly appealing to the figure of romance, and perhaps also because personal photos and ads might, consciously or otherwise, reflect the long-established conventions and language-games of traditional dating, we conclude that the practices constructed by the website are ambiguous, in that they may conjure up a variety of forms of love and relationships. While a market-based commodification of relationships might be more foregrounded than a more romantic understanding, their simultaneous presence may lead either to the user being very confused about the relationship the site offers to initiate, or privileging the figure they wish.

Another feature of digital language is its ability to deliver a whole range of data upon a few clicks. We hypothesize that such an overabundance of information is likely to add to the user's confusion. Although the website strongly pushes toward basing contact decisions upon the affinity score, the easy availability of so much data is likely to invite users to explore further in the partner profile. As a result, the user is likely to be quickly overwhelmed by the profusion of data, and confused about the criteria which are really important to them. This is all the more likely as both romance and market figures are simultaneously activated by the website, focusing attention on "rational" criteria, but also simultaneously suggesting (possibly unconscious) fantasies arising from the personal photographs and ad, or data regarding, for instance, occupation or religion.

After the first contact, the relationship will use habitus-based language-games that will, at best, progressively enable the discovery of the "real" other and the development of mutual understanding and possible intimacy, and at worst, the ending of the relationship after the first face-to-face meeting. All in all, the original digital language gives rise to confusions, frustrations, and challenges for the development of further language-games and partnership.

Discussion

In this section, we first discuss our findings vis-a-vis prior research on online dating, and more specifically, on its market versus romance debate. We then reinterpret our findings in terms of a reification process that ultimately serves the interests of the industry to the detriment of users.

Prior online dating research and the market-romance debate

We have suggested that both the coexistence of market- and romance-associated language features in matchaffinity.com, and the overabundance of data it presents the user with, were likely to result in confusion. This is aligned with prior online dating research findings evidencing the "more-means-worse effect" (Wu and Chiou, 2009; Lee and Chiou, 2016): an overabundance of options results in excessive searching, and leads to poorer choices. Schwartz (2004) has also argued for a similar, more general "more-is-less" effect: too much choice induces psychological stress. This might explain the divergence in prior research regarding the commodification of love (Illouz, 2007, 2012 and others) versus the resistance of the mythical ideal of romantic love whatever the market form (Bergström, 2013, 2019). Here, drawing on our mixed findings (the dominance of market-related digital language along with the persistence of romantic languages features), we suggest that the users' downplaying of the market might be a counterintuitive paradoxical effect of the confusion generated by, precisely, the digital language of the market place: by creating psychological distress, excessive and ambiguous data kills the system, and defeats the conceptual figure of the market. This conclusion is consistent with prior research findings that the well-established opposition between love/romance and market (Dröge and Voirol, 2011) is still a vivid perception, as exemplified in Bergström's research, where many users "express[ed] unease about [the profile-based selection] that they associate with the world of *consumption*" (Bergström, 2019, p. 111, emphasis added). If the market and romance are two irreconcilable categories in users' minds, they are all the more likely to privilege the latter as the market induces mental overload.

We also suggest that the market metaphor misses an important difference between a market of commodities (Illouz, 2007; Kaufmann, 2010) and online dating. Beyond its facade, a dating website is not only about choosing but also largely about being chosen. Bergström's (2019) evidence that young women use dating websites to test their attractiveness suggests that narcissistic reassurance might be an important stake for users. Considering these two last points, what online dating provides in abundance – perhaps more so than actual relationships – is hope for a romantic relationship and narcissistic reassurance.

To sum up, our analysis enables a bridging of the two opposed views that online dating results either in a commodification of love or in the disregard of market aspects associated with the vividness of the myth. In scrutinizing the language used on our website, we suggest that, paradoxically, the ambiguity and overabundance of the market-related digital language of the website diverts users from its logic, ensuring the survival of the myth of romance.

A world of reified lovers

The translation of users' subjective experience into scores and categories takes away all the living part of their experience. As we have seen with the earlier example of food preferences in Figure 12.4, users' singular, complex, shifting, and possibly ambivalent preferences are translated into predetermined categories. The same is true for users' views (you can choose whether you like "hot sex" or not, but you cannot express preferences depending on the time and context). After completing the test, the user can be very surprised to discover that the person displayed on the website does not fit their self-perception, resulting in possible negative feelings of having been interpreted (in the psychoanalytical sense) and reduced to some aspects of themselves. We could hypothesize that, more than their being treated as products on a market, users may resent this reduction of their selves. In some other social places of encounter, for instance, nightclubs or parties, while the market metaphor is at least implicit (see also the English slang "meat market"), the (admittedly illusory) feeling that they can potentially express the entirety of their selves may prevent a similar feeling of being objectified.

The website argues that compatibility "naturally emerges in every romantic relationship" (see Figure 12.2, quote 5) – however, this is very debatable. Partners may be passionate, but unable to reconcile some divergent aspects of their personality or lifestyle – in such cases, the relationship might be strong, but unlikely sustainable. Conversely, potential partners might be very similar but lack the sparks of romance. The website denies potential conflicts not only between partners but also between forms of partnership.

Both objectification and the denial of conflict pertain to the reification process (Lukács, 1971), whose ultimate consequence is the irrefutability and then the maintenance of the existing social order, which serves the interests of some parties at the expense of others. Here, we have demonstrated how the singular subjectivity of users was objectified, and how conflict was denied – the first steps of a reification process. If we add other research findings highlighting the disillusions, or even the wounds (Illouz, 2012) brought by online dating, or else the persistence of traditional gender inequalities in the partnership market (for instance, the fact that, in virtual as in real life, senior women are not considered very attractive) (Bergström, 2019), we see how, all things together, users are likely to be the losing actors of the online dating game and the dating service companies whose business is flourishing[9] the winners. Maybe disillusioned users keep on playing it because, as we have suggested, the game provides abundant hope.

Conclusion

In this last section, we recapitulate our contribution, present the limitations of our study, and suggest subsequent avenues for future research.

Contribution

In this article, we have addressed the market versus romance debate that has been hitherto unresolved in online dating research. Drawing on Wittgenstein's

(1922, 1953) successive conceptions of language, our analysis of matchaffinity.com shows that, while traditional dating is a matter of complex habitus-based language-games, the website makes use of what we have labelled and described as a digital language. This digital language provides the user with a vast amount of data upon which to base their choice of partner – thereby conjuring up the figure of the market. Nonetheless, the idea of romance finds expression in texts and photographs displayed on the website. Our conclusions are that both the co-presence of romance and market figures and the overabundance of data generate confusion. This confusion, we contend, explains the divergence between scholars about whether or not market has commodified love: when the user is lost in ambiguities and too many data, the mythical figure of romantic love retains its allure and strength. Dating websites seem to be markets for hope, more than for actual relationships, and to detrimentally reify users, at their own profits. Thus our research not only adds to an understanding of divergent prior online dating research but, by studying another type of platforms than the ones previously scrutinized, complement the body of research on digitalization and datafication, as well as more general mechanisms of contemporary social life (reification). We have also evidenced that the digital professionalization of the partnership market leads to the implementation of project management-oriented organizational processes.

Limitations and further research

First, our conclusions rely on the analysis of a single website. Other websites, which do not put as strong an emphasis on compatibility, may use less categories or less computed numbers or diagrams – meaning that conclusions might not necessarily be generalizable. Second, we have conducted an analytical demonstration, which needs validation through empirical studies that shed light on whether and how, in practice, the affinity scores and reports determine partner choice. It might be that users perceive a sense of freedom to contact whoever they want that overrides the pressure toward compatibility, either because they are genuinely autonomous or because they do not trust (or understand) these numbers and diagrams.

Such empirical research could also encompass the later steps of the encounter (written exchanges, face-to-face meeting, etc.), to gauge the enduring influence of the digital language (and of the "interpretation" of the other on its basis) on the ongoing relationship. More empirical research is also needed because the market versus romance debate is probably set in very different terms according to the website considered. While all dating websites have the facade of a market, they may be perceived differently according to their functionalities and target demographics. Matchaffinity.com combined market and romance figures, and, as such, was an ideal case study for shedding light on this debate, but what about websites that discursively foreground casual relationships, or those displaying a limited amount of data?

Another limitation of our work relates to the heterogeneity of existing research debating the romance versus market issue, which includes both analytical works (often at the macro, society, and capitalism level) and empirical locally situated investigations. Additionally, local contexts are unequally represented in empirical works: France, where Bergström has been investigating the subject for more than ten years, is overrepresented. It might also be the case that, given the tendency for sociological research to be published in the local language, we have missed non-English-language publications.

Finally, the romance versus market debate, which is ultimately a matter of users' perceptions and practices, remains subject to many intersectional influences. Bergström (2019), for example, has shown that dating practices are also a matter of social class and gender. It could be of interest to study how class, gender, or other social characteristics (ethnicity, religion, place of living) impact on dating site users' practices, and on their construction of the romance versus market issue. Finally, our analysis draws on work by scholars who, most often implicitly, focus on Western dating practices. In other cultural contexts, different constructions of partnership might hold sway – even in the West, there might be some divergence from one context to another. Since many websites have sister versions all over the world, it might be of interest (and relatively easy) to compare users' practices in different countries.

Notes

1 See Pew Research Center (2016) about the United States or Bergström (2016a) about France.
2 The authors are grateful to Sylvie Heumez for her help in material collection and to the participants and discussants of conferences where a former version of this text has been presented (EGOS 2019 Edinburgh; ARC 2019 Odense; and CMS 2010 Naples). The first author is also indebted to the ESSEC Research Centre for funding.
3 The site also accepts female users "looking for a woman" and male users "looking for a man," but, by default, it assumes heteronormativity and targets heterosexual individuals.
4 Here, we use "figure" in the everyday meaning of "form" or "character."
5 Page numbers are those of the English version of the article.
6 Wittgenstein did not use the term "digital" but his binary logic concept, based on Russel, has central aspects of technical digitization (encoding phenomena in binary, discrete information) (Nørreklit et al. 2019).
7 Similarly, in the "love stories" pages, some users are reporting on successful experiences of romantic love at first glance, such as illustrated by the following quotes: "We hit it off immediately sparks flew and we neither of us wanted to leave" (sic) or "As our first dance said, I knew I loved him before I met him."
8 However, photos and personal ads are subjected to website moderation and research has shown that there are many similarities in the ads (Illouz, 2007), if only because the sites give advice on the subject.
9 See, for instance, https://www.statista.com/outlook/372/100/online-dating/worldwide and https://www.statista.com/outlook/371/100/matchmaking/worldwide (retrieved on 29 December 2019).

References

Alaimo, C., & Kallinikos, J. (2017). Computing the everyday: Social media as data platforms. *The Information Society*, 33(4): 175–191.

Barthes, R. (1964). Rhétorique de l'image, *Communications*, 4, 41–42. (English translation: Rhetoric of the image). In Barthes, R. (Ed.), *Image-Music-Text*. New York: Noonday Press, 1977.

Bergström, M. (2011a). La toile des sites de rencontres en France. Topographie d'un nouvel espace social en ligne. *Réseaux*, 166: 225–260.

Bergström, M. (2011b). Casual dating online. Sexual norms and practices on French heterosexual dating sites. *Zeitschrift für Familienforschung (Journal of Family Research)* 23(3): 319–336.

Bergström, M. (2013). La loi du supermarché ? Sites de rencontres et représentations de l'amour. *Ethnographie française*, 43(3): 433–442 (English translation available on Cairn International databasis: The law of the supermarket? Online dating and representations of love, p. I-IX).

Bergström, M. (2015). L'âge et ses usages sexués sur les sites de rencontres en France (années 2000). *Clio*, 42: 125–146 (English translation available on Cairn International databasis: Gendered attitudes to age on online dating sites (France, 2000s)).

Bergström, M. (2016a). Sites de rencontre: Qui les utilise en France ? Qui y trouve son conjoint ? *Population & Sociétés*, 530: 1–4.

Bergström, M. (2016b). (Se) correspondre en ligne. L'homogamie à l'épreuve des sites de rencontres. *Sociétés contemporaines*, 104: 13–40.

Bergström, M. (2019). *Les nouvelles lois de l'amour. Sexualité, couple et rencontres au temps du numérique*. Paris: La Découverte.

Bialecki, M., O'Leary, S., & Smith, D. (2017). Judgement devices and the evaluation of singularities: The use of performance ratings and narrative information to guide film viewer choice. *Management Accounting Research*, 35: 56–65.

De Rougemont, D. (1983). *Love in the Western world*. Princeton, NJ: Princeton University Press (Original edition: L'amour et l'Occident. Paris, Plon, 1939).

Dröge, K., & Voirol, O. (2011). Online dating: the tensions between romantic love and economic rationalization. *Zeitschrift für Familienforschung (Journal of Family Research)*, 23(3): 337–357.

Finkel, E.J., Eastwick, P.W., Karney, B.R., Reis, H.T., & Sprecher, S. (2012). Online dating: A critical analysis from the perspective of psychological science. *Psychological Science in the Public Interest*, 13(1): 3–66.

Hancock, J.H., & Toma, C.L. (2009). Putting your best face forward: the accuracy of online dating photographs. *Journal of Communication*, 59: 367–386.

Heino, R.D., Ellison, N.B., & Gibbs, J.L. (2010). Relationshopping: investigating the market metaphor in online dating. *Journal of Social and Personal Relationships*, 27(4): 427–447.

Illouz, E. (2007). *Cold intimacies, emotions and late capitalism*. Cambridge, UK and Malden, MA: Polity Press.

Illouz, E. (2012). *Why Love Hurts*. Cambridge, UK and Malden, MA: Polity Press.

Jeacle, I., & Carter, C. (2011). In TripAdvisor we trust: rankings, calculative regimes and abstract systems. *Accounting, Organizations & Society*, 36(4/5): 293–309.

Kaufmann, J.C. (2010). *Sex@mour. Les nouvelles clés des rencontres amoureuses*. Paris: Armand Colin.

Lardellier, P. (2012). *Les réseaux du coeur. Sexe, amour et séduction sur Internet*. Paris: François Bourin Editeur.

Lee, C.C, & Chiou, W.B. (2016). More eagerness, more suffering from search bias: accuracy incentives and need for cognition exacerbate the detrimental effects of excessive searching in finding romantic partners online. *Journal of Behavioral Decision Making*, 29: 3–11.

Lukács, G. (1971). *History and Class Consciousness*. London: Merlin Press.

Modell, J. (1991). *Into One's Own: From Youth to Adulthood in the United States, 1920–1975*. Berkeley, CA.: University of California Press.

Myers West, S. (2017). Data capitalism: redefining the logics of surveillance and privacy. *Business & Society*, 58(1): 20–41.

Nørreklit, L., Jack, L., & Nørreklit, H. (2019). Moving towards digital governance of university scholars: instigating a post-truth university culture. *Journal of Management and Governance*, 23(4): 869–899.

Pew Research Center (2016). *15% of American adults have used online dating sites or mobile dating apps*. Retrieved from https://www.pewresearch.org/internet/topics/online-dating/, on 29th December 2019.

Roscoe, P., & Chillas, S. (2014). The state of affairs: critical performativity and the online dating industry. *Organization*, 21(6): 797–820.

Rose, N. (1992). Governing the enterprising self. In Heelas, P., & Morris, P. (Eds), *The Values of the Enterprise Culture: The Moral Debate*. London: Routledge, pp. 141–164.

Rosenfeld, M., & Thomas, R. (2012). Searching for a mate: the rise of the internet as a social intermediary. *American Sociological Review*, 77(4): 523–547.

Schwartz, B. (2004). The Tyranny of Choice. *Scientific American*, 290(4): 70–75.

Schwartz, S.H. (1992). Universals in the content and structure of values: theory and empirical tests in 20 countries. In Zanna, M. (Ed.), *Advanced in Experimental Social Psychology* (vol. 25). New York: Academic Press, pp. 1–65.

Scott, S.V., & Orlikowski, W.J. (2012). Reconfiguring relations of accountability: Materialization of social media in the travel sector. *Accounting, Organizations & Society*, 37(1): 26–40.

Shorter, E. (1975). *The Making of the Modern Family*. New York: Basic Books.

Toma, C.L., & Hancock, J.H. (2016). Looks and lies: the role of physical attractiveness in online date self-presentation and deception. *Communication Research*, 37(3): 335–351.

Wittgenstein, L. (1922). *Tractatus Logico-Philosophicus*. London: K. Paul, Trench, Trubner.

Wittgenstein, L. (1953). *Philosophical Investigations*. Oxford: Blackwell.

Wu, P.L., & Chiou, W.B. (2009). More options lead to more searching and worse choices in finding partners for romantic relationships online: an experimental study. *CyberPsychology and Behavior*, 12(3): 315–318.

Zuboff, S. (2015). Big other: surveillance capitalism and the prospects of an information civilization. *Journal of Information Technology*, 30: 75–89.

Zuboff, S. (2019). *The Age of Surveillance Capitalism: The Fight for a Human Future at the New Frontier of Power*. London: Profile Books.

Chapter 13

Conclusion

A traversal between autonomy and heteronomy can be identified in the sense of a synoptic perspective. In the tradition of Enlightenment thinking, man is no longer helplessly at the mercy of the world. In the appropriation of the world, the individuals experience themselves as effective. The individual makes a difference. It is not exposed to the world. Instead, the individuals can shape the world and give themselves a place. This form of expansive learning experiences a dialogical potentation with digital media's production and action orientation. Learning becomes more fluid through the media structure. People can connect at low thresholds. Never before has learning been such a collective and interactive process as it has become possible through digital media. Such learning also requires management – knowledge is not locked away in books and is freely accessible. Questions can be discussed in an open power-free exchange. But this also means appropriate management of the learning process.

Conversely, management processes as such are becoming more fluid. Project teams can connect from any part of the globe. Geographical distance no longer separates, which also changes the way we work. As the home office phenomenon in the wake of the Corona pandemic has also shown, working is more decentralized than ever before. Appropriate concepts need to be developed, implemented, and evaluated. The contributions in this volume provide a heuristic background for this. This emancipative perspective on learning and management, together with the decentralizing elements, is contrasted with a heteronomous perspective. Digital media standardize learning through query tools, exam protocols, and performance tracking to an unprecedented extent. Performance can be constantly evaluated. These effects are so powerful that they permeate all walks of life. The evaluation practice evokes a permanent self-optimization that can indeed be interpreted as learning. The logic of quality management also inscribes itself more firmly into the lifeworld through the assessments. The consideration of organizational learning through an infinite quality management process unfolds repressive effects. This outlines the poles of emancipation/self-determination versus repression/heteronomy. These poles constitute the field of tension that the contributions to this volume illuminate with specific approaches in the context of learning and management of digital media.

DOI: 10.4324/9781003188728-16

Index

Note: Page numbers in *italics* indicate a figure and page numbers in **bold** indicate a table on the corresponding page.

abstraction in agile frameworks 13–16
action and agility 19–25; facts, values, and possibilities in 22–25; integration of actor-world relationship in 20–22; understanding and 26–27
actor-loop 32–33
actors, agile 12–13; actor-reality construction in COVID-19 pandemic 167–171; actor-world relational construction 165–167, *166*; agile self 34–35; communication and 25–33; four dimensions actor-world relationship and 20–22; having dialogue with themselves 16–17, 36n3; pragmatic constructivism (PC) and (*see* pragmatic constructivism (PC)); using facts, values, and possibilities 22–25, 36n7
Adler, P. S. 38–39
Agamben, G. 60
Agile Alliance 104
agile cognition 9, 12; communication in 25–33; conceptual illusions in 18–19; creating ideas in 18; creative cognition and 16–18; critical assessment in 18; factors influencing 15–16; questions in 17–18
agile frameworks: abstraction and change in 13–16; creative cognition in 16–18
agile management 1; agile-oriented media pedagogy and 104–105; in customer-oriented corporate structures 103–104; defined 102–104; paranoiac versus 90–94; *see also* management
Agile Manifesto 104; on agile self 34; face-to-face communication principle in 27; focus on individuals in interaction in 19; principles in 10–11; on synchronization of communicative tools 15; value preferences in 9–10
agile self 34–35
agility: action and 19–25; cognitive process in 10; defined 103; implemented in university management 91–93; principles of 10–11; value preferences in 9–10
Ajana, B. 59–60
Andrejevic, M. 185–186
Anthropocene age 65, 66
anti-capitalism 183
Apple, M. W. 181–182
apprenticeship 109
Aristotle 74
autocratic cognition 12

Balslev, J. 131
Barbrook, R. 184
Barcan, R. 70, 93
Baudrillard, J. 100–101
behaviorist theory 107
Bergström, M. 191, 194–195, 211
Biesta, G. 63
big data 7, 67n1; Anthropocene age and 65, 66; biopolitics and promises attached to 58–60; desire to turn the world into objects than can be manipulated and 64–65; Earth forgetfulness and 65; introduction to 56–57; machines for 63–64; meaning and capacity of life and 65–66; and school life in Danish context 61–62; toward dialogical life-friendly small data machines and 66, 67n2

Bildung 56
biopolitics and big data 58–60
Bjur, W. 127
Boltanski, L. 182–183
Borys, B. 38–39
Bourdieu, P. 73
Bröckling, U. 182

Californian ideology 184
Cameron, A. 184
capitalism: consumer 179–181; neoliberal 181–185; new spirit of 182–183
Caravantes, G. 127
chamber of delusions 79–80, 84–90
Chiapello, È. 182–183
Chillas, S. 194
co-authorship 30, 31–33
Cocherell, L. 127
collaborative learning 110–111; decision-making in 120; digital tools for 121; as interactive and social process 118, 118–119; monitoring in 121; phases of 119–120; review in 121; roles in 120; tasks in 120–121; teacher's role in 121–122; time management in 120
communication 25–33; agile 30–31; dialog as principle of digital 99–102; narratives and synergy 29; transformation disrupting integration and 29–30; understanding in 26–29
Community of Practice 109
competition 182
complex adaptive systems 143
conceptual frameworks 14–15
conceptual habitus 83–84, 86–87
conceptual illusions 18–19
connectivism 1, 111–115, **114**
consumer capitalism 179–181
COVID-19 pandemic 159–160, 171–173; actor-reality construction in 167–171; agile learning for faster integration of dimensions of reality with 164–165; attempting integration in first phase of 167–169; attempting integration in second phase of 169–170; big data and 58; digital language in times of crisis and 162–163; mis- and disinformation facilitating nonintegrated learning and 170–171; new remote work and 40, 41, 42, 44, 52; pragmatic constructivism (PC) and (see pragmatic constructivism (PC))
Craig, R. 70

creative cognition 16–18
critical assessment in agile cognition 18
customer-oriented corporate structures 103–104

Danish Evaluation Institute (EVA) 131–133
dating platforms: analyzing scripts on 197; brief history of partnership and love and 193; contribution and future research on 209–211; discussion of research results on 207–209; historical perspectives and online dating research and 192–195; introduction to 190–192; matchaffinity.com 197–207, 199–203, 205; tensions between market and romance in research on 193–195; theory and methodological analysis of 195–197
Dean, J. 180
de-location 100
De Rougemont, D. 193
Dewey, J. 63
dialogue 16–17, 36n3; as principle of digital communication 99–102
digital age, the: concepts of agile management in 102–104; dating 101–102; decentralized communication infrastructure of 99–100; features of 100–101
digital competence 114–115
digitalization: accelerating processes 128; of dating platforms (See dating platforms); failures in 126–127; incorporation phase in 130; isolation phase in 129–130; as magic 135–138; methodological analysis of education sector 130–135; narrative of neoliberal 183–185; transcendence phase in 130
digital language 77–81; chamber of delusion and 79–80; crowding out conceptual habitus and ethics 78–79; dating platforms and 195–197; ordinary language under attack by language puritanism and 77–78; shaping paranoiac management action 80–81
digital management: by Excel spreadsheet 81–84; paranoiac 90–91
double-loop understanding 31–33
Downes, S. 113
Dröge, K. 194, 195

Earth forgetfulness 65
eduScrum 153–154, 155

Engeström, Y. 109
entrepreneurial self 181–187; neoliberal digitization and 183–185; new spirit of capitalism and 182–183; social web and 185–187
ethos 74–75
Excel spreadsheet, digital management by 81–84
explanation and understanding 27

facts as knowledge 22–25, 36n7
flexibility in new remote work 39, 43–44
Ford, H. 179
Fordism 179–181
Fordist self 181
formalizations in new remote work 39–40, 40; changing procedures in 42–43; enabling 43–44, 51–53
Fowler, M. 116
fractals 142
Frazer, J. G. 127
Frege, G. 77

Gartner 128
Gilles, D. 102–103
global transparency 38–39, 44
group work 110
Guevara, C. 180

habitus 73; conceptual 83–84, 86–87; digital language crowding out conceptual 78–79; digital management by Excel spreadsheet and 81–84; language-games and 73–74, 195–197
Hacking, I. 58
Heidegger, M. 65
Heino, R. D. 194
Highsmith, J. 116
Hume, D. 24

Illouz, E. 194
inconsistency as conceptual illusion 19
Instagram 102
integration of dimensions in actor-world relationship 20–22; COVID-19 pandemic and 167–171
internal transparency 39
IT revolution: challenge of 7–9; magic and 134; transformation in 5–7

Kaerlein, T. 184
Kaufmann, J. C. 194

Kop, R. 115
Kure, N. 136

language-games 126; habitus and 73–74, 195–197; management narration through logos and 74–75; pragmatic reality constructs in 75–76; scripts and dialectics in 76–77
language puritanism 78–79
Larsen, M. V. 128
Lave, J. 109
law of contiguity 129, 134, 135
learning 1–2, 214; agile 108, 117–118, 164–165; agile management and 102–104; Agile Manifesto and 104; agile-oriented media pedagogy and 104–105; collaborative 110–111, *118*, 118–122; as connecting information 111–115, **114**; connectivism theory of 1, 111–115, **114**; dialog as principle of digital communication and 99–102; digital competence in 114–115; digitalization as magic in 130–135; introduction to theories of 107–108; Lightschools® and (see Lightschools®); from the professional world 115–118, **117**; social constructivism theory of 107–108, 109–111, **110**, 120; as social-mediated process 108–111, **110**
legitimate peripheral participation (LPP) 109
Lembo, D. 117
Leontiev, A. N. 109
Lewis, T. 60
Lightschools®: 13 common principles of 144–145; as complex adaptive system 143; distributed living, learning, and co-creating among people using 147–149; distributed living, learning, and co-creating among spaces using 149–152; eduScrum and 153–154, 155; emergent curriculum of 142–144; fractal organization of 142; introduction to 140–141; measurement of development and impact of 146–147; natural time and PDRAC-spiral with 152–153; potential development habits with 145–146; project-based learning and 153; run up chart and impediments in 156–157; sprints in 154–155; stories and tasks in 155–156
local transparency 44

logical positivism 77–78
logos 74–75

magic: digitalization as 135–138; in management 127–128; Marcell Mauss' theory of 128–130
Magic of Organizational Life, The 128
Malinowski, B. 135–136
management 214; defined 179; by Excel spreadsheet 81–83; Fordist 179–181; neoliberal mentality of the entrepreneurial self and 181–182; new spirit of capitalism and 182–183; *See also* agile management
"Manifesto for Agile Software Development" 104
matchaffinity.com 197–207, *199–203, 205*
Mau, S. 58
Mauss, M. 128–130
McCoy, C. 83
McLuhan, M. 100
metaphysics 24
Monett, D. 117
monitoring in project-based learning 121
mutual understanding 30–31
Myers West, S. 190

narrative/narration: of neoliberal digitization 183–185; ordinary language of 77–78; pragmatics of 75–76; synergy and 29; through logos 74–75
neoliberal digitization 183–185
neoliberalism 181–182
New Public Management 135, 136
Nørreklit, H. 136

O'Reilly, T. 101–102

paranoiac management 80–81, 86, 87–90; versus agile governance 90–94; by digital technology 90–91
participatory appropriation 109
pathos 74–75
PDRAC-spiral 152–153, 154–155
Piaget, J. 108, 122n1
Popper, K. 132
positivism 24; logical 77–78
possibilities, knowledge of 22–25
post-truth culture 80
pragmatic constructivism (PC) 160; agile learning for faster integration of dimensions of reality and 164–165; meaning of language for action and 161–162; tentative framework based on theoretical background of 165–167, *166*
pragmatics 75–76
professional world, learning from 115–118, **117**
project-based learning (PBL) 119; decision-making in 120; digital tools for 121; *Lightschools*® 153; monitoring in 121; phases of 119–120; review in 121; roles in 120; tasks in 120–121; teacher's role in 121–122; time management in 120
project management, agile 116–117
puritanism, language 78–79

reductionist scripting 77
remote work, new: enabling formalizations in 43–44, 51–53; flexibility in 39, 43–44; formalizations in 39–40, *40*, 42–44; further research agenda and concluding remarks on 53; global transparency in 38–39, 44; how procedures can be different in 42–43; how student supervision and instruction remain enabled for individuals in 46–48; how we can miss the point when changing processes in 48–51; illustrations of 44–51; internal transparency in 39; introduction to 38–41, *40*; repair in 39, 43; values and meanings driving action at organizational level in 45–46; what has changed in 41–42
repair in new remote work 39, 43
"Requiem of the Media" 100–101
Røge, K. 136
Rogoff, B. 109
"Role of Religion and Magic, The" 135
Roscoe, P. 194
Rosenbaum, H. 83

Salza, P. 117
school digitization, Denmark: advantages and disadvantages of 62; background on 61–62; new trends in 61; school as democratic community and 62–63
scripts and dialectics 76–77
Searle, J. 79–80
self: agile 34–35; entrepreneurial 181–187; Fordist 181
Sieber, S. 117
Siemens, G. 113

small data machines 66, 67n2
social constructivism theory 107–108, 109–111, **110**, 120
Social Media 185–187
Social Web 185–187
Starkey, L. 115
Steinert, H. 180
Stewart, J. C. 117–118
symbolic scripts 76–77

tasks in project-based learning 120–121
Taylor, F. 180
Tesar, M. 117
time management 120
topic-loop 32
Tractus Logico-Philosophicus 77–78, 94
transformation: challenge of 7–9; communication in 25–33; conceptual resilience and 14–15; disrupting integration 29–30; IT and 5–7
trust 28–29

understanding 26–29; action and 26–27; co-authorship and double-loop 31–33; explanation and 27; mutual 30–31; value and 27–29
university management 86–87; agility implementation in 91–93; chamber of delusions and 79–80, 84–90; by Excel spreadsheet 81–84; generalization and further research on 93–94; habitus-based language-games versus digital language in 73–81; introduction to 70–72; methodological analysis of 72–73; by paranoiac management action 80–81, 86, 87–90; by systematic intimidation of culprit 87–90

Vacca, M. 117
values 22–25; and meanings driving action at organizational level in new remote work 45–46; understanding and 27–29
Voirol, O. 194, 195
Vygotsky, L. S. 108

Web 2.0 101–102
Wenger, E. 109
WhatsApp 102
Why-what-How (WwH) emergent curriculum 143–144
Wikipedia 102
Wittgenstein, L. 72, 73, 77–79, 94, 161; dating platforms research and 192, 195–196, 209–210

Yunus, M. 141

zone of proximal development (ZPD) 108

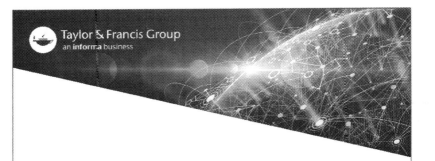

Printed in the United States
by Baker & Taylor Publisher Services